The History
of the

Khalifahs
Who Took
The Right Way

being a translation of the chapters on
al-Khulafa' ar-Rashidun
from
Tarikh al-Khulafa'
of
Jalal ad-Din as-Suyuti
Translated by ᶜAbdassamad Clarke

Publi
Ta-Ha Publishers Ltd.
1, Wynne Road
London SW9 0BB

Published by:

Ta-Ha Publishers Ltd.
1 Wynne Road
London SW9 0BB

By: Jalal ad-Din as-Suyuti
General Editor: Afsar Siddiqui
Translated by: Abdassamad Clarke

British Library Cataloguing in Publication Data
As-Suyuti, Jalal ad-Din
History of the Khalifahs Who Took the Right Way, The
I. Title

ISBN 1 897940 25 4

Typeset by: Bookwright.
Printed & Bound by: Deluxe Printers Tel: 0181-965-1771

Contents

May Allah bless the Prophet, his Family and Companions and grant them peace.

This is a new translation of the chapters on *al-Khulafa' ar-Rashidun* from as-Suyuti's *Tarikh al-Khulafa'*. These chapters shine with a genuine light.

I have continued beyond the first four *khulafa'* to include al-Hasan ibn ᶜAli ibn Abi Talib, may Allah be pleased with him, because as-Suyuti saw him as the fifth of the *Khulafa'*. It was he who legitimately transferred the *khilafah* to Muᶜawiyah, may Allah be pleased with him.

The translation lacks the majority of references to the books which are the sources of the *hadith* quoted, because whoever is interested will find the Arabic text easily available.

Furthermore the translation stays as close as possible to the original Arabic at the risk of a slight awkwardness in the English. Where necessary I have added within parentheses whatever seemed necessary for an understanding of the book.

The history outlined in these pages is further illuminated by a work which is even greater than it, but is itself an exposition that assumes a knowledge of what is in these pages, that is *al-ᶜAwasim min al-Qawasim* ('The Defence Against Disaster') by Qadi Abu Bakr ibn al-ᶜArabi, may Allah show mercy to him. Whereas as-Suyuti gives the most authentic traditions relating to these *khilafahs*, Qadi Abu Bakr truly lays bare the real significance of many of the events which as-Suyuti so expertly relates.

Abu Bakr as-Siddiq

may Allah be pleased with him

A bu Bakr as-Siddiq, may Allah be pleased with him, was the *khalifah* of the Messenger of Allah, may Allah bless him and grant him peace. His name was ᶜAbdullah ibn Abi Quhafah ᶜUthman ibn ᶜAmir ibn ᶜAmr ibn Kaᶜb ibn Saᶜd ibn Taym ibn Murrah ibn Kaᶜb ibn Lu'ayy ibn Ghalib, al-Qurashi, at-Tayyimi, whose genealogy connects to that of the Messenger of Allah, may Allah bless him and grant him peace, in Murrah.

An-Nawawi said in his *Tahdhib:* What I have said, that the name of Abu Bakr as-Siddiq was ᶜAbdullah, is correct and well known. It is said also that his name was ᶜAteeq, but the truth upon which the generality of the men of knowledge agree is that ᶜAteeq (the one set free) was an affectionate nickname and not his own name and he was given that name on account of his having been set free from the Fire as has been narrated in the *hadith* of at-Tirmidhi; and it is also said, on account of his face's *ᶜitaqah*, that is to say its goodness and beauty, as Musᶜab ibn az-Zubayr, al-Layth ibn Saᶜd and a whole group said; and it has also been said that it is because there is nothing in his genealogy to be found fault with.

Musᶜab ibn az-Zubayr and others said, 'The *ummah* agree unanimously on his being named as-Siddiq because he hastened to affirm the Messenger of Allah, may Allah bless him and grant him peace, and adhered steadfastly to truthfulness, and he was not remiss nor did he hesitate in any state or condition. He made exalted stands in Islam, among which was his story on the Night of the Isra', his steadfastness and his replying to the *kuffar* about it. There is also his emigration with the Messenger of Allah, may Allah bless him and grant him peace, leaving his family and children, and his remaining by the Prophet, may Allah bless him and grant him peace, in the Cave and on the rest of the journey (of the *Hijrah*). Then there are his words on the Day of Badr, and on the Day of Hudaybiyah when the matter of delaying entry into Makkah seemed unclear to others. There is his weeping when the Messenger of Allah, may Allah bless him and grant him peace, said, "Allah has given a slave the choice between this life and the next (and he has chosen the next)." Later there is his steadfastness on the day of the death of the Messenger of Allah, may Allah bless him and grant him peace, his addressing the people and his stilling them. There is his undertaking the matter of the oath of allegiance for the benefit of the Muslims, and then his diligence in sending the army of Usamah ibn Zaid to Syria and his determination on that. Then there is the stand he took over those who reneged (on their Islam) and his exchange of views with the other Companions until he overcame their arguments with his proofs, and Allah expanded their breasts as He had expanded his breast to the reality and truth, which was to fight the renegades. Then there is his equipping the armies to go to Syria to conquer it and his support of them. Then he sealed all of that by an important action which was one of his best deeds and most majestic of his virtues—his appointment of ʿUmar, may Allah be pleased with him, as *khalifah* of the Muslims, (and his perceptiveness concerning him, his bequeathing to him, and his entrusting the *ummah* to Allah, so that Allah, the Mighty and Exalted, made him succeed among them as the best *khalifah*; and for ʿUmar, who was one of his good actions, were realised the establishment of Islam, the strengthening of the *deen* and the fulfillment of the promise of Allah, the Exalted, that He would make it manifest over the *deen*, all of it.) How many qualities, stations and virtues of as-Siddiq there are which just cannot be numbered.'

The above is from an-Nawawi.

I say: I want to expand upon the introduction to as-Siddiq somewhat, mentioning about him much that I have discovered of his life, and to arrange that in sections.

His name and affectionate nickname

Ibn Kathir said that all admit that his name was ᶜAbdullah ibn ᶜUthman, except for the narration of Ibn Saᶜd on the authority of Ibn Sirin which asserts his name to have been ᶜAteeq whereas the truth is that that was his affectionate nickname. Then there is some disagreement as to the time of his being so named, and the reason for it; for some say that it was on account of the ᶜ*itaqah* of his countenance, that is, its beauty—but Abu Nuᶜaym al-Fadl ibn Dukayn said that it was on account of his priority in merit— and also it is said on account of the nobility of his pedigree, that is its purity, as there is nothing in his lineage that can be accounted a stain; and it is said too he was first so named and afterwards called ᶜAbdullah.

Al-Qasim ibn Muhammad questioned ᶜA'ishah, may Allah be pleased with her, as to the name of Abu Bakr, and she replied, 'ᶜAbdullah.' Then he said, 'The people call him ᶜAteeq.' She answered, 'Abu Quhafah had three sons whom he named ᶜAteeq, Muᶜtaq and Muᶜaytaq.'

Musa ibn Talhah said: I said to my father Talhah, 'Why was Abu Bakr called ᶜAteeq?' He said, 'His mother had no son surviving and when she gave birth to him, she faced towards the House (the Kaᶜbah) with him and exclaimed, "O Allah if this one is ᶜAteeq (free) from death then give him to me."'

Ibn ᶜAbbas said: He was only called ᶜAteeq because of the beauty of his face.

ᶜA'ishah, may Allah be pleased with her, said, 'Abu Bakr's name which his family called him by was ᶜAbdullah, but the name ᶜAteeq became the dominant usage.' In a version, 'But the Prophet, may Allah bless him and grant him peace, called him ᶜAteeq.'

ᶜA'ishah, may Allah be pleased with her, said, 'By Allah, I was in my house one day and the Messenger of Allah, may Allah bless him and grant him peace, and his companions were in the courtyard, a curtain between me and them. Abu Bakr came up and the Prophet, may Allah bless him and grant him peace, said, "Whoever is pleased to look upon one who is free from the Fire then let him look upon Abu Bakr." The name which his family knew him by was ᶜAbdullah but ᶜAteeq became the dominant usage.'

ᶜA'ishah, may Allah be pleased with her, said, 'Abu Bakr entered upon the Messenger of Allah, may Allah bless him and grant him peace, who said, "Abu Bakr, you are the one Allah has freed from the Fire." From that day he was known as ᶜAteeq.'

ᶜAbdullah ibn az-Zubayr said, 'Abu Bakr's name was ᶜAbdullah, then the Messenger of Allah, may Allah bless him and grant him peace, said to him, "You are Allah's freed one from the Fire." So he was known as ᶜAteeq.'

As for the name as-Siddiq, it is said about it, 'He was given the affectionate nickname in the *Jahiliyyah*, because of the truthfulness for which he was known.' It has been said also, 'Because of his haste in affirming the Messenger of Allah, may Allah bless him and grant him peace, in that of which he informed.'

Al-Hasan al-Basri and Qatadah said: The first time that he became known for it was the morning after the Night of the *Isra*'.

ᶜA'ishah, may Allah be pleased with her, said: The idolators came to Abu Bakr and said, 'What do you think of your Companion? He claims that he was taken this night to *Bait al-Maqdis* (Jerusalem).' He replied, 'Did he say that?' They said, 'Yes.' He said, 'He has definitely told the truth. I believe and affirm him in matters more remote than that, the news from heaven in the early part of the morning and in the evening.' For that reason he was called as-Siddiq.

Abu Hurairah said: When the Messenger of Allah, may Allah bless him and grant him peace, returned on the night in which he was made to travel (to Jerusalem), and he was at Dhu Tuwa, he said, 'Jibril, my people will not believe me.' He (Jibril) said, 'Abu Bakr will believe you, and he is as-Siddiq.'

An-Nazzal ibn Sabrah said: That man, Allah named him as-Siddiq on the tongue of Jibril and on the tongue of Muhammad, may Allah bless him and grant him peace. He was the deputy of the Messenger of Allah, may Allah bless him and grant him peace, for the prayer; he was contented with him for our *deen* and so we were pleased with him for our worldly affairs.

Abu Yahya said: I cannot count the number of times that I heard ᶜAli say upon the *mimbar*, 'Truly Allah named Abu Bakr through the tongue of His Prophet, a *siddiq*.'

Hakim ibn Saᶜd said: I heard ᶜAli say, and he swore upon it, 'Allah definitely revealed from heaven the name of Abu Bakr, as-Siddiq.'

In the *hadith* of Uhud, 'Be still, for there are only upon you a Prophet, a *siddiq* and two martyrs.'

'Abu Bakr's mother was the daughter of his father's paternal uncle (she was his father's cousin). Her name was Salma bint Sakhr ibn ᶜAmir ibn Kaᶜb. She was given the *kunya* (surname) Umm al-Khayr (Mother of the Best),' said az-Zuhri.

His birth and early life

He was born two years and some months after the birth of the Prophet, may Allah bless him and grant him peace, and he died when he was sixty-three years old.

Ibn Kathir said: As for that which Yazid ibn al-Asamm said, that the Prophet, may Allah bless him and grant him peace, said to Abu Bakr, 'Am I greater (older) or you?' And he said, 'You are greater than me but I have more years than you,' it is a *mursal* (reaching back only as far as one of the Followers) *ghareeb* (unusual, in having a singular isnad) tradition, and what is well known is the opposite (i.e. the Prophet, may Allah bless him and grant him peace, was older), and it is true only of al-ᶜAbbas (that he was some years younger than the Prophet, may Allah bless him and grant him peace).

His early life was in Makkah, which he only left for trade, and he had great wealth among his people, complete manliness, and munificence, and courtesy among them, as Ibn ad-Daghniyyah said, 'You join ties of kinship, you are truthful, you attain what others are denied, you support those in need, you help in difficult times, and you are hospitable to the guest.'

An-Nawawi said: He was one of the chiefs of Quraysh in the *Jahiliyyah*, one of their counsellors, beloved among them, and the wisest in the direction of their affairs. Then when Islam came he preferred it over everything else, and entered into it perfectly and completely.'

Ma'ruf ibn Kharrabudh said: Abu Bakr as-Siddiq, may Allah be pleased with him, was one of ten men of Quraysh who united preeminence in *Jahiliyyah* and Islam. He had responsibility for the settlement of blood-money and debts. That was because Quraysh had no king to whom all affairs could be referred. Rather in each tribe there was a general area of responsibility which resided in its chief; so that Banu Hashim had responsibility for giving (the pilgrims) to drink, and feeding them (by collecting from the tribes of Quraysh), meaning that no-one ate or drank except from their food and drink. Banu 'Abd ad-Dar had responsibility for being the door-keepers and guardians (of the Ka'bah) and for the banner and council, i.e. no-one could enter the House without their permission, and whenever Quraysh fastened on the banner of war, the Banu 'Abd ad-Dar bound it for them, and whenever they assembled together for a matter, either to confirm or annul it, their assembly could not be anywhere but in the House of Council, nor decided upon except there, and it belonged to Bani 'Abd ad-Dar.'

Abu Bakr was the most abstinent of men in the *Jahiliyyah*

'A'ishah, may Allah be pleased with her, said: By Allah, Abu Bakr never spoke poetry (i.e. he never 'composed' poetry) either in the *Jahiliyyah* or in Islam, and he and 'Uthman gave up drinking wine in the *Jahiliyyah*.

She said, may Allah be pleased with her: Abu Bakr had forbidden himself wine in the *Jahiliyyah*.

'Abdullah ibn az-Zubayr said: Abu Bakr never ever spoke poetry.

Abu'l-'Aliyyah ar-Riyahi said: It was said to Abu Bakr as-Siddiq in a gathering of the companions of the Messenger of Allah, may Allah bless him and grant him peace, 'Did you drink wine in the Jahiliyyah?' He said, 'I seek refuge in Allah.' Someone said, 'Why?'

He replied, 'I tried to protect my honour and guard my manliness, for whoever drinks wine will lose his honour and his manliness.' He said: That reached the Messenger of Allah, may Allah bless him and grant him peace, and he said, 'Abu Bakr has told the truth, Abu Bakr has told the truth,' twice.

His description

ᶜA'ishah, may Allah be pleased with her, said that a man said to her, 'Describe Abu Bakr to us.' She said, 'A fair man, of slender build, thin cheeked and with a stoop; he could not keep his lower garment from slipping over his loins; gaunt-faced, eyes deep-set, with a prominent forehead, and the backs of his hands fleshless. This is his description.'

ᶜA'ishah, may Allah be pleased with her, said that Abu Bakr used to dye with Henna and *katam*.

Anas said: The Messenger of Allah, may Allah bless him and grant him peace, went to Madinah and there was no-one among his companions having hair of mixed white and black except Abu Bakr, so he dyed it with Henna and *katam*.

His acceptance of Islam

Abu Saᶜid al-Khudri said: Abu Bakr said, 'Am I not the most suitable of people for it (the *khilafah*)? Am I not the first to accept Islam? Am I not the one of such-and-such? Am I not the one of such-and-such?'

Al-Harith related that ᶜAli, may Allah be pleased with him, said: The first among men to accept Islam was Abu Bakr.

Zaid ibn Arqam said: The first to perform the prayer with the Prophet, may Allah bless him and grant him peace, was Abu Bakr as-Siddiq.

Abu Arwa ad-Dawsi the Companion, may Allah be pleased with him, said: The first to accept Islam was Abu Bakr as-Siddiq.

Ash-Shaᶜbi said: I asked Ibn ᶜAbbas, 'Who was the first person to accept Islam?' He said, 'Abu Bakr as-Siddiq. Did you not hear the words of Hassan (ibn Thabit)?:

"When you recall the distress of a trusted brother, then remember your brother Abu Bakr for what he did.

The best of creation, most fearfully obedient of them, and the most just, except for the Prophet, and the most certain to fulfil what he has undertaken,

The second, the follower whose assembly is praised, and the first of the men of them who affirmed the Messenger.'"

Furat ibn as-Sa'ib said: I asked Maimun ibn Mihran, 'Is ᶜAli better in your view or Abu Bakr and ᶜUmar?' He shook until his staff fell from his hand and replied, 'I never thought that I would live to a time when anyone would be compared with them. Their good deeds belong to Allah! They were the head of Islam.' I said, 'ᶜAli was the first to accept Islam or Abu Bakr?' He said, 'By Allah, Abu Bakr believed in the Prophet, may Allah bless him and grant him peace, at the time of Buhayra the monk when he passed by him.'

There is a disagreement as to him and Khadijah (which of them was first to accept Islam) until (it is said that) he married her to him, may Allah bless him and grant him peace, and all of that before the birth of ᶜAli.

A whole group of the Companions and the Followers said that he was the first to accept Islam, and some of them claimed that there was a consensus on that. It has been said, 'The first to accept Islam was ᶜAli.' It has also been said, 'Khadijah.' The reconciliation between these apparently conflicting statements is that Abu Bakr was the first man to accept Islam, ᶜAli was the first of the children to accept Islam, and Khadijah was the first woman to accept Islam.

Salim ibn Abi'l-Jaᶜd said: I said to Muhammad ibn al-Hanafiyyah, 'Was Abu Bakr the first person to accept Islam?' He said, 'No.' I said, 'So how did Abu Bakr excel and precede others so much so that no-one else is mentioned but Abu Bakr?' He said, 'Because he was the best of them in Islam from the moment he accepted Islam until the moment he met his Lord.'

Muhammad ibn Saᶜd ibn Abi Waqqas said to his father Saᶜd, 'Was Abu Bakr the first of you to accept Islam?' He said, 'No.

More than five people accepted Islam before him, but he was the best of us in Islam.'

Ibn Kathir said: It is clear that the people of his house, may Allah bless him and grant him peace, believed before anyone; his wife Khadijah, his freed slave Zaid, Zaid's wife Umm Ayman, ᶜAli and Waraqah.

ᶜIsa ibn Yazid said: Abu Bakr as-Siddiq said, 'I was sitting in the courtyard of the Kaᶜbah and Zaid ibn ᶜAmr ibn Nufayl was seated, then Umayyah ibn Abi's-Salt passed by him and said, "How are you, seeker after good?" He said, "Well." He said, "And have you found?" He said, "No," so he said,

"Every *deen* on the Day of Rising, except that which Allah has decreed, will perish.

But as for this Prophet who is awaited, will he be from us or from you?" And I had not heard before that of a prophet who was awaited and who would be sent. So I went to Waraqah ibn Naufal who used to look much towards heaven, and was much astonished of heart. I stopped him and told him the story. He said, "Yes, my nephew. We are the people of books and sciences, but this Prophet who is awaited is from the midst (noblest) of the Arabs genealogically—and I have a knowledge of genealogy—and your people are midmost (noblest) of the Arabs in terms of lineage." I said, "Uncle, and what will the Prophet say?" He said, "He will say what is said to him, except that he will not oppress nor be oppressed nor seek the oppression (of anyone)." So that when the Messenger of Allah, may Allah bless him and grant him peace, was sent I believed in him and affirmed him.'

Muhammad ibn ᶜAbd ar-Rahman ibn ᶜAbdullah ibn al-Husayn at-Tamimi narrated that the Messenger of Allah, may Allah bless him and grant him peace, said, 'I have never invited anyone to Islam except that he had an aversion to it, and irresolution and deliberation, except for Abu Bakr. He did not delay when I reminded him and he was not irresolute.' Al-Baihaqi said: This was because he used to see the proofs of the prophethood of the

Messenger of Allah, may Allah bless him and grant him peace, and hear the traces of it before his invitation (to Islam), so that when he invited him he had already reflected and thought about it, and he submitted and accepted Islam at once.

Abu Maisarah said that the Messenger of Allah, may Allah bless him and grant him peace, used to hear someone calling him when he went out, 'Muhammad!' When he heard the voice he would turn back in flight and he told it in confidence to Abu Bakr who was his friend in *Jahiliyyah*.

Ibn ᶜAbbas said: The Messenger of Allah, may Allah bless him and grant him peace, said, 'I never spoke to anyone about Islam but that they refused me and rejected my words except for the son of Abu Quhafah. I never spoke to him about something but that he accepted it and was steadfast in it.'

Abu'd-Darda' said: The Messenger of Allah, may Allah bless him and grant him peace, said, 'Will you leave me my companion? (Will you leave me my companion?). I said, "People, I am the Messenger of Allah to you all," and you said, "You are lying." Abu Bakr said, "You have told the truth."'

His companionship and expeditions

The ᶜ*ulama'* say: Abu Bakr accompanied the Prophet, may Allah bless him and grant him peace, from the moment he accepted Islam until his death, not leaving him in a journey or in residence, except for that which he, may Allah bless him and grant him peace, authorised him to go out on, such as the *Hajj* and fighting expeditions. He was present at all the battles with him, emigrated with him, leaving his family and children, longing for Allah and His Messenger, may Allah bless him and grant him peace. He was his close companion in the cave. He, exalted is He, said, '*The second of two when the two of them were in the cave, when he said to his companion, "Do not be sad. Truly Allah is with us."* (Qur'an 9: 40). He undertook to help the Messenger of Allah, may Allah bless him and grant him peace, more than once. He gave splendid service in the battles, and was firm

y of Uhud and the Day of Hunain when all of the
d fled, as we will show in the section on his bravery.
airah said: The angels made each other to rejoice on
of Badr, saying, 'Do you not see as-Siddiq with the
r of Allah, may Allah bless him and grant him peace, in
r?'
d: The Messenger of Allah, may Allah bless him and
n peace, said to me and Abu Bakr on the Day of Badr,
e of you is Jibril and with the other is Mika'il.'
in said that ᶜAbd ar-Rahman ibn Abi Bakr was, on the
adr, with those who associate partners with Allah. When
) accepted Islam he said to his father, 'You were ex-
) me (*ahdafta*) as a target on the Day of Badr, but I
away from you and did not kill you.' Abu Bakr said,
er, if you had been exposed to me as a target I would not
rned away from you.' Ibn Qutaibah said: The meaning of
1 is *ashrafta* – you were high or open, exposed and close.
is said of a tall building, '*Hadaf* (literally – target).'

His bravery and that he was the bravest of the Companions

ᶜAli said, 'Tell me who is the bravest of men?' They said, 'You.' He
said, 'As for me, I never encountered anyone but that I took my due
from him, but tell me who is the bravest of men?' They said, 'We
don't know. Who is it?' He said, 'Abu Bakr. On the Day of Badr we
made a shelter from the sun for the Messenger of Allah, may Allah
bless him and grant him peace, and then we said, "Who will be with
the Messenger of Allah, may Allah bless him and grant him peace,
so that none of the idolators may fall upon him?" By Allah, none of
us drew near except for Abu Bakr who brandished a sword over
the head of the Messenger of Allah, may Allah bless him and grant
him peace. No-one fell upon him but that he in turn fell upon him.
So he is the bravest of men.'

ᶜAli, may Allah be pleased with him, said: I saw the Messenger
of Allah, may Allah bless him and grant him peace, and Quraysh

grabbed him. One held him and another threw him down and they were saying, 'Are you the one who has made the gods into one god?' By Allah, none of us approached except Abu Bakr, striking this one, and restraining that one, and throwing down another, saying, 'Woe to you! Will you kill a man because he says, "My Lord is Allah?"' Then ᶜAli raised a cloak which he was wearing and wept until his beard was wet and said, 'I adjure you by Allah! Is the believer of the people of Firᶜawn better or Abu Bakr?' People were silent. He said, 'Will you not answer? By Allah, an hour of Abu Bakr is better than a thousand hours of the like of the believer of the people of Firᶜawn. He was a man who concealed his *iman*, and this was a man who was open about his *iman*.'

ᶜUrwah ibn az-Zubayr said: I asked ᶜAbdullah ibn ᶜAmr ibn al-ᶜAs about the worst thing that the idolators did to the Messenger of Allah, may Allah bless him and grant him peace. He said, 'I saw ᶜUqbah ibn Abi Muᶜayt who came to the Prophet, may Allah bless him and grant him peace, while he was praying, and he placed his cloak about his neck and seriously tried to throttle him. Then Abu Bakr came and defended him and said, "Would you kill a man because he says, 'My Lord is Allah,' and he has come to you with clear signs from your Lord?"'

Abu Bakr said, 'On the Day of Uhud everyone fled from the Messenger of Allah, and I was the first to return.' The rest of the *hadith* is in the *Musnad* which Al-Haytham ibn Kulayb narrated.

ᶜA'ishah, may Allah be pleased with her, said: When the companions of the Prophet, may Allah bless him and grant him peace, gathered, and they were thirty-eight men, Abu Bakr pressed upon the Messenger of Allah, may Allah bless him and grant him peace, to be open and public. He said, 'Abu Bakr, we are few.' Abu Bakr wouldn't stop urging the Messenger of Allah, may Allah bless him and grant him peace, until the Messenger of Allah, may Allah bless him and grant him peace, made things public. The Muslims went into every corner of the Mosque (of Makkah), every man among his own kinsfolk, and Abu Bakr stood up among the people addressing them, so that he was the first public speaker to invite people to Allah and His Messenger. The idolators leapt upon Abu Bakr and the Muslims, and they beat them, in every corner of the Mosque, very severely. (The conclusion of this *hadith* will come in the biography of ᶜUmar, may Allah be pleased with him.)

ᶜAli, may Allah be pleased with him, said: When Abu Bakr accepted Islam, he was open about his Islam and he invited people to Allah and to His Messenger, may Allah bless him and grant him peace.

His spending his wealth on the Messenger of Allah and that he was the most generous of the Companions

Allah, exalted is He, says, '*And he will be averted from it (the Fire) who has the most fearful obedience, the one who gives his wealth purifying himself,*' (Qur'an 92: 17-21) to the end of the *surah*. Ibn al-Jawzi said: They agree unanimously that this was revealed about Abu Bakr.

Abu Hurairah said: The Messenger of Allah, may Allah bless him and grant him peace, said, 'No wealth ever benefitted me as did the wealth of Abu Bakr.' Abu Bakr wept and said, 'Are I and my wealth for any but you, Messenger of Allah?' ᶜA'ishah, may Allah be pleased with her, narrated the like of it. Ibn Kathir said: And it is narrated in *hadith* of ᶜAli, Ibn ᶜAbbas, Anas, Jabir ibn ᶜAbdullah and Abu Saᶜid al-Khudri, may Allah be pleased with all of them. Saᶜid ibn al-Musayyab also narrated it and added, 'And the Messenger of Allah, may Allah bless and grant peace to him and his family, used to make use of the wealth of Abu Bakr as he did of his own wealth.'

ᶜA'ishah, may Allah be pleased with her, and ᶜUrwah ibn az-Zubayr said: Abu Bakr, may Allah be pleased with him, accepted Islam on the day that he did and he had forty thousand *dinars* (and in a wording—forty thousand *dirhams*) and he spent them on the Messenger of Allah, may Allah bless him and grant him peace.

Ibn ᶜUmar, may Allah be pleased with both of them, said: Abu Bakr accepted Islam, may Allah be pleased with him, on the day that he did, and in his house there were forty thousand *dirhams*. Then he emigrated to Madinah and he had nothing but five thousand *dirhams*. He had spent all of that on freeing slaves and helping the cause of Islam.

ᶜA'ishah, may Allah be pleased with her, said that Abu Bakr freed seven (slaves) each one of whom was being tortured for the sake of Allah.

Ibn ᶜUmar said: I was with the Prophet, may Allah bless him and grant him peace, and Abu Bakr as-Siddiq was with him, and he had on a large (coarse goat-skin) cloak which he had fastened over his breast with a skewer, and then Jibril, peace be upon him, descended upon him and said, 'Muhammad, how is it that I see Abu Bakr and he has on a large (coarse goat-skin) cloak which he has fastened over his breast with a skewer?' He said, 'Jibril, he spent his wealth upon me before the Conquest (of Makkah).' He said, 'Allah sends greetings of peace to him and says to say to him, "Are you pleased with Me in this poverty of yours or displeased?" Abu Bakr said, 'Am I displeased with my Lord? I am pleased with my Lord. I am pleased with my Lord. I am pleased with my Lord.'

Ibn ᶜAbbas, may Allah be pleased with both of them (he and his father al-ᶜAbbas), related from the Prophet, may Allah bless him and grant him peace, that he said, 'Jibril, peace be upon him, descended upon me and he had on a large piece of coarse cloth fastened on him, so I said to him, "Jibril, what is this?" He said, "Allah, exalted is He, has ordered the angels that they should fasten in the heaven as Abu Bakr fastens on earth."' Ibn Kathir said: This is very much to be rejected. If it were not that many people hand down this one and the one before it, it would be better to completely avoid them.

ᶜUmar ibn al-Khattab said: The Messenger of Allah, may Allah bless him and grant him peace, ordered us to give *sadaqah* and that agreed with the property that I had so I said, 'Today I will outdo Abu Bakr if I am ever to outdo him,' and I brought half of my wealth. The Messenger of Allah, may Allah bless him and grant him peace, said, 'What have you left for your family?' I said, 'I have left the like of it.' Then Abu Bakr came with every-thing that he had, and he said, 'Abu Bakr, what have you left for your family?' He said, 'I have left for them Allah and His Messen-ger.' I said, 'I will never ever outdo him in anything.'

Al-Hasan al-Basri said that Abu Bakr came to the Prophet, may Allah bless him and grant him peace, with his *sadaqah* and con-cealed it. He said, 'Messenger of Allah, this is my *sadaqah*, and, Allah can return to me (for more).' Then ᶜUmar came with his *sadaqah* openly and said, 'Messenger of Allah, this is my *sadaqah* and I can return to Allah (for more).' The Messenger of Allah, may Allah bless him and grant him peace, said, 'The difference between your two *sadaqahs* is the same as the difference be-tween your words.'

Abu Hurairah said: The Messenger of Allah, may Allah bless him and grant him peace, said, 'I have never been under obliga-tion to anyone but that I have repaid him, except for Abu Bakr, for he has put obligations on me which Allah will repay him for on the Day of Rising. No-one's wealth has ever benefitted me as has Abu Bakr's wealth.'

Abu Bakr as-Siddiq, may Allah be pleased with him, said: I came with my father Abu Quhafah to the Prophet, may Allah bless him and grant him peace, who said, 'You should have left the *shaykh* until I could come to him.' I said, 'Rather it is more correct that he should come to you.' He said, 'We would rather be protective of him for the favours we are obliged to his son for.'

Ibn ᶜAbbas said: The Messenger of Allah, may Allah bless him and grant him peace, said, 'No-one has shown greater favour to me than Abu Bakr. He shared himself and his wealth with me and he married me his daughter.'

His knowledge and that he was the most knowledgeable of the Companions and the most intelligent of them

An-Nawawi said, in his *Tahdhib*, and from his own writing I transmit: Our companions proved the vastness of his knowledge by his words, may Allah be pleased with him, in the well established *hadith* which is in the two *Sahih* collections, 'By Allah, I will fight whoever distinguishes between *salah* and *zakah*. By Allah, if they refuse me as much as the halter of a camel which they used to pay to the Messenger of Allah, may Allah bless him and grant him peace, I will fight them over their refusal.' Shaykh Abu Ishaq saw a proof, in this and other things, in his *Tabaqat*, that Abu Bakr as-Siddiq, may Allah be pleased with him, was the most knowledgeable of the Companions, because they all failed to understand the judgement on this issue except for him, then it became clear to them because of his discussions with them that his words were the correct position, so they came back to that.

Ibn ᶜUmar was asked, 'Who used to give *fatwa* for people at the time of the Messenger of Allah, may Allah bless him and grant him peace?' He said, 'Abu Bakr and ᶜUmar, may Allah be pleased with them. I don't know of anyone other than them.'

Abu Saᶜid al-Khudri said: The Messenger of Allah, may Allah bless him and grant him peace, addressed people and said, 'Allah, the Blessed and Exalted, has given a slave the choice between the world and that which is with Him. That slave has chosen that which is with Allah, exalted is He.' Then Abu Bakr wept and said, 'We would ransom you with our fathers and our mothers.' We were astonished at his weeping because the Messenger of Allah informed about a slave who had been given a choice. But the Messenger of Allah, may Allah bless him and grant him peace, was the one given the choice, and Abu Bakr was the most knowledgeable of us.

The Messenger of Allah, may Allah bless him and grant him peace, said, 'The most generous of people to me with his company and his wealth is Abu Bakr. If I were to take an intimate friend other than my Lord I would have taken Abu Bakr, but there is the brotherhood of Islam and its affection. Let no door remain open but for the door of Abu Bakr.'

The above are the words of an-Nawawi.

Ibn Kathir said: As-Siddiq, may Allah be pleased with him, was the best read of the Companions, meaning that he was the most knowledgeable of them in the Qur'an, because he, may Allah bless him and grant him peace, put him forward as *imam* of the prayer for the Companions, may Allah be pleased with him and them, along with his words, 'The best read in the Book of Allah will lead the people.'

ᶜA'ishah, may Allah be pleased with her, said: The Messenger of Allah, may Allah bless him and grant him peace, said, 'It is not fitting for a people among whom is Abu Bakr that another than him should lead them (as *imam*: the word having the meaning of both leading, and leading the prayer).'

He was, along with that, the most knowledgeable in the *Sunnah*. When the Companions referred to him on several occasions, he produced transmissions of *sunnahs* from the Prophet, may Allah bless him and grant him peace, he had memorised and which he produced at the moments when they were needed, and which they didn't have. How could that not be when he had persevered in accompanying the Messenger, may Allah bless him and grant him peace, from the very beginning of his being sent until his death? Along with that he was one of the most intelligent of the slaves of Allah and one of the most comprehending. However, there are not many *hadith* traced back with a chain of transmission to him, only because of the short time he lived and the speed of his death after the Prophet, may Allah bless him and grant him peace. If he had lived for long, his narrations would have been very extensive. None of the transmitters left a *hadith* that he transmitted without narrating it. But none of the Companions from his time, needed to transmit from him what they shared with him in the narration of, so they only transmitted from him what they themselves didn't have.

Maimun ibn Mihran said: Abu Bakr, when a dispute was brought to him, used to look in the Book of Allah. Then if he found there the basis for a judgement between the disputants he would give judgement on that basis. If there was nothing in the Book and he knew a *sunnah* on that matter from the Messenger of Allah, may Allah bless and grant him and his family peace, he would give judgement by that. If he could not find the right way he would go out and ask the Muslims, and say, 'Such and such has come to me, so do you know whether the Messenger of Allah, may Allah bless him and grant him peace, gave any judgement on that?' Perhaps a group would gather around him, everyone of them mentioning a judgement of the Messenger of Allah, may Allah bless him and grant him peace. Abu Bakr would say, 'Praise belongs to Allah Who has put among us those who preserve and memorise from our Prophet.' If he was unable to find a *sunnah* about it from the Messenger of Allah, may Allah bless him and grant him peace, he would gather the leaders and the best of the people and seek their counsel. If they would agree on a view he would give judgement by that. ᶜUmar, may Allah be pleased with him, used to do that. If he was unable to find some way in the Qur'an and the *Sunnah*, he would look to see if Abu Bakr had given a judgement on it. If he found that Abu Bakr had already given judgement on it he would pass judgement on the basis of that judgement. If not, he would call the leaders of the Muslims and if they would agree unanimously on a matter he would give judgement on that basis.

As-Siddiq, may Allah be pleased with him, was, along with that, the most knowledgeable in the genealogies of the Arabs, particularly of Quraysh. A Shaykh of the Ansar said: Jubayr ibn Mutᶜim used to be the most knowledgeable of Quraysh in the genealogies of Quraysh and of the Arabs in general and he used to say, 'I only took genealogies from Abu Bakr as-Siddiq, and Abu Bakr as-Siddiq was the most learned in genealogy of the Arabs.'

Along with that, as-Siddiq had reached the limit in the interpretation of dreams. He used to interpret dreams in the time of the Messenger of Allah, may Allah bless him and grant him peace. Muhammad ibn Sirin, and he was the foremost in this knowledge by general consensus, said: Abu Bakr was the most able of this *ummah* after the Prophet, may Allah bless him and grant him peace, to draw a meaning (from a dream).

Samurah said: The Messenger of Allah, may Allah bless him and grant him peace, said, 'I have been commanded to interpret the dream (and to tell it or teach it) to Abu Bakr.'

Ibn Kathir said: He was one of the clearest and most eloquent of people.

Az-Zubayr ibn Bakkar said: I heard one of the people of knowledge saying, 'The most eloquent of those of the Companions of the Messenger of Allah who gave the *khutbah* were Abu Bakr and ᶜAli ibn Abi Talib, may Allah be pleased with both of them.' In the *hadith* of *as-Saqifah* we will relate the words of ᶜUmar, may Allah be pleased with him. He was one of the most knowing of mankind of Allah and the most fearful of Him. Some of his words on that and on the interpretation of dream and some of his *khutbahs* we will place together in an independent section.

One of the proofs that he was the most knowledgeable of the Companions is the *hadith* of the Treaty of Hudaybiyah when ᶜUmar asked the Messenger of Allah, may Allah bless him and grant him peace, 'For what reason should we accept disgrace in our *deen*?' The Prophet, may Allah bless him and grant him peace, answered him. Then he went to Abu Bakr and asked him the same question that he had asked the Messenger of Allah, may Allah bless him and grant him peace, and he answered him just as the Prophet, may Allah bless him and grant him peace, had answered him word for word.

Along with that, he was the most penetrating of the Companions in his views and the most perfect of them in intellect. ᶜAbdullah ibn ᶜAmr ibn al-ᶜAs said: I heard the Messenger of Allah, may Allah bless him and grant him peace, saying, 'Jibril came to me and said, "Allah orders you to seek the counsel of Abu Bakr."'

Muᶜadh ibn Jabal told that when the Prophet, may Allah bless him and grant him peace, wanted to send Muᶜadh to the Yemen he sought the counsel of men of his companions among whom were Abu Bakr, ᶜUmar, ᶜAli, Talhah, az-Zubayr and Usayd ibn Hudayr. The people talked and every man had his own view. He said, 'What do you think, Muᶜadh?' I (Muᶜadh) said, 'I think the same as that which Abu Bakr said.' The Prophet, may Allah bless him and grant him peace, said, 'Allah dislikes in the heaven that Abu Bakr should make a mistake.' Ibn Abi Usamah related it in his *Musnad*, 'Allah, in the heaven, dislikes that Abu Bakr as-

Siddiq should make a mistake on the earth.' Sahl ibn Saᶜd as-Saᶜidi said: The Messenger of Allah, may Allah bless him and grant him peace, said, 'Allah dislikes that Abu Bakr should make a mistake.' The men who transmitted it are all trustworthy.

His memorisation of the Qur'an

An-Nawawi said, in his *Tahdhib.* As-Siddiq was one of the Companions who memorised all of the Qur'an.

A large group have mentioned this also, of them Ibn Kathir in his *Tafsir.* As for the tradition of Anas, 'Four gathered together (i.e. memorised entirely) the Qur'an in the time of the Messenger of Allah, may Allah bless him and grant him peace,' what he meant was 'of the Ansar' as I made clear in the book *Al-Itqan.* As for that which ash-Shaᶜbi said, 'Abu Bakr as-Siddiq, may Allah be pleased with him, died without gathering (memorising) all of the Qur'an,' it is rejected, or it can be interpreted that he meant by 'gathering', i.e. in a *mushaf* with the organisation (of *surahs* and *ayat*) which ᶜUthman gave it, may Allah be pleased with him.

That he was the most eminent of the Companions and the best of them

The people of the *Sunnah* are unanimous that the best of mankind after the Messenger of Allah, may Allah bless him and grant him peace, were Abu Bakr, then ᶜUmar, then ᶜUthman, then ᶜAli, then the rest of the ten (who were given the good news of the Garden by the Prophet, may Allah bless him and grant him peace), then the rest of the people of Badr, then the rest of the people of Uhud, then the rest of the people of the oath of allegiance (of Hudaybiyah), then the rest of the Companions. Mansur al-Baghdadi relates that there is consensus on this.

Ibn ᶜUmar said, 'We were choosing between people in the time of the Messenger of Allah, may Allah bless him and grant him peace, so we chose Abu Bakr, then ᶜUmar (ibn al-Khattab), then ᶜUthman (ibn ᶜAffan) may Allah be pleased with them all.'

At-Tabarani added, in *al-Kabir*, 'And the Prophet came to know of that but did not deny it.'

Ibn ᶜUmar said: We, while the Messenger of Allah, may Allah bless him and grant him peace, was among us, used to prefer Abu Bakr, ᶜUmar, ᶜUthman and ᶜAli.

Abu Hurairah said: We, the gatherings of the Companions of the Messenger of Allah, may Allah bless him and grant him peace, while we were considerable numbers, used to say, 'The best of this *ummah* after our Prophet are Abu Bakr, then ᶜUmar, and then ᶜUthman,' and then we would be silent.'

Jabir ibn ᶜAbdullah said: ᶜUmar said to Abu Bakr, 'O best of mankind after the Messenger of Allah, may Allah bless him and grant him peace.' Abu Bakr said, 'If you say that, then I heard him saying, "The sun has not risen over a man better than ᶜUmar."'

Muhammad ibn ᶜAli ibn Abi Talib said: I said to my father, 'Who is the best of mankind after the Prophet, may Allah bless him and grant him peace?' He said, 'Abu Bakr.' I said, 'Then who?' He said, 'ᶜUmar.' I was afraid that he would say ᶜUthman so I said, 'Then you?' He said, 'I am nobody but a man among the Muslims.'

ᶜAli said: The best of this *ummah* after our Prophet are Abu Bakr and ᶜUmar. Adh-Dhahabi said: This is *mutawatir* from ᶜAli (it was narrated by a large number of people directly from him to other people so that it reached later generations from large numbers of people), so may Allah curse *ar-Rafidah* (literally 'the rejectors' i.e. the *Shiᶜah*), how ignorant they are!

ᶜUmar ibn al-Khattab said: Abu Bakr, our master, the best of us and the most beloved to the Prophet, may Allah bless him and grant him peace, said, '....'

ᶜAbd ar-Rahman ibn Abi Layla said that ᶜUmar ascended the *mimbar* and said, 'Definitely the best of this *ummah* after our Prophet is Abu Bakr. Whoever says anything else is an inventor of falsehood. May there be upon him that which is upon the inventor of falsehood.' Also Ibn Abi Layla said: ᶜAli said, 'Anyone who prefers me over Abu Bakr and ᶜUmar, I will lash with the *hadd* punishment due to the inventor of falsehood.'

Abu'd-Darda', said that the Messenger of Allah, may Allah bless him and grant him peace, said, 'The sun has not risen nor has it set over anyone better than Abu Bakr, unless he were a prophet.' In a differently worded version, '...over any of the Muslims, after the prophets and messengers, better than Abu Bakr.' Jabir, in his wording, related, 'The sun has not risen over anyone of you better than him.' There are other texts which support it from other angles and which require that it be a sound or good *hadith*. Ibn Kathir indicated that his judgement was that it was sound.

Salamah ibn al-Akwa^c said: The Messenger of Allah, may Allah bless him and grant him peace, said, 'Abu Bakr as-Siddiq is the best of mankind, unless it be a prophet.' Sa^cd ibn Zurarah said: The Messenger of Allah, may Allah bless him and grant him peace, said, 'The *Ruh al-Quds,* Jibril, informed me that, "The best of your *ummah* after you is Abu Bakr."'

^cAmr ibn al-^cAs said: I said, 'Messenger of Allah, which of the people is most beloved to you?' He said, '^cA'ishah.' I said, 'Of the men?' He said, 'Her father.' I said, 'Then who?' He said, 'Then ^cUmar ibn al-Khattab.' This *hadith* has been narrated without, 'Then ^cUmar,' in narrations of Anas, Ibn ^cAmr and Ibn ^cAbbas.

^cAbdullah ibn Shaqiq said: I said to ^cA'ishah, 'Which of the companions of the Messenger of Allah were most beloved to the Messenger of Allah, may Allah bless him and grant him peace?' She said, 'Abu Bakr.' I said, 'Then who?' She said, 'Then ^cUmar.' I said, 'Then who?' She said, 'Abu ^cUbaidah ibn al-Jarrah.'

Anas said: The Messenger of Allah, may Allah bless him and grant him peace, said about Abu Bakr and ^cUmar, 'These two are the lords of the mature adults of the people of the Garden, of the first ones and the last ones, except for the prophets and the messengers.' There is recorded the like of it of ^cAli, and of Ibn ^cAbbas, Ibn ^cUmar, Abu Sa^cid al-Khudri and Jabir ibn ^cAbdullah.

^cAmmar ibn Yasir said: Whoever preferred anyone of the companions of the Messenger of Allah, may Allah bless him and grant him peace, over Abu Bakr and ^cUmar has belittled the *Muhajirun* and the *Ansar*.

Az-Zuhri said: The Prophet, may Allah bless him and grant him peace, said to Hassan ibn Thabit, 'Have you said anything about Abu Bakr?' He said, 'Yes.' He said, 'Say it and I will listen.' He said,

'And the "*second of the two*" in the glorious cave,
The enemy went round about it when he ascended the mountain.
The love of the Messenger of Allah (for him) they already knew,
Of creation he held not equal any man.'

And the Prophet, may Allah bless him and grant him peace, laughed until his back teeth were visible, then said, 'You have told the truth, Hassan; he is as you said.'

Anas ibn Malik said: The Messenger of Allah, may Allah bless him and grant him peace, said, 'The most merciful of my *ummah* towards my *ummah* is Abu Bakr, the most severe of them in the matter of Allah is ʿUmar, the most truly modest of them is ʿUthman, the most knowledge of them of the *halal* and the *haram* is Muʿadh bin Jabal, the most knowledgeable in the laws of inheritance is Zayd ibn Thabit, the best read of them (in Qur'an reading) is Ubayy ibn Kaʿb, and every *ummah* has a trusted one and the trusted one of this *ummah* is Abu ʿUbaidah ibn al-Jarrah.' Ibn ʿUmar added (in his narration) to it, 'and the most decisive of them (as Qadi) is ʿAli.' Shaddad ibn Aus added to it, 'and Abu Dharr is the most abstinent of my *ummah* and the most truthful of them, Abu'd-Darda' is the most given to worship of my *ummah* and has the most fearful obedience of them, and Muʿawiyah ibn Abi Sufyan is the most forbearing of my *ummah* and the most liberally generous.'

Our Shaykh al-Khafiji was asked about these distinguishing characteristics and whether they negated the ones previously given and he replied that there was no contradiction.

Those *ayat* which have been revealed in praise of him or in affirmation of him or other matters concerning him

Know that I have seen a book written by one of the scholars on the names of those about whom Qur'an was revealed but it was not accurate or comprehensive, so I composed on that subject a copious, comprehensive and accurate book and I excerpt from it here that which pertains to as-Siddiq, may Allah be pleased with him.

Allah, exalted is He, says, *'The second of the two when the two of them were in the cave, when he said to his companion, "Do not be sad, truly Allah is with us." So Allah sent down His tranquility upon him.'* (Qur'an 9: 40) The Muslims are unanimously agreed that the companion who is mentioned here is Abu Bakr, and there will come a tradition from him on it.

Ibn ᶜAbbas said, about His words, exalted is He, *'Then Allah sent down His tranquility upon him,'* he said, 'upon Abu Bakr. (As for) the Prophet, may Allah bless him and grant him peace, tranquility was always upon him.'

Ibn Masᶜud said that Abu Bakr bought Bilal from Umayyah ibn Khalf and Ubayy ibn Khalf with a cloak and ten pieces of silver (approximately an ounce each), then set him free for the sake of Allah. Then Allah revealed, *'By the night when it covers...'* up to His words, *'... truly your endeavours are different,'* (Qur'an 96: 1-4) meaning the endeavours of Abu Bakr, Umayyah and Ubayy.

ᶜAmir ibn ᶜAbdullah ibn az-Zubayr said: Abu Bakr used to set free (slaves) upon (their acceptance of) Islam, in Makkah. He would set free old women and women generally whenever they accepted Islam. His father said, 'Son, I see you freeing weak people. Why do you not free strong men who would stand with you, protect you and repel (attackers) from you.' He said, 'Father, I wish for that which is with Allah.' He (ᶜAmir) said: Some of my family told me that this *ayah* was revealed about him, *'So as for he who gives and has fearful obedience ...'* (Qur'an 96: 5-21) to its end.

ᶜUrwah said that Abu Bakr as-Siddiq, may Allah be pleased with him, freed seven, each of whom was being tortured for

Allah, and that about him was revealed, *'And the most fearfully obedient will be averted from it (the Fire)...'* (Qur'an 96: 18-21) to the end of the *surah*.

ᶜAbdullah ibn az-Zubayr said: This *ayah, 'And there is not for anyone with him a benefit to be recompensed,'* ('i.e. he does not do good as a recompense for a favour that someone has shown him, rather he does it spontaneously purely for the Face of Allah' *Tafsir* Ibn Juzayy) (Qur'an 96: 19) was revealed about Abu Bakr as-Siddiq, may Allah be pleased with him.

ᶜA'ishah, may Allah be pleased with her, said that Abu Bakr never used to break an oath until Allah revealed the atonement for breaking an oath.

Usayd ibn Safwan who enjoyed companionship (of the Prophet, may Allah bless him and grant him peace) said: ᶜAli said, *'"And the one who came with the truth (al-haqq)"* (Qur'an 39: 33) is Muhammad *"and he affirmed it"* (Ibid) refers to Abu Bakr as-Siddiq.' Ibn ᶜAsakir said: The narration is this way, *'with al-haqq (truth)'* (rather than *as-sidq* [sincerity or truthfulness] the usual reading in Qur'an) and perhaps it was a variant reading of ᶜAli.

Ibn ᶜAbbas spoke about His words, exalted is He, *'And take their counsel in the matter.'* (Qur'an 3: 159) He said, 'It was revealed about Abu Bakr and ᶜUmar.'

Ibn Shawdhab said: *'And for him who fears the standing (before) his Lord there are two gardens,'* (Qur'an 55: 46) was revealed about Abu Bakr, may Allah be pleased with him.

Ibn ᶜUmar and Ibn ᶜAbbas each said about His words, exalted is He, *'And the right-acting of the believers,'* (Qur'an 66: 4) that they were revealed about Abu Bakr and ᶜUmar.

Mujahid said: When *'Truly Allah and His angels send blessings on the Prophet,'* (Qur'an 33: 56) was revealed, Abu Bakr said, 'Messenger of Allah, Allah has not sent down on you good but that we share in it,' and then this *ayah* was revealed, *'He is the One Who sends blessings upon you (the muminun) and His angels (send blessings upon you).'* (Qur'an 33: 43)

ᶜAli ibn al-Hussein said that this *ayah* was revealed about Abu Bakr, ᶜUmar and ᶜAli, *'And We wrest away that which is in their*

breasts of malice, as brothers on couches, facing each other.'
(Qur'an 15: 47)

Ibn ᶜAbbas said: There was revealed about Abu Bakr *'And We have counselled man with good treatment of his parents,'* up to His words, *'the promise of sincerity which they were promised.'* (Qur'an 46: 15-16)

Ibn ᶜUyaynah said: Allah reproached all of the Muslims concerning the Messenger of Allah, may Allah bless him and grant him peace, excepting only Abu Bakr alone, for he was definitely excluded from the reproach. Then he recited, *'If you do not help him then Allah has already helped him when the ones who disbelieve expelled him as the second of two, when they two were in the cave.'* (Qur'an 9: 40).

The *ahadith* related on his merit coupled with ᶜUmar, apart from what has already been mentioned

Abu Hurairah said: I heard the Messenger of Allah say, may Allah bless him and grant him peace, 'While a shepherd was in the middle of his flock, a wolf rushed upon it and carried off from it a sheep and the shepherd pursued it. The wolf turned to him and said, "Who will look after it on the Day of Rising, the day when there will be no other shepherd than me?" And as a man was driving an ox which he had laden it turned to him and said, "I was not created for this, but I was created for tillage,"' and the people said, 'Glory be to Allah, that an ox should talk?' The Prophet, may Allah bless him and grant him peace, said, 'I believe in that and Abu Bakr and ᶜUmar (believe),' and Abu Bakr and ᶜUmar weren't there at that time, i.e. they weren't in the gathering. He bore witness to their belief in that, perhaps meaning the perfection of their belief.

Abu Saᶜid al-Khudri said: The Messenger of Allah, may Allah bless him and grant him peace, said, 'There has been no prophet but that he had two deputies from the people of heaven and two deputies from the people of earth. As for my two deputies from the people of heaven, they are Jibril and Mika'il, and as for my two deputies from the people of earth they are Abu Bakr and ᶜUmar.'

Saᶜid ibn Zaid said: I heard the Messenger of Allah, may Allah bless him and grant him peace, saying, 'Abu Bakr is in the Garden, ᶜUmar is in the Garden, ᶜUthman is in the Garden, ᶜAli is in the Garden, ...' and he mentioned all of the ten (who were promised the Garden).

Abu Saᶜid said: The Messenger of Allah, may Allah bless him and grant him peace, said, 'The ones of the highest ranks, those beneath them will see as you see the stars rising over the horizon of the sky, and Abu Bakr and ᶜUmar are among them.' It is also recorded in *ahadith* of Jabir ibn Samurah and Abu Hurairah.

Anas said that the Messenger of Allah, may Allah bless him and grant him peace, used to come out to his companions of the *Muhajirun* and the *Ansar* while they were sitting, among them Abu Bakr and ᶜUmar, and none of them would lift their eyes to him except for Abu Bakr and ᶜUmar. They used to gaze upon him and he would gaze upon them and they would smile at him and he would smile at them.

Ibn ᶜUmar said that the Messenger of Allah, may Allah bless him and grant him peace, went out one day and entered the mosque, with Abu Bakr and ᶜUmar, one on his right hand side and the other on his left hand side, he holding their hands. He said, 'Like this we will be raised up on the Day of Rising.' It is also recorded from Abu Hurairah.

Ibn ᶜUmar said: The Messenger of Allah, may Allah bless him and grant him peace, said, 'I will be the first over whom the earth will split open, then Abu Bakr and ᶜUmar.'

ᶜAbdullah ibn Hantab said that the Prophet, may Allah bless him and grant him peace, saw Abu Bakr and ᶜUmar and said, 'These two are hearing and sight.' It is also recorded from *hadith* of Ibn ᶜUmar and Ibn ᶜAmr.

Abu Arwa ad-Dawsi said: I was with the Prophet, may Allah bless him and grant him peace, (seated) and then Abu Bakr and ᶜUmar came up, so he said, 'Praise belongs to Allah Who has helped me through you two.' It has been transmitted also in a *hadith* of al-Bara' ibn ᶜAzib.

ᶜAmmar ibn Yasir said: The Messenger of Allah, may Allah bless him and grant him peace, said, 'Oh Jibril, tell me of the merits of ᶜUmar ibn al-Khattab.' He said, 'Even if I were to tell you his merits for the length of time that Nuh remained among his people the merits of ᶜUmar would not be exhausted, and truly ᶜUmar is one of the good actions of Abu Bakr.'

ᶜAbd ar-Rahman ibn Ghanam said that the Messenger of Allah, may Allah bless him and grant him peace, said to Abu Bakr and ᶜUmar, 'If you two were to agree on a counsel I would not oppose you.' It is also recorded from a *hadith* of al-Bara' ibn ᶜAzib.

Ibn ᶜUmar was asked, 'Who used to give *fatwa* in the time of the Messenger of Allah, may Allah bless him and grant him peace?' He said, 'Abu Bakr and ᶜUmar and I know of no others apart from them.' Al-Qasim ibn Muhammad said: Abu Bakr, ᶜUmar, ᶜUthman and ᶜAli used to give *fatwa* in the time of the Messenger of Allah, may Allah bless him and grant him peace.

Ibn Masᶜud, may Allah be pleased with him, said that the Messenger of Allah, may Allah bless him and grant him peace, said, 'Truly, every prophet has an elect from his *ummah* and my elect from my *ummah* are Abu Bakr and ᶜUmar.'

ᶜAli said: The Messenger of Allah, may Allah bless him and grant him peace, said, 'May Allah show mercy to Abu Bakr. He wed me his daughter, and he carried me to the abode of the *Hijrah*, and he set Bilal free. May Allah show mercy to ᶜUmar. He says the truth even if it is bitter. The truth has left him without a friend. May Allah show mercy to ᶜUthman. The angels are shy of him. May Allah show mercy to ᶜAli. O Allah, make the truth turn with him wherever he turns.'

Sahl, may Allah be pleased with him, said: When the Prophet, may Allah bless him and grant him peace, came back from the Farewell Hajj he ascended the *mimbar* and praised Allah, then said, 'People, Abu Bakr has never harmed me, so know that about him. People, I am pleased with him, and with ᶜUmar, ᶜUthman, ᶜAli, Talhah, az-Zubayr, Saᶜd, ᶜAbd ar-Rahman ibn ᶜAuf, and the first emigrants (*muhajirun*), so know that of them.'

Ibn Abi Hazim said: A man came to ᶜAli ibn al-Hussein and said, 'What was the position of Abu Bakr and ᶜUmar with the Messenger of Allah, may Allah bless him and grant him peace?' He said, 'Just like their position with respect to him this very hour.' (They are buried right beside the Prophet, may Allah bless him and grant him peace).

Bistam ibn Muslim said: The Messenger of Allah, may Allah bless him and grant him peace, said to Abu Bakr and ᶜUmar, 'No-one shall have command over you after me.'

Anas related, as a *marfuᶜ hadith*, 'Love of Abu Bakr and ᶜUmar is *iman* (belief) and hatred of them is *kufr* (disbelief).'

Ibn Masᶜud said: Love of Abu Bakr and ᶜUmar and a knowledge of them is (a part) of the *Sunnah*.

Anas related as a *marfuᶜ*, 'I hope for my *ummah* in their love for Abu Bakr and ᶜUmar what I hope for them in the saying, "No god but Allah."'

The *ahadith* related on his merit alone apart from what has already been mentioned

Abu Hurairah said: I heard the Messenger of Allah saying, 'Whoever spends two of a pair of anything in the way of Allah will be called from one of the doors of the Garden, "Slave of Allah, this is good." Whoever was one of the people of prayer will be called from the door of prayer, whoever was one of the people of *jihad* will be called from the door of *jihad*, whoever was one of the people of *sadaqah* will be called from the door of *sadaqah*, and whoever was one of the people of fasting will be called from the door of fasting.' Abu Bakr said, 'There will not be any need left with one who is called from these doors. Will anyone be called from them all, Messenger of Allah?' He said, 'Yes, and I hope that you are one of them, Abu Bakr.'

Abu Hurairah, may Allah be pleased with him, said: The Messenger of Allah, may Allah bless him and grant him peace, said, 'As for you, Abu Bakr, you will be the first of my *ummah* to enter the Garden.'

Abu Saᶜid, may Allah be pleased with him, said: The Messenger of Allah, may Allah bless him and grant him peace, said,

'Truly, one of the most generous people to me, with his company and his property, is Abu Bakr, and if I were to take an intimate friend apart from my Lord I would have taken Abu Bakr as an intimate friend, but there is the brotherhood of Islam.' This *hadith* has been narrated by transmissions from Ibn ᶜAbbas, Ibn az-Zubayr, ibn Masᶜud, Jundub ibn ᶜAbdullah, al-Bara', Kaᶜb ibn Malik, Jabir ibn ᶜAbdullah, Anas, Abu'l-Waqid al-Laythi, Abu'l-Maᶜalli, ᶜA'ishah, Abu Hurairah, and Ibn ᶜUmar, may Allah be pleased with all of them, and their paths of transmission have been enumerated in *ahadith* which are *mutawatir* (narrated by a number of Companions to large numbers of others).

Abu'd-Darda' said: I was sitting with the Prophet, may Allah bless him and grant him peace, when Abu Bakr came up and greeted and said, 'There was something between me and ᶜUmar ibn al-Khattab, and I was hasty with him, then later I regretted and I asked him to forgive me, but he refused, so I have come to you.' He said, 'May Allah forgive you, Abu Bakr,' three times. Later, ᶜUmar relented and went to the house of Abu Bakr but did not find him. He came to the Prophet, may Allah bless him and grant him peace. The face of the Prophet, may Allah bless him and grant him peace, became flushed until Abu Bakr grew afraid and fell down on his knees saying, 'Messenger of Allah, by Allah, I was more in the wrong than him,' twice. The Prophet, may Allah bless him and grant him peace, said, 'Truly, Allah sent me to you and you said, "You lie," and Abu Bakr said, "You have told the truth," and he shared himself and his wealth with me. Will you leave me my companion?' saying this last twice. He was not caused any hurt after that. Ibn ᶜUmar, may Allah be pleased with him, related the like of it, in which he said: Then the Messenger of Allah, may Allah bless him and grant him peace, said, 'Do not cause me hurt in my companion, for Allah sent me with guidance and the life-transaction of the Truth. You said, "You lie!" and Abu Bakr said, "You have told the truth." If it was not that Allah named him a "companion" I would have taken him as an intimate friend. But there is the brotherhood of Islam.'

Al-Miqdam said that: ᶜAqil ibn Abi Talib and Abu Bakr insulted each other. Abu Bakr was a genealogist, except that he refrained because of his (ᶜAqil's) kinship to the Prophet, may Allah bless him and grant him peace, and turned away from him. He complained to the Prophet, may Allah bless him and grant him peace. Then the Prophet, may Allah bless him and grant him peace, stood among the people and said, 'Will you not leave me my companion? What is your business compared to his business? For, by Allah, there is not one man of you but that upon the door of his house there is a darkness, except for the door of Abu Bakr, for upon his door there is light. By Allah, you said, "You lie!" and Abu Bakr said, "You have told the truth!" and you withheld your wealth and he was liberal to me with his wealth, and you abandoned me and he shared with me and followed me.'

Ibn ᶜUmar, may Allah be pleased with both of them, said: The Messenger of Allah, may Allah bless him and grant him peace, said, 'Whoever trails his robe haughtily, Allah will not look upon him on the Day of Rising.' So Abu Bakr said, 'One of the two sides of my robe hangs loosely unless I repeatedly correct that.' The Messenger of Allah, may Allah bless him and grant him peace, said, 'You don't do it out of haughtiness.'

Abu Hurairah, may Allah be pleased with him, said: The Messenger of Allah, may Allah bless and grant him and his family peace, said, 'Who of you has started today fasting?' Abu Bakr said, 'I did.' Then he said, 'Who of you has followed a funeral cortege?' Abu Bakr said, 'I have.' He said, 'Who of you has fed a bereft person today?' Abu Bakr said, 'I have.' He said, 'Who of you has visited a sick person today?' Abu Bakr said, 'I have.' The Messenger of Allah, may Allah bless him and grant him peace, said, 'They are not gathered together in a man but that he will enter the Garden.' This *hadith* has been transmitted in narrations of Anas ibn Malik and ᶜAbd ar-Rahman ibn Abi Bakr. In the *hadith* of Anas, at the end of it there is, 'The Garden has become obligatory for you.' In the *hadith* of ᶜAbd ar-Rahman, its wording is: The Messenger of Allah, may Allah bless him and grant him peace, performed the dawn prayer, then turned his face to his companions and said, 'Who of you has started today fasting?' So ᶜUmar said, 'Messenger of Allah, I did not decide to fast yester-day, so I have not begun today fasting.' Abu Bakr said, 'But I did decide to fast yesterday so I have begun today fasting.' He said, 'Has anyone of you today visited a sick person?' So ᶜUmar said, 'Messenger of Allah, we haven't left (the mosque after the dawn prayer) yet. How could we have visited a sick person?' Abu Bakr said, 'It reached me that my brother ᶜAbd ar-Rahman ibn ᶜAuf is complaining (of an illness) so I made my way to him to see how he is this morning.' He said, 'Has anyone of you fed a bereft person today?' ᶜUmar said, 'Messenger of Allah, we haven't left yet.' Abu Bakr said, 'I entered the mosque and there was a beg-gar, then I found a piece of barley bread in ᶜAbd ar-Rahman's (his son's) hand, so I took it and gave it to him.' Then he said, 'You! So rejoice in the Garden.' Then he said a word which pleased ᶜUmar, and he (ᶜUmar) claimed that he had never meant to do a good action but that Abu Bakr had preceded him to it.

Ibn Masᶜud, may Allah be pleased with him, said: I was in the mosque praying and the Messenger of Allah, may Allah bless him and grant him peace, entered, with him Abu Bakr and ᶜUmar. He found me making supplication and said, 'Ask and you will be given it.' Then he said, 'Whoever loves to recite the Qur'an freshly, then let him recite with the recitation of Ibn Umm ᶜAbd (an affectionate name for Ibn Masᶜud).' I returned to my house and Abu Bakr came to me to give me the good news (of what the Prophet, may Allah bless him and grant him peace, had said). Then ᶜUmar came and found Abu Bakr coming out having beaten him to it, so he said, 'Truly, you always outdo with good.'

Rabiᶜah al-Aslami, may Allah be pleased with him, said: There were some words between me and Abu Bakr, and he said to me something I disliked, and then he regretted it and said to me, 'Rabiᶜah repeat the like of it back to me so that it can be retalia-tion.' I said, 'I will not do it.' Abu Bakr said, 'You must say it or I will appeal to the Messenger of Allah, may Allah bless him and grant him peace, for help against you.' I said, 'I am not going to do it.' So Abu Bakr, may Allah be pleased with him, went off to the Prophet, may Allah bless him and grant him peace, and I went off following him. Some people from Aslam came and said to me, 'May Allah show mercy to Abu Bakr. For what reason is he appealing to the Messenger of Allah, may Allah bless him and grant him peace, for help against you and he was the one who said to you what he said?' So I said, 'Do you grasp who this is? This is Abu Bakr as-Siddiq. This is the "*second of the two*" (Qur'an 9: 40), and this is the white-haired one of the Muslims. Beware that he should turn and see you supporting me against him and so become angry, then come to the Messenger of Allah, may Allah bless him and grant him peace, who will become angry because of his anger, and then Allah will become angry, because of their anger and Rabi^cah will be destroyed.' They said, 'What do you tell us to do?' He said, 'Go back.' Abu Bakr, may Allah be pleased with him, went and I alone followed him, until he came to the Messenger of Allah, may Allah bless him and grant him peace, and told him the story just as it was. He raised his head to me and said, 'Rabi^cah, what is it with you and as-Siddiq?' So I said, 'Messenger of Allah such and such happened, and he said to me a word which I disliked, and then he said to me, "Say as I said so that it will be retaliation," and I refused.' Then the Messenger of Allah, may Allah bless him and grant him peace, 'Right! Do not repeat it back to him, but rather say, "Allah has forgiven you, Abu Bakr."' So I said to him, 'May Allah forgive you, Abu Bakr.' (Al-Hasan said: So Abu Bakr, may Allah be pleased with him, turned away and he was weeping).

Ibn ^cUmar, may Allah be pleased with both of them, said that the Messenger of Allah, may Allah bless him and grant him peace, said to Abu Bakr, 'You are my companion at the *hawd* (Pool) and my companion in the cave.'

Ibn ^cAbbas, may Allah be pleased with him, said: The Messenger of Allah, may Allah bless him and grant him peace, said, 'Abu Bakr was my companion and my solace in the cave.'

Hudhayfah, may Allah be pleased with him, said: The Messenger of Allah, may Allah bless him and grant him peace, said, 'There are in the Garden birds the likes of Bactrian camels.' Abu Bakr, 'Truly, they must be blessed, Messenger of Allah.' He said,

'More blessed than them is whoever eats them, and you are one of those who will eat them.' This *hadith* has been narrated in a transmission of Anas.

Abu Hurairah, may Allah be pleased with him, said: The Messenger of Allah, may Allah bless him and grant him peace, said, 'I was made to ascend to heaven. I did not pass by a heaven but I found in it my name, "Muhammad is the Messenger of Allah and Abu Bakr as-Siddiq is his successor."' Its *isnad* is weak but it has been narrated also in *hadith* of Ibn ᶜAbbas, Ibn ᶜUmar, Anas, Abu Saᶜid, and Abu'd-Darda', may Allah be pleased with all of them, with weak *isnads*, yet which support and strengthen each other.

Saᶜid ibn Jubayr, may Allah be pleased with him, said: I recited in the presence of the Prophet, may Allah bless him and grant him peace, *'O you self made tranquil!'* (Qur'an 89: 28-30) and Abu Bakr said, 'Messenger of Allah, this is beautiful.' So the Messenger of Allah, may Allah bless him and grant him peace, said, 'Certainly the angel will say it to you at the time of death.'

ᶜAmir ibn ᶜAbdullah ibn az-Zubayr, may Allah be pleased with him, said: When, *'And if we had decreed for them, "Kill yourselves!"'* (Qur'an 4: 66) to the end of the *ayah* was revealed, Abu Bakr said, 'Messenger of Allah, if you had ordered me to kill myself I would have done it.' He said, 'You have told the truth.'

Ibn Abi Mulaykah said: The Messenger of Allah, may Allah bless him and grant him peace, and his companions entered a pool and he said, 'Let every man swim to his companion.' He said: So every man swam until there only remained the Messenger of Allah, may Allah bless him and grant him peace, and Abu Bakr. So the Messenger of Allah, may Allah bless him and grant him peace, swam to Abu Bakr until he embraced him, and said, 'If I were to take an intimate friend until I meet Allah I would have taken Abu Bakr as an intimate friend, but he is my companion.' It is recorded also, connected back through Ibn ᶜAbbas.

Sulayman ibn Yasar said: The Messenger of Allah, may Allah bless him and grant him peace, said, 'The qualities of good are three hundred and sixty qualities. Whenever Allah wishes good for a slave He puts in him one of those qualities by which he enters the Garden.' Abu Bakr said, 'Messenger of Allah, is there in me anything of them?' He said, 'Yes, a summing of them all.'

Sadaqah al-Qurashi related from a man that he said: The Messenger of Allah, may Allah bless him and grant him peace, said, 'The qualities of good are three hundred and sixty.' So Abu Bakr said, 'Messenger of Allah, do I have anything of them?' He said, 'All of them are in you, so therefore joy to you, Abu Bakr.'

Mujammaᶜ ibn Yaᶜqub al-Ansari related from his father that he said: The circle of the Prophet, may Allah bless him and grant him peace, was numerous and tightly gathered together until it became like walls. Abu Bakr's seat would be empty, and no-one of the people would aspire to it. When Abu Bakr came he would sit in that spot, and the Prophet, may Allah bless him and grant him peace, would turn his face to him, and direct his discourse to him, and people would listen.

Anas, may Allah be pleased with him, said: The Prophet, may Allah bless him and grant him peace, said, 'Love of Abu Bakr and gratitude to him are a duty on everyone of my *ummah*.' The like of it is in a *hadith* of Sahl ibn Saᶜd.

ᶜA'ishah, may Allah be pleased with her, in a *hadith* which is *marfuᶜ*, said: People, all of them, will be taken to account except for Abu Bakr.

That which has been related from the Companions and the right-acting early generations on his merit

Jabir, may Allah be pleased with him, said: ᶜUmar ibn al-Khattab said, 'Abu Bakr is our lord (*sayyid*).'

ᶜUmar, may Allah be pleased with him, said, 'If the *iman* of Abu Bakr were to be weighed against the *iman* of the inhabitants of the Earth, he would outweigh them.'

ᶜUmar, may Allah be pleased with him, said, 'Abu Bakr was a surpassing outstripper.' And ᶜUmar said, 'I would that I were a hair upon the chest of Abu Bakr.' And he said, 'I would love to be in the Garden in such a position that I could see Abu Bakr.'

And he said, 'Certainly the scent of Abu Bakr was sweeter than the scent of musk.'

ᶜAli entered upon Abu Bakr when he was shrouded and said, 'No-one who will meet Allah with his pages (of the records of his deeds) is more beloved to me than this shrouded one.'

ᶜAbd ar-Rahman ibn Abi Bakr as-Siddiq said: The Prophet, may Allah bless him and grant him peace, said, 'ᶜUmar ibn al-Khattab told me that he never attempted to be before Abu Bakr in a good action but that Abu Bakr was before him in it.'

ᶜAli said: By the One in Whose hand is my self, we never strove to be first in a good action but that Abu Bakr was before us in it.

ᶜAli said: The best of mankind after the Messenger of Allah, may Allah bless him and grant him peace, are Abu Bakr and ᶜUmar. Love of me will never be united with hatred of Abu Bakr and ᶜUmar in the heart of a believer.

Ibn ᶜUmar said: Three of Quraysh are the most handsome faced of Quraysh and the best of them in character, and the surest hearted of them. If they were to tell you something they would not lie to you. If you told them something they would not call you a liar; Abu Bakr as-Siddiq, Abu ᶜUbaydah ibn al-Jarrah and ᶜUthman ibn ᶜAffan.

Ibrahim an-Nakhaᶜi said: Abu Bakr was named, '*Al-Awwah* – Compassionate (literally: one saying "Ah" and sighing a great deal for pity for people),' because of his pity and his mercy.

Ar-Rabiᶜ ibn Anas said: It is recorded in the First Book, 'The likeness of Abu Bakr as-Siddiq is the likeness of rain, wherever it falls it is of benefit.'

Ar-Rabiᶜ ibn Anas said: We considered the companions of the prophets and we couldn't find a prophet who had a companion the like of Abu Bakr as-Siddiq. Az-Zuhri said: One of the merits of Abu Bakr is that he never doubted about Allah for an hour.

Az-Zubayr ibn Bakkar said: I heard one of the people of knowledge saying, 'The orators (who gave the *khutbah*) among the companions of the Messenger of Allah, may Allah bless him and grant him peace, were Abu Bakr as-Siddiq and ᶜAli ibn Abi Talib, may Allah be pleased with both of them.'

Abu Husayn said: There was not born to Adam among his descendants anyone better than Abu Bakr, after the prophets and messengers. Abu Bakr took a stand on the Day of *ar-Riddah* (repudiation of Islam by many of the Arab tribes on the death of the Prophet, may Allah bless him and grant him peace) which was like the stand of one of the prophets.

Section

Ash-Sha‘bi said: Allah singled out Abu Bakr with four qualities with which he did not single out any other person: He named him as-Siddiq and named no-one apart from him as-Siddiq; and he was the Companion of the Cave along with the Messenger of Allah, may Allah bless him and grant him peace; his close companion on the *Hijrah;* and the Messenger of Allah, may Allah bless him and grant him peace, ordered him to lead the prayer while the Muslims were witnesses to that.

Ja‘far said: Abu Bakr used to listen to the intimate conversation of Jibril with the Prophet, may Allah bless him and grant him peace, without seeing him.

Ibn al-Musayyab said: Abu Bakr was, in relation to the Prophet, may Allah bless him and grant him peace, in the position of a deputy and he would take his counsel in all his affairs. He was his second in Islam, and his second in the Cave, his second in the shelter on the Day of Badr, and his second in the grave. The Messenger of Allah, may Allah bless him and grant him peace, would not prefer anyone over him.

The *ahadith* and *ayat* which indicate his *khilafah,* and the words of the *imams* on that

Hudhayfah, may Allah be pleased with him, said: The Messenger of Allah, may Allah bless him and grant him peace, said, 'Follow the lead of the two who come after me, Abu Bakr and ‘Umar.' It is also recorded in a *hadith* of Ibn Mas‘ud, may Allah be pleased with him.

ᶜAbdullah ibn ᶜUmar, may Allah be pleased with him, said: I heard the Messenger of Allah, may Allah bless him and grant him peace, saying, 'There will be twelve *khalifahs* after me; Abu Bakr will not last except for a little.' There is unanimous agreement on the authenticity of the first part of this *hadith*, as it is narrated by many different paths. Its explanation has been given earlier in the introduction of the book. In the two *Sahih* books in the preceding *hadith* there is that he, may Allah bless him and grant him peace, when he gave a *khutbah* close to his death, said, 'There is a slave whom Allah has given a choice ...' and in the end of which there is, 'And let not a door remain but that it is closed except for the door of Abu Bakr.' And in a wording of the two of them (al-Bukhari and Muslim), 'Let there not remain in the mosque a passageway except the passageway of Abu Bakr.' The men of knowledge say, 'This is an indication of the *khilafah* because he would go out by it (the door and passageway) to take the lead in the prayer for the Muslims.' This has been narrated of a *hadith* of Anas, may Allah be pleased with him, and its wording is, 'Close these doors which open into the mosque except for the door of Abu Bakr.' And it is recorded in *hadith* of ᶜA'ishah, may Allah be pleased with her, Ibn ᶜAbbas, Muᶜawiyah ibn Abi Sufyan, and Anas.

Jubayr ibn Mutᶜim, may Allah be pleased with him, related from his father that he said: A woman came to the Prophet, may Allah bless him and grant him peace, and he told her to come back to him later. She said, 'What do you think if I come and don't find you?' as if she were saying, 'Death.' He said, 'If you don't find me then come to Abu Bakr.'

Anas, may Allah be pleased with him, said: Banu Mustaliq sent me to the Messenger of Allah, may Allah bless him and grant him peace, (saying), 'Ask him, "To whom should we pay our *sadaqat* (*zakah*) after you?"' So I came to him and asked him and he said, 'To Abu Bakr.'

Ibn ᶜAbbas, may Allah be pleased with both of them, said: A woman came to the Prophet, may Allah bless him and grant him peace, to ask him about something. He said to her, 'Return (another time).' She said, 'Messenger of Allah, if I return and I don't find you?' (referring to his death). He said, 'If you come and don't find me, then come to Abu Bakr, for he is the *khalifah* after me.'

ʿA'ishah, may Allah be pleased with her, said: The Messenger of Allah, may Allah bless him and grant him peace, said to her, 'Call your father (Abu Bakr) and your brother so that I can write something, for I fear that some desirous person will covet, and someone will say, "I am more worthy," and Allah and the believers refuse all except Abu Bakr.'

ʿA'ishah also said: The Prophet, may Allah bless him and grant him peace, said to me in his sickness in which he died, 'Call ʿAbd ar-Rahman ibn Abi Bakr and I will write a testament for Abu Bakr so that no-one will disagree about him after me.' Then later he said, 'Leave it. I seek refuge with Allah that the believers should disagree about Abu Bakr.'

ʿA'ishah, may Allah be pleased with her, was asked, 'Who would the Prophet, may Allah bless him and grant him peace, have left as *khalifah* if he had left a *khalifah?'* She said, 'Abu Bakr.' It was said to her, 'Then who after Abu Bakr?' She said, 'ʿUmar.' It was said to her, 'Who after ʿUmar?' She said, 'Abu ʿUbaydah ibn al-Jarrah.'

Abu Musa al-Ashʿari, may Allah be pleased with him, said: The Prophet, may Allah bless him and grant him peace, became ill and his illness became severe. So he said, 'Command Abu Bakr and let him lead the people in prayer.' ʿA'ishah said, 'Messenger of Allah, he is a man who has a tender heart. If he stands in your place he will not be able to lead the people in prayer.' He said, 'Command Abu Bakr and let him lead the people in prayer.' She repeated what she had said and so he said, 'Command Abu Bakr and let him lead the people in prayer; truly you are the female companions of Yusuf.' So the messenger came to him (Abu Bakr) and he led the people in prayer in the lifetime of the Prophet, may Allah bless him and grant him peace. In some of the versions of the *hadith* of ʿA'ishah, may Allah be pleased with her, she said, 'I persisted in that with the Messenger of Allah, may Allah bless him and grant him peace. All that carried me to do that was it did not occur to me in my heart that people could ever love a man who stood in his position after him. It was only that I was of the view that never would anyone stand in his position but that people would take a bad omen from it, and so I wished that the Messenger of Allah, may Allah bless him and grant him peace, might turn from Abu Bakr.'

Ibn Zamᶜah, may Allah be pleased with him, said that the Prophet, may Allah bless him and grant him peace, ordered them to perform the prayer and Abu Bakr was not there, so that ᶜUmar stepped forward and he prayed (as *imam*). The Prophet, may Allah bless him and grant him peace, said, 'No! No! No! Allah and the Muslims refuse any but Abu Bakr. Let Abu Bakr lead the people in prayer.'

Ibn ᶜUmar said: ᶜUmar said, 'Allahu Akbar.' The Prophet, may Allah bless him and grant him peace, heard his 'Allahu Akbar', raised his head in anger and said, 'Where is Ibn Abi Quhafah?'

The men of knowledge say: In this *hadith* there is the clearest of proofs that as-Siddiq was absolutely the best of the Companions, and the one having most right to the *khilafah*, and the most worthy of them for leadership.

Al-Ashᶜari said: It is known of necessity that the Prophet, may Allah bless him and grant him peace, ordered as-Siddiq that he should lead the people in prayer in the presence of the *Muhajirun* and the *Ansar*. Along with his saying, 'He must lead the people who is the best read of them in the Book of Allah,' it proves that he (Abu Bakr) was the best read of them, i.e. the most knowledgeable of them in the Qur'an.

The Companions themselves sought to prove by this that he was the one with the most right to the *khilafah*, among them ᶜUmar – and his words will follow in the section on the act of pledging allegiance – and among them ᶜAli.

ᶜAli said: Truly the Prophet ordered Abu Bakr to lead the people in prayer and indeed I was present, and I was not absent and was not ill; and we were pleased for our wordly affairs with the one the Prophet, may Allah bless him and grant him peace, was pleased with for our *deen*.

The men of knowledge say that Abu Bakr was recognised for his fitness for the *imamah* during the time of the Prophet, may Allah bless him and grant him peace.

Sahl ibn Sa^cd said: There was fighting among Bani ^cAmr ibn ^cAuf and it reached the Prophet, may Allah bless him and grant him peace, so he came to them after the mid-day prayer in order to make peace between them. He said to Bilal, 'If it is the time of the prayer, and I don't come, then order Abu Bakr to lead the people in prayer.' When it was time for the afternoon prayer Bilal announced the prayer (with the *iqamah*) and then ordered Abu Bakr, so he led the prayer.

Hafsah, may Allah be pleased with her, said to the Prophet, may Allah bless him and grant him peace, 'When you were ill you gave precedence to Abu Bakr.' He said, 'I am not the one who gives precedence to him, but it is Allah Who gives him precedence.'

^cAli, may Allah be pleased with him, said: The Prophet, may Allah bless him and grant him peace, said to me, 'I asked Allah to give precedence to you three times, but He refused me, save to give precedence to Abu Bakr.'

Al-Hasan said: Abu Bakr said, 'Messenger of Allah, I still see myself (in dream) treading in people's courtyards.' He said, 'You will be, of men, a way (*sabeel*).' He said, 'And I saw on my breast something like two small dark marks.' He said, 'Two years.'

Abu Bakrah said: I came to ^cUmar, and there were people with him eating. He threw a look among the hindmost of the people to a man and said, 'What do you find in what you read of the books from before you?' He said, 'The *khalifah* of the Prophet, may Allah bless him and grant him peace, is his Siddiq.'

Muhammad ibn az-Zubayr said: ^cUmar ibn ^cAbd al-^cAziz sent me to al-Hasan al-Basri to ask him some things. So I came to him and said, 'Satisfy me regarding that which people disagree about. Did the Prophet, may Allah bless him and grant him peace, appoint Abu Bakr as *khalifah*?' So al-Hasan who was seated drew himself up and said, 'Is it in any doubt? You have no father (a proverbial Arabic expression)! By Allah, the One Whom there is no god but Him, he definitely appointed him as *khalifah*. He was certainly more knowing of Allah, and more fearfully obedient of Him, and more strongly fearful of Him than that he should die upon it without making him take the command.'

Abu Bakr ibn ʿAyyash said: Ar-Rashid said to me, 'Abu Bakr, how did the people appoint Abu Bakr as *khalifah*?' I said, 'Amir al-Muminin, Allah was silent, and His Messenger was silent and the *muminun* were silent.' He said, 'By Allah, you have only increased me in confusion.' He said, 'Amir al-Muminin, the Prophet, may Allah bless him and grant him peace, was sick for eight days and Bilal entered upon him and said, "Messenger of Allah, who should lead the people in prayer?" He said, "Order Abu Bakr to lead the people in prayer." So Abu Bakr led the people in prayer for eight days while the revelation was still descending. So the Messenger of Allah, may Allah bless him and grant him peace, was silent because of the silence of Allah, and the *muminun* were silent because of the silence of the Messenger of Allah, may Allah bless him and grant him peace.' So he (Ibn ʿAyyash) astonished him (ar-Rashid), and he said, 'May Allah bless you.'

A group of the men of knowledge deduced the *khilafah* of as-Siddiq from *ayat* of the Qur'an. Al-Hasan al-Basri said, concerning His words, exalted is He, *'O you who believe, whoever of you reneges on his deen then Allah will bring a people whom He loves and who love Him, ...'* (Qur'an 5: 54) – 'It means Abu Bakr and his companions, for, when the Arabs reneged on their Islam, Abu Bakr and his companions waged *jihad* against them until they made them return to Islam.'

Qatadah said, 'When the Prophet, may Allah bless him and grant him peace, died, the Arabs reneged (on their Islam).' Then he mentioned Abu Bakr's fighting them until he said, 'We used to say that this *ayah* was revealed about Abu Bakr and his companions, *"Then Allah will bring a people whom He loves and who love Him."* (Qur'an 5: 54)'

Juwaybir said, concerning His words, exalted is He, *'Say to those who were left behind of the desert Arabs, "You will be called to (fight) a people of great power ..."* (Qur'an 48: 16) 'They were Banu Hanifah.' Ibn Abi Hatim and Ibn Qutaybah said, 'This *ayah* is a proof of the *khilafah* of as-Siddiq, because he was the one who called people to fight them.'

The Shaykh Abu'l-Hasan al-Ash°ari said: I heard Abu'l-°Abbas ibn Shurayh saying, 'The *khilafah* of as-Siddiq is in the Qur'an in this *ayah* (above).' He said, 'Because the people of knowledge unanimously agree that there was not, after its revelation, any fight which they were called to except for Abu Bakr's calling them, and the people, to fight those who reneged (on their Islam) and refused the *zakah*.' He said, 'That indicates the necessity of the *khilafah* of Abu Bakr and the obligation of obedience to him, since Allah informs us that the one who turns away from that will be punished painfully.' Ibn Kathir said: And whoever explains the '*people of great power*' as being the Persians and the Byzantines then as-Siddiq is the one who equipped and prepared the armies to go against them, and the completion of their affair was left to °Umar and °Uthman who are two branches of as-Siddiq. And Allah, exalted is He, says, '*Allah has promised the ones who believe and do right actions that He will definitely appoint them as khulafa' in the land, ...*' (Qur'an 24: 55) up to the conclusion of the *ayah*. This *ayah* fits the *khilafah* of as-Siddiq.

°Abd ar-Rahman ibn °Abd al-Hamid al-Mahdi said: The granting of authority to Abu Bakr and °Umar is in the Book of Allah. Allah, exalted is He, says, '*Allah has promised the ones who believe and do right actions that He will definitely appoint them as khulafa' in the land, ...*' up to the conclusion of the *ayah*.

Abu Bakr ibn °Ayyash said: Abu Bakr as-Siddiq is the *khalifah* of the Messenger of Allah, may Allah bless him and grant him peace, in the Qur'an, because Allah, exalted is He, says, '*For the poor emigrants who were expelled from their homes and their properties seeking bounty from Allah and contentment, and they help Allah and His Messenger. Those they are the truthful.*' (Qur'an 59: 8). The ones Allah named '*truthful*' are not liars, and they said, '*Khalifah* of the Messenger of Allah.' Ibn Kathir said: A good deduction.

Ash-Shafi°i said: People are unanimously agreed on the *khilafah* of Abu Bakr as-Siddiq. That is because people were hard pressed after the Messenger of Allah, may Allah bless him and grant him peace, but they did not find under the expanse of the sky one better than Abu Bakr, so they gave him authority over them.

Mu°awiyah ibn Qurrah said: The Companions of the Messenger of Allah, may Allah bless him and grant him peace, never doubted that Abu Bakr was the *khalifah* of the Messenger of Allah, may Allah bless him and grant him peace, and they would not call him anything but the *khalifah* of the Messenger of Allah, may Allah bless him and grant him peace, and they never agreed unanimously on a mistake or a misguidance.

Ibn Mas°ud, may Allah be pleased with him, said: What the Muslims view as good is with Allah good. And what the Muslims view as bad is with Allah bad. The Companions all held the view that they should appoint Abu Bakr as the *khalifah*.

Murrah at-Tayyib said: Abu Sufyan ibn Harb came to °Ali and said, 'What is it with this authority that it is among the very least of Quraysh and the humblest of them?' meaning Abu Bakr, 'By Allah, if I had wished I would have filled it against him with horses and men.' He said that °Ali said, 'How long you have been at enmity with Islam and its people, Abu Sufyan, and that did not hurt it at all. We found Abu Bakr worthy of it (the *khilafah*).'

The oath of allegiance to him

°Umar ibn al-Khattab, may Allah be pleased with him, addressed the people upon his return from the Hajj and said in his *khutbah*: It has reached me that so-and-so of you said, 'If °Umar were to die I would pledge allegiance to so-and-so.' Let no man deceive himself by saying, 'The pledge of allegiance to Abu Bakr was made suddenly and unexpectedly.' It was like that but Allah protected (us) from the evil of it. There is not among you today one, behind whom the necks of competitors stop short (an Arabic expression) like Abu Bakr. He was one of the best of us when the Messenger of Allah, may Allah bless him and grant him peace, died. °Ali and az-Zubayr and those with them stayed back in the house of Fatimah. The *Ansar* all stayed away from us in the roofed gallery of Bani Saʿidah. The *Muhajirun* gathered around Abu Bakr, so I said to him, 'Abu Bakr, let us be off to our brethren, the *Ansar.*' So we went off until two good men met us and mentioned to us what the people had done. They said, 'Where do you intend (going) *Muhajirun*?' I said, 'We want our brethren the *Ansar.*' They said, 'You must not approach them, but decide your own affair, *Muhajirun.*' I said, 'By Allah, we will go to them.' We went on until we came to them in the roofed gallery of Bani Saʿidah and there they were all gathered, and right in the middle of them a man all muffled up. I said, 'Who is this?' They said, 'Saʿd ibn ʿUbadah.' I said, What is wrong with him?' They said, 'He is in pain.' When we sat down, their speaker stood, praised Allah as He is worthy and said, 'And now, we are the *Ansar* of Allah, and the battalion of Islam and you, *Muhajirun*, are a handful of us, and a party of you have come at a leisurely pace wishing to uproot us and exclude us from the command.' When he became silent I wanted to speak. I had prepared a speech that pleased me and which I wanted to deliver in the presence of Abu Bakr. I used to fear in him a lack of incisiveness and he was milder, more forbearing than me and more dignified. Then Abu Bakr said, 'Gently.' I disliked to anger him, and he was more knowledgeable than me. By Allah, he did not leave a word that had pleased me in my prepared speech but that he said it in his spontaneous talk, the like of it and better than it until he was silent. He said, 'Now, as for that good which you have mentioned about yourselves, you are worthy of it, but the Arabs will never recognise this command except among this section of Quraysh. They are the midmost (noblest) of the Arabs by descent and by tribe, and I am contented for you with either of these two men, (so pledge allegiance to) whichever of them you wish.' He took hold of my hand and the hand of Abu ʿUbaydah ibn al-Jarrah (and he was seated between us) and I disliked nothing he had said apart from that. It was, by Allah, such that if I were to be put forward and my head struck off, that not approaching me because of any guilt, it would have been more beloved to me than that I should assume command over a people among whom was Abu Bakr. Then a speaker from them said, 'I am of those by means of whose counsel people seek relief and one having a family that will aid and defend me (literally, 'I am their much-rubbed little rubbing post and their honoured little palm-tree'). Let there be from us an *amir* and from you an *amir,* Quraysh.' Then the confusion increased and voices were raised until I became afraid of dissension, so I said, 'Stretch out your hand, Abu Bakr,' and he stretched out his hand and I swore allegiance to him, the *Muhajirun* swore allegiance to him, then the *Ansar* swore allegiance to him. By Allah, we did not find in that for which we assembled a matter more fitting than the pledge of allegiance to Abu Bakr. We feared that if we separated from the people and there was no pledge of allegiance that they would conclude a pledge of allegiance after we had gone, and we would have to pledge allegiance on a basis which we were not pleased with, or we would have to oppose them so that there would be strife over that.

Ibn Mas'ud said: When the Messenger of Allah, may Allah bless him and grant him peace, was taken, the *Ansar* said, 'Let there be from us an *amir* and from you an *amir.*' 'Umar ibn al-Khattab, may Allah be pleased with him, came to them and said, '*Ansar,* do you not know that the Messenger of Allah, may Allah bless him and grant him peace, ordered Abu Bakr to lead the people (in *salah*)? So which of you would be pleased to give himself precedence over Abu Bakr?' The *Ansar* said, 'We seek refuge with Allah that we should give ourselves precedence over Abu Bakr.'

Abu Sa'id al-Khudri said: The Messenger of Allah, may Allah bless him and grant him peace, died and the people assembled in the house of Sa'd ibn 'Ubadah and among them were Abu Bakr and 'Umar, and the public speakers of the *Ansar* stood up and one of them began to speak, saying, 'You men of the *Muhajirun,* whenever the Messenger of Allah, may Allah bless him and his family and grant them peace, appointed one of you to any position of authority, he paired one of us with him; we think therefore that a man from us and a man from you should be appointed to this command.' The public speakers of the *Ansar* followed each other on that same theme. Then Zaid ibn Thabit stood up and said, 'Do you not know that the Messenger of Allah, may Allah bless him and grant him peace, was one of the *Muhajirun* and his *khalifah* is one of the *Muhajirun* and we were the *Ansar* of the Messenger of Allah and we shall be the *Ansar* of the *khalifah* of the Messenger of Allah just as we were his *Ansar.*' He took the hand of Abu Bakr and said, 'This is your man,' then ᶜUmar swore allegiance to him and then the *Muhajirun* and the *Ansar*. Abu Bakr ascended the *mimbar* and looked at people's faces and did not find az-Zubayr, so he called for az-Zubayr and he came. He (Abu Bakr) said, 'You said, son of the aunt of the Messenger of Allah, may Allah bless him and grant him peace, and his disciple, that you want to break the staff of the Muslims.' So he said, 'There is no blame on you *Khalifah* of the Messenger of Allah,' and he stood and pledged allegiance to him. Then he looked at the faces of the people and could not see ᶜAli so he summoned him and he came. He said, 'You said, son of the uncle of the Messenger of Allah, may Allah bless him and grant him peace, and his relation through marriage to his daughter, that you want to break the staff of the Muslims.' So he said, 'There is no blame on you, *Khalifah* of the Messenger of Allah,' and he pledged allegiance to him.

Anas ibn Malik said: When Abu Bakr was pledged allegiance in the assembly hall, then, on the morrow, he sat upon the *mimbar* and ᶜUmar stood and spoke before Abu Bakr, praised Allah, and said, 'Allah has gathered your authority to the best of you, the Companion of the Messenger of Allah and the "*second of the two when they two were in the cave*" (Qur'an 9: 40), so stand and pledge allegiance to him,' and the people pledged allegiance to Abu Bakr with a general and public allegiance after the allegiance made in the assembly hall. Then Abu Bakr spoke, praised Allah, and said, 'And now, people, I have been put in authority over you and I am not the best of you. So if I do right then help me, and if I do wrong then put me straight. Truthfulness is a sacred trust and lying is a betrayal. The weak one among you is strong as far as I am concerned until I restore to him his right, *insha'Allah*, and the strong one of you is weak until I take what is due from him, *insha'Allah*. No people forsake *jihad* in the way of Allah but that Allah delivers a humiliating blow to them. Nor does indecency ever spread among a people but that Allah envelops them in trials. Obey me as long as I obey Allah and His Messenger, and if I disobey Allah and His Messenger then you do not owe me obedience. Stand up for your prayer, may Allah have mercy upon you.'

ᶜAbd ar-Rahman ibn ᶜAuf said: Abu Bakr gave an address (*khutbah*) and said, 'By Allah, I was never eager for a position of command for even as long as a day or a night, and I never desired it, and I have never asked Allah for it in secret nor openly. However I was afraid of dissension. I will have no rest in command. I have been invested with a mighty matter which I have not the energy for, nor the power, except it be by Allah's strengthening.' ᶜAli and az-Zubayr said, 'We were not angry except that we were too late for the counsel, and we see Abu Bakr as the person most fitted for it. He was the Companion of the Cave. We know his honour and his excellence. The Messenger of Allah, may Allah bless him and grant him peace, ordered him to lead the people in prayer while he was yet alive.'

Ibrahim at-Tamimi said: When the Messenger of Allah, may Allah bless him and his family and grant them peace, died, ᶜUmar came to Abu ᶜUbaydah ibn al-Jarrah and said, 'Stretch out your hand so that I can pledge allegiance to you. You are the trusted one of this *ummah* according to the tongue of the Prophet, may Allah bless him and grant him peace.' So Abu ᶜUbaydah said to ᶜUmar, 'I never thought you weak in your mind before this, since I became a Muslim. Would you pledge allegiance to me when among you there is as-Siddiq, the "*second of the two*"?'

Muhammad ibn Abi Bakr said that Abu Bakr said to ᶜUmar, 'Stretch out your hand so that I can pledge allegiance to you.' ᶜUmar said to him, You are better than me.' Abu Bakr said to him, 'You are stronger than me,' and he repeated it, but ᶜUmar said, 'My strength shall be for you along with your merit,' and he swore allegiance to him.

Humayd ibn ᶜAbd ar-Rahman ibn ᶜAuf said: The Messenger of Allah, may Allah bless him and grant him peace, died while Abu Bakr was with some of the people of Madinah, so he came and uncovered his face and kissed him and said, 'May my father and mother be your ransom, how sweet you are in life and death. Muhammad has died, by the Lord of the Kaᶜbah!' and he mentioned the rest of the *hadith* then he said: Abu Bakr and ᶜUmar went off in haste until they came to them. Then Abu Bakr spoke and he didn't leave out anything that Allah had revealed about the *Ansar* nor anything that the Messenger of Allah, may Allah bless him and grant him peace, had mentioned about them but that he mentioned it, and he said, 'You know that the Messenger of Allah, may Allah bless him and grant him peace, said, "If mankind were to travel in one valley and the *Ansar* were to travel in another valley, I would travel in the valley of the *Ansar*." You know, Saᶜd, that the Messenger of Allah, may Allah bless him and grant him peace, said while you were seated, "Quraysh are the authorities of this matter, and the best of mankind will follow the best of them and the worst of them will follow the worst of them."' So Saᶜd said to him, 'You have told the truth. We are the deputies and you are the commanders.'

Abu Saᶜid al-Khudri said: When Abu Bakr was pledged allegiance, he saw some dejection among people and so he said, 'What is holding you back? Am I not the one with the most right to this command? Am I not the first to accept Islam? Am I not ...? Am I not ...?' and he mentioned various qualities.

Ar-Rafiᶜ at-Ta'i said: Abu Bakr told me about his pledge of allegiance and what the *Ansar* had said, and what ᶜUmar had said, and he said, 'So they pledged allegiance to me and I accepted it from them. I was afraid that there would be dissension and, after it, reneging (from Islam).' He (Ar-Rafiᶜ) said to Abu Bakr, 'What made you take upon yourself the governance of the people and you forbade me taking command of (even) two people?' He said, 'I could not find any escape from that. I was afraid of division in the *ummah* of Muhammad, may Allah bless him and grant him peace.'

Qais ibn Abi Hazim said, 'I sat with Abu Bakr as-Siddiq a month after the death of the Messenger of Allah, may Allah bless him and grant him peace,' and he mentioned his story. 'Then the cry went up among people, "The prayer is summoned." People gathered and he ascended the *mimbar* then said, "I would love that someone other than me would take care of this authority for me. If you take me to task by the *sunnah* of your Prophet I am not up to it. He was protected from *the shaytan*, and revelation used to descend upon him from heaven."'

Al-Hasan al-Basri said: When Abu Bakr was pledged allegiance he stood addressing the people and said, 'Now, I have been put in charge of this authority and I dislike it. By Allah, I would love that one of you would take care of it for me. If you charge me with acting among you with the like of the action of the Prophet, may Allah bless him and grant him peace, I cannot undertake that. The Prophet, may Allah bless him and grant him peace, was a slave whom Allah honoured with revelation and protected him by it (from error). I am only human. I am no better than any of you. Take care of me, and if you see me going straight then follow me and if you see me deviating then set me straight. Know that I have a *shaytan* who seizes upon me; when you see me becoming angry then avoid me, so that I do not leave traces and marks on your hairs and your skins.'

ᶜUrwah said: When Abu Bakr was appointed, he addressed people with a *khutbah*. He praised Allah and said, 'Now, I have been appointed in command over you and I am not the best of you. However the Qur'an was revealed, the Prophet, may Allah bless him and grant him peace, laid down as customary different *sunnahs* and we were taught, so we learnt. So, know, people, that the most acute of sharp intellect is (he who has) the most fearful obedience (*tuqa*); that the most incapable (form) of incapacity is wickedness; that the strongest of you, as far as I am concerned, is the weak one until I take his right for him; and that the weakest of you, as far as I am concerned, is the strong one until I take from him what he is due (to give). People, I am only a follower, I am not an innovator, so that if I do well, help me and if I deviate then put me straight. I say these words of mine and I seek the forgiveness of Allah for me and for you.' Malik said, 'No-one will ever be an *imam* (i.e. *amir*) unless on this condition.'

Abu Hurairah, may Allah be pleased with him, said: When the Messenger of Allah, may Allah bless him and grant him peace, died, Makkah was shaken with an earthquake and Abu Quhafah heard that and said, 'What is this?' They said, 'The Messenger of Allah, may Allah bless him and grant him peace, has died.' He said, 'A momentous thing. Who has undertaken the command after him?' They said, 'Your son.' He said, 'Are Banu ᶜAbd Manaf and Banu al-Mughirah contented with that?' They said, 'Yes.' He said, 'No-one may put down what they raise up and no-one may raise up what they put down.'

ᶜA'ishah, Ibn ᶜUmar, Saᶜid ibn al-Musayyab and others relate that Abu Bakr was pledged allegiance on the day that the Messenger of Allah, may Allah bless him and grant him peace, died, on Monday the 12th night of Rabiᶜ al-Awwal in the eleventh year of the *Hijrah.*

Ibn ᶜUmar said: Abu Bakr never sat on that place upon which the Messenger of Allah, may Allah bless him and grant him peace, sat upon the *mimbar* until he met Allah. ᶜUmar did not sit on the place Abu Bakr sat until he met Allah and ᶜUthman did not sit in ᶜUmar's place until he met Allah.

That which happened in his *khilafah*

Those weighty matters which happened in his days were the despatch of Usamah's army; fighting against the people who reneged (on Islam) and against those who refused the *zakah*; Musaylimah the Liar; and the collection of the Qur'an.

ᶜUmar, may Allah be pleased with him, said: When the Messenger of Allah, may Allah bless him and grant him peace, died there reneged whoever reneged of the Arabs and they said, 'We will pray but we will not produce the *zakah*.' I went to Abu Bakr and said, '*Khalifah* of the Messenger of Allah, be conciliatory with the people and be gentle and mild with them, for they are only on the level of wild animals.' He said, 'I hoped for your help and you have come to me holding back your help. Tyrannical in *Jahiliyyah* and granting licence in Islam. What did you think I should conciliate them with? With composed verses and forged magic? Away, away! The Prophet, may Allah bless him and grant him peace, has gone and revelation is cut off. By Allah, I will fight them as long as the sword remains in my hand, even if they refuse me a hobbling rope (of a camel).' ᶜUmar said: I found him more penetrating on the matter than me, more resolute, and he collected the people together on matters which appeared little and unimportant to many because of their inconvenience to them when I was appointed in command over them.

ᶜA'ishah, may Allah be pleased with her, said: When the Messenger of Allah, may Allah bless him and grant him peace, died then hypocrisy raised its head, the Arabs reneged and the *Ansar* secluded themselves. If that which descended on my father had come down on the immovable mountains it would have broken them. They did not disagree on a point but that my father was prompt with its utility and its judgement. They said, 'Where should the Prophet, may Allah bless him and grant him peace, be buried?' We could not find anyone with knowledge of that. Then Abu Bakr said, 'I heard the Messenger of Allah, may Allah bless him and grant him peace, saying, "No Prophet dies but that he is buried beneath the bed upon which he died."' She said: They disagreed about his inheritance and could find no-one with knowledge on that point, then Abu Bakr said, 'I heard the Messenger of Allah, may Allah bless him and grant him peace, saying, "We, the company of the Prophets, we are not inherited from. What we leave is a *sadaqah*."'

Some of the men of knowledge said: This was the first disagreement which happened among the Companions, may Allah be pleased with them. Some said, 'We will bury him in Makkah, his city in which he was born', and others said, 'No, in his mosque,' and others said, 'No, in *al-Baqiᶜ*', and others said, 'In *al-Bait al-*

Maqdis, the burial ground of the Prophets', until Abu Bakr told them of the knowledge that he had. Ibn Zunjawayh said: This *sunnah* was one which was uniquely As-Siddiq's among all of the *Muhajirun* and *Ansar* and they had recourse to him for it.

Abu Hurairah, may Allah be pleased with him, said: 'By the One Whom there is no god but Him, if Abu Bakr had not been appointed *khalifah* then Allah would not have been worshipped.' Then he said it a second time and then he said it a third time. Someone said to him, 'How so, Abu Hurairah?' So he said, 'The Messenger of Allah, may Allah bless him and grant him peace, directed Usamah ibn Zaid, along with seven hundred men, to Syria. When they arrived at Dhu Khushub the Prophet, may Allah bless him and grant him peace, died, the Arabs around Madinah reneged on their Islam and the companions of the Messenger of Allah, may Allah bless him and grant him peace, gathered around him and said, "Bring these back. Do you direct these against the Byzantines while the Arabs around Madinah have reneged?" He said, "By the One Whom there is no god but Him, even if dogs were dragging the wives of the Prophet, may Allah bless him and grant him peace, by their feet I would not return an army which the Messenger of Allah had sent out, nor undo a standard which he had tied!" He sent Usamah and every tribe he would pass by which was wishing to renege would say (to themselves), "If these (the people of Madinah) did not have power, the like of these (the army) would not have come out from them, so let us leave them alone until they meet the Byzantines." They met them, defeated them, killed them and returned safely, so that they (the tribes) remained firm in Islam.'

ᶜUrwah said: The Messenger of Allah, may Allah bless him and grant him peace, began to say in his illness, 'Despatch the army of Usamah,' so that it travelled until it reached al-Jurf (three miles from Madinah on the road to Syria). His (Usamah's) wife, Fatimah bint Qais, sent a message to him saying, 'Do not hasten, because the Messenger of Allah, may Allah bless him and grant him peace, is heavily afflicted.' He did not proceed until the Messenger of Allah, may Allah bless him and grant him peace, died. When he died, he returned to Abu Bakr and said, 'The Messenger of Allah, may Allah bless him and grant him peace, sent me while we were not in this state of yours. I fear that the Arabs will reject (their Islam), and if they reject, they are the first to be fought. If they do not reject, I will carry on, because with me are the chiefs of the people and the best of them.' Abu Bakr addressed the people and said, 'By Allah, that birds (of prey) were to snatch me away is more beloved to me than that I should give anything precedence over the command of the Messenger of Allah, may Allah bless him and grant him peace.' Then he sent him.

Adh-Dhahabi said: When the death of the Prophet, may Allah bless him and grant him peace, became well known in the districts, many groups of the Arabs reneged on their Islam and refused the *zakah* so Abu Bakr as-Siddiq prepared to fight them. ʿUmar and others counselled him to avoid fighting them, so he said, 'By Allah, if they refused me a hobbling cord or a young she-goat which they used to pay to the Messenger of Allah, may Allah bless him and grant him peace, I would fight them over its refusal.' ʿUmar said, 'How can you fight people when the Messenger of Allah, may Allah bless him and grant him peace, said, "I have been ordered to fight people until they say: There is no god but Allah, and that Muhammad is the Messenger of Allah, and whoever said it, his property and his blood are safe from me except for its *due* (punishment for crimes) and his reckoning is up to Allah."?' Abu Bakr said, 'By Allah, I will fight whoever makes a distinction between the prayer and the *zakah*, for the *zakah* is what is *due* on property, and he said, "Except for its *due*."' ʿUmar said, 'By Allah, it was only that I saw that Allah had expanded the breast of Abu Bakr to fighting and I knew that it was right.'

ʿUrwah said: Abu Bakr went out with the *Muhajirun* and the *Ansar* until he reached a swamp opposite Najd and the nomadic Arabs fled with their families. The people spoke to Abu Bakr and said, 'Go back to Madinah, to the children and women, and put a man in command of the army,' and they persisted until he returned, putting Khalid ibn al-Walid in command. He said to him, 'If they submit in Islam and pay the *sadaqah* (the *zakah*) then whoever of you wishes to return may return,' and Abu Bakr went back to Madinah.

Ibn ᶜUmar said: When Abu Bakr set out and was mounted on his camel, ᶜAli ibn Abi Talib took hold of its reins and said, 'Where are you going, *Khalifah* of the Messenger of Allah? I say to you that which the Messenger of Allah, may Allah bless him and grant him peace, said to you on the Day of Uhud, "Sheath your sword, and do not cause us grief and concern for your person," and return to Madinah, for, by Allah, if we are caused to grieve because of you there will not be any order in Islam ever.'

Handhalah ibn ᶜAli al-Laythi said that Abu Bakr sent Khalid and ordered him to fight people over five matters, whoever abandoned one of them, he was to fight him just as he was to fight whoever abandoned all five: The *shahadah* that there is no god but Allah and that Muhammad is His slave and messenger, the establishment of the prayer, the production of the *zakah*, the fast of Ramadan and the pilgrimage of the House. Khalid and those with him went out in *Jumada al-Akhirah* and fought Banu Asad and Ghatafan. They killed whomever they killed and captured whomever they captured, and the rest returned to Islam. In this event ᶜUkkashah ibn Mihsan and Thabit ibn Aqram were martyred.

In Ramadan of this year, Fatimah, may Allah be pleased with her, the daughter of the Messenger of Allah, may Allah bless him and grant him peace, died, the Mistress (*Sayyidah*) of the world's women, and her age was twenty-four years old. Adh-Dhahabi said: The Messenger of Allah, may Allah bless him and grant him peace, had no descendants but through her (because the issue of his daughter Zaynab became extinct, az-Zubayr ibn Bakkar said). Umm Ayman died a month before her. In *Shawwal* ᶜAbdullah ibn Abi Bakr died. Then Khalid went with his army to *al-Yamamah* to fight Musaylimah the Liar, towards the end of the year. The two hosts met, the siege lasted some days, and then the Liar was killed, may Allah curse him. Wahshi the one who killed Hamzah killed him. A great number of the Companions were martyred there: Abu Hudhayfah ibn ᶜUtbah, Salim the freed slave of Abu Hudhayfah, Shujaᶜ ibn Wahb, Zaid ibn al-Khattab, ᶜAbdullah ibn Sahl, Malik ibn ᶜAmr, at-Tufail ibn ᶜAmr ad-Dawsi, Yazid ibn Qais, ᶜAmir ibn al-Bukayr, ᶜAbdullah ibn Makhramah, as-Sa'ib ibn ᶜUthman ibn Madhᶜun, ᶜUbad ibn Bishr, Maᶜan ibn ᶜAdi, Thabit ibn Qais ibn Shamas, Abu Dujanah Simak ibn Harb and a large number totalling seventy (of the Companions). Musaylimah, on the day of his death, was one hundred and fifty years old, his birth having been before the birth of ᶜAbdullah, the father of the Prophet, may Allah bless him and grant him peace.

In the twelfth year, as-Siddiq sent al-ᶜAla' ibn al-Hadrami to Bahrain who had reneged. So they met at *Jawatha* and the Muslims were victorious. He sent ᶜIkrimah ibn Abi Jahl to Oman who had reneged, and he sent al-Muhajir ibn Abi Umayyah to the people of Nujayr. He sent Ziyad ibn Labid al-Ansari to a group of those who had reneged. In that year Abu'l-ᶜAs ibn ar-Rabiᶜ died, the husband of Zaynab, the daughter of the Prophet, may Allah bless him and grant him peace, also as-Saᶜb ibn Juthamah al-Laythi, and Abu Marthad al-Ghanawi. In that year, after finishing fighting the people who had reneged, as-Siddiq, may Allah be pleased with him, sent Khalid ibn al-Walid to the land of Basra and he raided Ubullah, captured it and took Mada'in Kisra, the one which is in Iraq, partly by treaty and partly by force. In that year Abu Bakr as-Siddiq undertook the *Hajj*, then returned and sent ᶜAmr ibn al-ᶜAs and the army to Syria; the battle of Ajnadayn happened in *Jumada al-Uwla* of the thirteenth year, and the Muslims were victorious. Abu Bakr was given the good tidings when he was close to death. ᶜIkrimah ibn Abi Jahl was martyred in it and Hisham ibn al-ᶜAs among a group of others. In that year there was the battle of *Marju's-Suffar*, the idolators were defeated and al-Fadl ibn al-ᶜAbbas, among others, was martyred.

The collection of the Qur'an

Zaid ibn Thabit said: Abu Bakr sent for me at the time of the slaughter of people of al-Yamamah and ᶜUmar was with him. Abu Bakr said, 'ᶜUmar came to me and said, "The slaughter of people was very extensive on the Day of al-Yamamah and I fear the killing will extend to the reciters in these engagements, so that a lot of Qur'an will disappear unless they gather it together. I believe that the Qur'an should be gathered."' Abu Bakr said, 'I said to ᶜUmar, "How can I do something that the Messenger of Allah, may Allah bless him and grant him peace, did not do?" ᶜUmar said, "It is, by Allah, good," and ᶜUmar did not give up returning to the matter until Allah expanded my breast to that, and I came to hold the view that ᶜUmar held.' Zaid said: ᶜUmar was sitting with him, not talking. Abu Bakr said, 'You are an intelligent young man and we have no doubts of you. You used to write the revelation for the Messenger of Allah, may Allah bless him and grant him peace; search out the Qur'an and collect it together.' By Allah, if he had imposed on me the responsibility of removing one of the mountains it would not have been heavier for me than what they ordered me to do of collecting the Qur'an. I said, 'How can the two of you do something which the Prophet, may Allah bless him and grant him peace, did not do?' So Abu Bakr said, 'It, by Allah, is good,' and he continued insisting on it until Allah expanded my breast to that which he had expanded the breasts of Abu Bakr and ᶜUmar. I searched out the Qur'an to collect it all together, from scraps (of paper), shoulder blade bones, palm branches and from the breasts of men, until I found two *ayat* from *Surah at-Tawbah* (The *Surah of* Repentance) along with Khuzaymah ibn Thabit which I found with no-one else, '*There has come to you a messenger from among yourselves ...*' (Qur'an 9: 128-129) to the end of the *surah*.

The pages upon which the Qur'an was collected were with Abu Bakr until Allah took him, then they were with ᶜUmar until Allah took him, then they were with Hafsah the daughter of ᶜUmar, may Allah be pleased with her.

ᶜAli said: The one with the greatest reward for the written copies of the Qur'an is Abu Bakr. Abu Bakr was the first to gather the Qur'an between two boards.

The things in which he was first

He was the first to accept Islam, the first to collect the Qur'an together, the first to name it a *mushaf* (written copy) – the proof of that has already been mentioned – and he was the first one to be named *khalifah*.

Abu Bakr ibn Abi Mulaykah said: It was said to Abu Bakr, '*Khalifah* of Allah!' He said, 'I am the *Khalifah* of the Prophet, may Allah bless him and grant him peace, and I am content with that.'

He was the first to rule the *khilafah* while his father was alive. **He was the first *khalifah* whose subjects allocated him a sum.** ᶜA'ishah, may Allah be pleased with her, said: When Abu Bakr was appointed *khalifah* he said, 'My people know that my profession is not incapable of providing for my family, and I have become occupied with the command and the affairs of the Muslims so the family of Abu Bakr will eat from this property while he works professionally for the Muslims.'

ᶜAta' ibn as-Sa'ib said: When Abu Bakr was pledged allegiance he arose in the morning and upon his forearm there were some garments and he was going to the market place. ᶜUmar said, 'Where are you going?' He said, 'To the market place.' He said, 'What are you going to do, when you have been put in charge of the affairs of the Muslims?' He said, 'What am I going to do to feed my family?' He said, 'Let us go. Abu ᶜUbaydah will allocate a sum for you.' So they went to Abu ᶜUbaydah and he said, 'I allocate you the supplies of a man among the *Muhajrun,* not the best of them nor the least of them, and the clothing of winter and summer. If you wear out something, return and take something in its place.' The two of them allocated him half a sheep everyday and what would clothe his head and his person.

Maimun said: When Abu Bakr was appointed *khalifah* they allocated him two thousand, so he said, 'Increase me, for I have dependents and you have kept me busy so that I cannot engage in trade,' so they increased him five hundred.

Al-Hasan ibn ᶜAli ibn Abi Talib said: When Abu Bakr was near to death, he said, 'ᶜA'ishah, look to the milch camel whose milk we used to drink, the bowl in which we used to prepare food, and the outer garments we used to wear, for we used to benefit from that when we were in charge of the command of the Muslims. When I die, return them to ʿUmar.' When Abu Bakr died she sent them to ʿUmar. ʿUmar said, 'May Allah show mercy to you, Abu Bakr! You have exhausted the one who comes after you.'

Abu Bakr ibn Hafs said: When he was close to death, Abu Bakr said to ʿA'ishah, may Allah be pleased with her, 'My little daughter, we were put in charge of the affairs of the Muslims, and we didn't take for ourselves a *dinar* nor a *dirham*, but we ate of the coarse flour of their food in our bellies, and we dressed with their rough clothing upon our backs. Nothing remains with us of the booty of the Muslims, neither a little nor a lot, but for this Abyssinian slave, this camel for drawing water, and this threadbare worn-out outer garment. When I die, send them to ʿUmar.'

He was the first one to make a bait al-mal (a building in which zakah and other revenues were stored while they were being distributed).

Sahl ibn Abi Khaythamah and others said that Abu Bakr had a *bait al-mal* at *as-Sunh* which no-one guarded. Someone said to him, 'Will you not put someone in charge of it to guard it?' He said, 'There is a lock on it,' and he used to give away what was in it until it was empty. When it was moved to Madinah, he changed it and put it in his house. Property came to him and he used to divide it up among the poorest of the people and he would divide it equally among them. He would buy camels, horses and weapons and put them there to be used in the way of Allah. He would buy outer garments which came from the outlying desert tracts and distribute them among the widows of Madinah. When Abu Bakr died and was buried, ʿUmar summoned the trustees, amongst them ʿAbd ar-Rahman ibn ʿAuf and ʿUthman ibn ʿAffan, and with them entered the *bait al-mal* of Abu Bakr. They opened the *bait al-mal* and found nothing in it, neither a *dinar* nor a *dirham*.

I say that this tradition refutes the words of al-ʿAskari in *Al-Awa'il* (Firsts), 'The first to take a *bait al-mal* was ʿUmar. The Prophet, may Allah bless him and grant him peace, had no *bait al-mal* nor had Abu Bakr, may Allah be pleased with him.' I had refuted this in my book which I composed on 'firsts', then later I saw that al-ᶜAskari alluded to this in another part of his book saying, 'The first to take charge of a *bait al-mal* was Abu ᶜUbaydah ibn al-Jarrah on behalf of Abu Bakr.'

Al-Hakim said: The first affectionate nickname in Islam was the nickname of Abu Bakr, may Allah be pleased with him, 'ᶜAteeq.'

Section

Jabir, may Allah be pleased with him, said: The Prophet, may Allah bless him and grant him peace, said, 'If the wealth of Bahrain were to come, I would give you so much and so much.' So when the wealth of Bahrain came after the death of the Prophet, may Allah bless him and grant him peace, Abu Bakr said, 'Whoever was owed anything by the Prophet, may Allah bless him and grant him peace, let him come to us.' I came and told him. He said, 'Take.' I took and found it to be five hundred. Then he gave me one thousand and five hundred.

Some examples of his forbearance and humility

Anisah said: Abu Bakr was settled among us for three years before he was appointed *khalifah* and a year afterwards, and the servant girls of the quarter would come to him with their flocks and he would milk them for them.

Maymun ibn Mihran said: A man came to Abu Bakr and said, 'Peace be upon you (*as-salamu alaika*—the singular form of address) *Khalifah* of the Messenger of Allah.' And he said, 'In among all of these.' (The man had greeted him exclusively of those present).

Abu Salih al-Ghiffari said that ᶜUmar ibn al-Khattab used to take care of an elderly blind woman in one of the outskirts of Madinah at night. He would draw water for her to drink, and would undertake her business. Sometimes when he came to her he would find that someone else had already beaten him to her and done what she wanted. He came to her more than one time so that the other might not beat him to her. ʿUmar lay in wait for him, and it was Abu Bakr who had come to her, and he was at that time *khalifah*. ʿUmar said, 'You are he, by my life!'

ʿAbd ar-Rahman al-Asbahani said: Al-Hasan ibn ʿAli came to Abu Bakr when he was upon the *mimbar* of the Prophet, may Allah bless him and grant him peace, and said, 'Come down from my father's seat.' He said, 'You have told the truth, it is your father's seat,' and he placed him in his lap and wept. ʿAli said, 'By Allah, this was not from my command.' He said, 'You have told the truth. By Allah, I did not suspect you.'

Section

Ibn ʿUmar said: The Messenger of Allah, may Allah bless him and grant him peace, appointed Abu Bakr to lead the *Hajj* in the first *Hajj* of Islam, then the Messenger of Allah, may Allah bless him and grant him peace, performed the *Hajj* the following year. When the Messenger of Allah, may Allah bless him and grant him peace, died and Abu Bakr was appointed *khalifah*, he put ʿUmar in charge of leading the *Hajj*, then Abu Bakr performed the *Hajj* the following year. When Abu Bakr died and ʿUmar was appointed *khalifah*, he put ʿAbd ar-Rahman ibn ʿAuf in charge of the *Hajj*, then ʿUmar continued to perform the *Hajj* every year until he died. ʿUthman was then appointed *khalifah*, and he put ʿAbd ar-Rahman ibn ʿAuf in charge of the *Hajj*.

His final illness, his death, his last testament and his appointment of ʿUmar as *khalifah*

Ibn ʿUmar said: The cause of Abu Bakr's death was the passing away of the Messenger of Allah, may Allah bless him and grant him peace. He was distressed and his body continued to waste away until he died.

Ibn Shihab related that Abu Bakr and al-Harith ibn Kaladah were eating a broth which Abu Bakr had been given. Al-Harith said to Abu Bakr, 'Lift your hand (from the dish) *Khalifah* of the Messenger of Allah. By Allah, in it there is a year's poison. I and you will die on the same day.' He took his hand away from it. Both of them became increasingly sick until they died on the same day at the end of the year.

Ash-Sha'bi said: What can we expect from this awful world when the Messenger of Allah, may Allah bless him and grant him peace, was poisoned and Abu Bakr was poisoned?

'A'ishah, may Allah be pleased with her, said: The beginning of Abu Bakr's illness was that he performed a *ghusl* on Monday the seventh of *Jumada al-Akhirah* which was a cold day. He had a fever for fifteen days and did not go out to the prayer. He died on the night of Tuesday eight days before the end of *Jumada al-Akhirah* in 13 A.H., when he was sixty-three years old.

Abu's-Safar said: They entered upon Abu Bakr during his illness and said, '*Khalifah* of the Messenger of Allah, shall we not call a doctor for you who will take a look at you?' He said, 'He has already taken a look at me.' They said, 'What did he say?' He said, 'Truly, I do what I will.'(see Qur'an 11: 108; 85: 16)

When Abu Bakr became seriously ill, he called for 'Abd ar-Rahman ibn 'Auf and said, 'Tell me about 'Umar ibn al-Khattab.' He said, 'You do not ask me about any matter but that you are more knowledgeable of it than me.' So Abu Bakr said, 'And even if ...?' 'Abd ar-Rahman ibn 'Auf said, 'He, by Allah, is better than your view of him.' Then he summoned 'Uthman ibn 'Affan and said, 'Tell me about 'Umar.' He said, 'You of all of us know best about him.' He said, 'Tell me that,' so he said, 'O Allah, my knowledge of him is that his inward is better than his exterior and that there is no-one like him among us.' He included in his counsel, along with the two of them, Sa'id ibn Zaid, Usayd ibn al-Hudayr and others of the *Muhajirun* and *Ansar*. Usayd said, 'O Allah, I know him to be the best after you. He is pleased for the good pleasure (of Allah), and displeased for the displeasure (of Allah). What he conceals is better than what he makes public. No-one stronger for this command than him will ever have authority over it.'

Some of the Companions entered upon him and one said to him, 'What will you say to your Lord when He asks you about your appointing ᶜUmar as *khalifah* over us when you have seen his toughness?' Abu Bakr said, 'By Allah, are you trying to frighten me? I will say, "O Allah, I have appointed as *khalifah* over them the best of Your people." Convey from me what I said to those behind you.' Then he called ᶜUthman and said, 'Write, "In the name of Allah, the Merciful, the Compassionate. This is the testament of Abu Bakr ibn Abi Quhafah at the end of his time in the world, as he was leaving it, and at the beginning of his time in the *Akhirah,* as he was entering it, where the disbeliever will believe, the wicked will be certain, and the liar will tell the truth. I have appointed after me as *khalifah* over you ᶜUmar ibn al-Khattab, so listen to him and obey him. I have not fallen short in my duty to Allah and His Messenger and His *deen* and to myself and you. If he is just, then that is my opinion of him and my knowledge of him. If he changes things, then every man has that which he earned. I intended good, and I do not know the hidden things, '*... and the ones who do wrong shall know what place of transformation they will be transferred to.*' (Qur'an 26: 227) Peace be upon you and the mercy of Allah and His blessings."' He asked for the writing and sealed it. Then he ordered ᶜUthman, he went out with the letter thus sealed, and people pledged allegiance and were pleased with it. Abu Bakr summoned ᶜUmar in private and advised him whatever he advised him. Then he left him and Abu Bakr raised his hands and said, 'O Allah, I only meant by that their good and feared dissension for them, and I have done for them what You know best, and I have exerted my intellect for them in arriving at a decision, and have appointed the best of them over them, and the strongest of them, and the most eager of them for that which would guide them. And there has come to me of Your command what has come to me (death), so put another in my place over them, for they are Your slaves, their forelocks are in Your hand. O Allah, put right their rulers, and make him one of Your *khalifahs* who take the right way, and put right his subjects for him.'

Ibn Mas^cud said: The most farsighted of people were three: Abu Bakr when he appointed ^cUmar as *khalifah*, the woman companion of Musa when she said, '*Hire him!*' (Qur'an 28: 26), and the chief minister (of Fir^cawn) when he said to his wife, '*Honour his (Yusuf's) dwelling place.*' (Qur'an 12: 21).

Yasar ibn Hamzah said: When Abu Bakr's illness grew serious he stood and looked over the people from a small window and said, 'I have made a covenant, so will you be contented with it?' So the people said, 'We will be content with it, *Khalifah* of the Messenger of Allah.' Then ^cAli stood and said, 'We will not be content unless it is ^cUmar.' He said, 'It is ^cUmar.'

^cA'ishah, may Allah be pleased with her, said: When death came to Abu Bakr, he said, 'What day is this?' They said, 'Monday.' He said, 'If I die tonight do not wait until tomorrow (to bury me), because the most beloved of days and nights to me is the closest to the Messenger of Allah, may Allah bless him and grant him peace.'

^cA'ishah, may Allah be pleased with her, said that Abu Bakr made a present to her of the fruit-cuttings of palm trees, twenty camel loads, from al-Ghabah. When death came to him he said, 'My little daughter, by Allah, there is no human being that I would more love to see wealthy than you, and there is no-one whose poverty after me is more grievous to me than you. I had given you as a gift twenty camel loads of fruit-cuttings of palm trees; if you had cut them and taken them they would have been yours, however today they are only the property of the ones who inherit, who are your two brothers and your two sisters, so divide them up by the Book of Allah.' She said, 'Father, even if it had been so much and so much I would have given it up. There is only Asma' (her sister), who is the other (sister)?' He said, 'The child who is in the womb of Kharijah's daughter; I think it is a girl.' In a version he said, 'The child who is in the womb of Kharijah's daughter; it occurs to me that it is a girl, so make her your concern.' Then she gave birth to Umm Kulthum.

^cUrwah said that Abu Bakr bequeathed one fifth of his property (the rest being divided according to the *shari^cah*), and said,

'I take from my wealth what Allah takes from the booty of the Muslims.' He also said that he (Abu Bakr) said, 'That I should bequeath a fifth is preferable to me than that I should bequeath a quarter, and that I should bequeath a quarter would be preferable to me than bequeathing a third. Whoever bequeathed a third leaves nothing.'

Ad-Dahhak said that Abu Bakr and ᶜAli both bequeathed a fifth of their properties to those who were not entitled to inherit from them of their close relatives.

ᶜA'ishah, may Allah be pleased with her, said: By Allah, Abu Bakr left neither a *dinar* nor a *dirham* of which Allah had struck the die.

ᶜA'ishah, may Allah be pleased with her, said: When Abu Bakr became grievously ill I quoted this verse:

'By your life, wealth does not avail the man,
When one day it (the spirit) rattles in the throat and the breast becomes constricted by it,'

and he uncovered his face and said, 'It is not like that. Rather say,

"And the agony of death comes in truth. That is what you used to turn away from." (Qur'an 50: 19)

Look out my two cloths and wash them, then bury me in them. The living has more need of the new than the dead.'

ᶜA'ishah, may Allah be pleased with her, said: I entered upon Abu Bakr when he was on the point of death and I said:

'Whoever's tears are ceaseless in sufficiency, in bitterness they will be poured out.'

So he said, 'Do not say this; rather say,

"And the agony of death comes in truth. That is what you used to turn away from."'

Then he said, 'On what day did the Messenger of Allah, may Allah bless him and grant him peace, die?' I said, 'Monday.' He said, 'I hope that it is between now and the night,' and he died on the night before Tuesday, and was buried before the morning.

Bakr ibn ᶜAbdullah al-Mazani said: When death came to Abu Bakr, ᶜA'ishah, may Allah be pleased with her, sat at his head and said:

'Every owner of camels must one day take them to drink, and every possessor of plunder must be despoiled.'

Abu Bakr understood it and said, 'It is not like that, my daughter, rather it is as Allah said:

"And the agony of death comes in truth. That is what you used to turn away from."'

ᶜA'ishah, may Allah be pleased with her, also said that she quoted this verse while Abu Bakr was dying:

'And a pure one, free from faults, from whose face the clouds draw drinking water,
Orphans love (him), a protection for the widows.'

Abu Bakr said, 'That was the Messenger of Allah, may Allah bless him and grant him peace.'

ᶜUbadah ibn Qais said: When death came to Abu Bakr he said to ᶜA'ishah, 'Wash these two cloths of mine and wrap me in them, for your father is one of two men: either dressed in the best way or stripped in the worst way.'

Ibn Abi Mulaykah said that Abu Bakr left as his last wish that his wife, Asma' bint ᶜUmays, should wash his body and that ᶜAbd ar-Rahman ibn Abi Bakr should help her.

Saᶜid ibn al-Musayyab said that ᶜUmar, may Allah be pleased with him, prayed over Abu Bakr between the grave (of the Prophet, may Allah bless him and grant him peace) and the *mimbar*, and said four *takbirs* over him.

ᶜUrwah and Qasim ibn Muhammad said that Abu Bakr left as his last wish to ᶜA'ishah that he should be buried by the side of the Messenger of Allah, may Allah bless him and grant him peace.

When he died, they dug a grave for him and put his head at the shoulder of the Messenger, may Allah bless him and grant him peace, and the niche (wherein the body was laid) touched the grave of the Messenger, may Allah bless him and grant him peace.

Ibn ᶜUmar said: ᶜUmar, Talhah, ᶜUthman and ᶜAbd ar-Rahman ibn Abi Bakr got down into Abu Bakr's grave (to place the body in the niche). Many people have said that he was buried at night.

Ibn al-Musayyab said that when Abu Bakr died, Makkah was shaken by an earthquake, and so Abu Quhafah said, 'What is this?' They said, 'Your son has died.' He said, 'A great misfortune! Who has undertaken the command after him?' They said, 'ᶜUmar.' He said, 'His companion.'

Mujahid said that Abu Quhafah returned the inheritance he received from Abu Bakr to the son of Abu Bakr and that Abu Quhafah only lived six months and some days after Abu Bakr. He died in *Muharram* of 14 A.H. when he was ninety-seven years of age.

The men of knowledge said: No-one took the *khilafah* during the life of his father except for Abu Bakr, and no father inherited from a *khalifah* except for Abu Bakr's.

Ibn ᶜUmar said: Abu Bakr ruled for two years and seven months.

Asmaᶜi said: Khufaf ibn Nudbah as-Salami said, mourning Abu Bakr:

> 'No living thing, tell it! has permanence, and all of the world, its business is annihilation.
> And property with the peoples is a deposit loaned and the condition on it is repayment.
> Man works and there is one lying in wait for him; the eye mourns him, and, the fire (excessive grief) of the brain.
> He becomes decrepit or he is slain or there overcomes him a sickness which afflicts him and for which there is no cure.
> Truly, Abu Bakr he is the succour (the rain) if Orion did not make vegetables to grow with water.
> By Allah, he does not reach his days the young wearer of a lower garment (common people) nor the wearer of an

upper garment (the élite).

Whoever works to reach his days, exerting himself, will isolate himself in an empty land.

What *hadith* with chains of transmission have been related from him

An-Nawawi said, in his *Tahdhib*: As-Siddiq related of the Messenger of Allah, may Allah bless him and grant him peace, one hundred and forty-two *hadith*. The reason for the small number of his narrations given the precedence of his companionship and his staying close to the Prophet, may Allah bless him and grant him peace, was that his death came before the spread of the *hadith* and the concern of the Followers for listening to them, acquiring them and memorising them.

ʿUmar, may Allah be pleased with him, mentioned in the previous *hadith* on the oath of allegiance that Abu Bakr left nothing which had been revealed about the *Ansar* or which the Messenger of Allah, may Allah bless him and grant him peace, had said about them but that he mentioned it. This is the best proof of the great amount of material he had memorised of the *Sunnah* and the vastness of his knowledge of the Qur'an. ʿUmar ibn al-Khattab transmitted from him, and ʿUthman ibn ʿAffan, ʿAli, Ibn ʿAuf, Ibn Masʿud, Hudhayfah, Ibn ʿUmar, Ibn az-Zubayr, Ibn ʿAmr, Ibn ʿAbbas, Anas, Zaid ibn Thabit, al-Bara' ibn ʿAzib, Abu Hurairah, ʿUqbah ibn al-Harith, his son ʿAbd ar-Rahman, Zaid ibn Arqam, ʿAbdullah ibn Mughaffal, ʿUqbah ibn ʿAmir al-Juhani, ʿImran ibn Husayn, Abu'l-Barzah al-Aslami, Abu Saʿid al-Khudri, Abu Musa al-Ashʿari, Abu't-Tufail al-Laythi, Jabir ibn ʿAbdullah, Bilal, ʿA'ishah his daughter, Asma' his daughter, and of the Followers: Aslam the freed slave of ʿUmar, Wasit al-Bajili and a number of others.

I have decided to enumerate his *hadith* here concisely, explaining after each *hadith* who made it public. I will treat each of them singly in their different paths of transmission in a *musnad* work devoted to that, *insha'Allah*.

1. The *hadith* of the *Hijrah* (the two Shaykhs [Al-Bukhari and Muslim] and others).

2. The *hadith* of the sea, 'It is completely pure, its water (for purification and cleansing), permitted its dead (to eat).' (ad-Daraqutni).

3. 'The *siwak* (tooth-stick) cleans the mouth and pleases the Lord.' (Ahmad).

4. 'That the Messenger of Allah, may Allah bless him and grant him peace, ate (meat of a) shoulder then later prayed and did not perform *wudu'* (washing to prepare for the prayer).' (Al-Bazzar and Abu Ya'la).

5. 'Let none of you make *wudu'* because of the taste of his food which is permitted for him to eat.' (Al-Bazzar).

6. 'The Messenger of Allah, may Allah bless him and grant him peace, forbade striking people at prayer.' (Abu Ya'la and al-Bazzar).

7. 'The last prayer which the Prophet, may Allah bless him and grant him peace, prayed was behind me in a single garment.' (Abu Ya'la).

8. 'Whoever it would please to recite the Qur'an freshly as it was revealed, then let him recite with the recitation of Ibn Umm 'Abd (i.e. Ibn Mas'ud).' (Ahmad).

9. He said to the Messenger of Allah, may Allah bless him and grant him peace, 'Teach me a prayer with which I can supplicate in my *salah.'* He said, 'Say, "O Allah I have wronged myself with a great wrong and none forgives wrong actions but You, so forgive me with a forgiveness from You and show mercy to me. Truly, You are the All-Forgiving, the Compassionate."' (Al-Bukhari and Muslim).

10. 'Whoever prayed the dawn prayer then he is in a covenant with Allah, so do not betray Allah with respect to His covenant. Whoever kills him, Allah will seek him out until He throws him in the Fire upon his face.' (Ibn Majah).

11. 'No Prophet has ever died until a man of his *ummah* led him in prayer.' (Al-Bazzar).

12. 'No man makes a wrong action then performs *wudu'* and does his *wudu'* well, then performs two *raka'at* and seeks Allah's

forgiveness but that He will forgive him.' (Ahmad, the authors of the four *Sunan*, and Ibn Hibban).

13. 'Allah has not made a prophet die but in the place he would love to be buried in.' (At-Tirmidhi).

14. 'May Allah curse the Jews and the Christians; they took the graves of their prophets as places of prostration.' (Abu Ya˓la).

15. 'The dead person has boiling water sprinkled on him for the tears of the living (i.e. the tears of wailing and mourning, particularly ritualised or professional mourning. The tradition is held not to refer to tears of sadness and sorrow).' (Abu Ya˓la).

16. 'Protect yourselves from the Fire even if it were with (giving) the half of a date, because it straightens that which is crooked, repels an evil death, and it stands with the hungry one in its stead with the satiated one.' (Abu Ya˓la).

17. The *hadith* of the obligations of *sadaqat* in its full length. (Al-Bukhari and others).

18. From Ibn Abi Mulaykah that he said: The reins fell from the hands of Abu Bakr as-Siddiq and he struck upon the foreleg of his camel and made it kneel down. They said to him, 'Why did you not tell us to give it back to you?' He said, 'My beloved, the Messenger of Allah, may Allah bless him and grant him peace, told me that I was not to ask people for anything.' (Ahmad).

19. 'The Messenger of Allah, may Allah bless him and grant him peace, told Asma' bint ˓Umays when she brought forth Muhammad ibn Abi Bakr to bathe herself and to enter *ihram* (for the *hajj*, as she gave birth on the way to Makkah).' (Al-Bazzar and at-Tabarani).

20. The Messenger of Allah, may Allah bless him and grant him peace, was asked, 'Which part of *hajj* is best?' He said, 'The raising of the voice (with *talbiyah*) and the shedding of blood (of animals brought to sacrifice).' (At-Tirmidhi and Ibn Majah).

21. That he kissed the (Black) Stone and said, 'If I had not seen the Messenger of Allah, may Allah bless him and grant him peace, kiss you I would not have kissed you.' (Ad-Daraqutni).

22. That the Messenger of Allah, may Allah bless him and grant him peace, sent an immunity to the people of Makkah, 'Let not

an idolator perform *hajj* after this year, nor let a naked person go around the House.' (Ahmad).

23. 'That which is between my house and my *mimbar* is one of the meadows of the Garden, and my *mimbar* is upon one of the fountains of the Garden.' (Abu Ya'la).

24. The full *hadith* of his going, may Allah bless him and grant him peace, to the home of Abu'l-Haytham ibn at-Tayyihan. (Abu Ya'la).

25. 'Gold for gold, like for like. And silver for silver, like for like. The one who gives increase or seeks increase is in the Fire.' (Abu Ya'la and al-Bazzar).

26. 'Cursed is whoever harms a believer or plots against him.' (At-Tirmidhi).

27. 'A mean person will not enter the Garden, nor a deceiver, nor a treacherous one, nor one of evil character. The first to enter the Garden is the slave when he obeys Allah and obeys his master.' (Ahmad).

28. 'The clientage (of a slave which includes inheriting from him as a relative) is for the one who sets free.' (Ad-Diya' al-Muqaddasi in *al-Mukhtarah*).

29. 'We (prophets) are not inherited from; that which we leave is a *sadaqah*.' (Al-Bukhari).

30. 'When Allah grants a prophet a means of subsistence (such as land yielding an income) and then later makes him die, He will appoint it for the one who undertakes it (the *khilafah*) after him.' (Abu Dawud).

31. 'He is ungrateful (*kafara*) to Allah who declares himself free of his lineage, even though it be in a minute way.' (Al-Bazzar).

32. 'You and that which is yours are for your father.' Abu Bakr said, 'He only meant by that maintenance.' (Al-Baihaqi).

33. 'Whoever's two feet become dusty in the way of Allah, Allah will forbid them from (entering) the Fire.' (Al-Bazzar).

34. 'I have been ordered to fight men until ...' (The two Shaykhs and others).

35. 'How excellent a slave of Allah and brother to his kinsfolk is Khalid ibn al-Walid, and (he is) one of the swords of Allah, may

Allah draw him against the disbelievers and hypocrites.' (Ahmad).

36. 'The sun has not risen over a man better than ᶜUmar. (At-Tirmidhi).

37. 'Whoever is put in charge of any affair of the Muslims and he appoints in command over them anyone out of favouritism, then there is the curse of Allah upon him, and Allah will not accept from him either repentance nor a ransom until He enters him into Jahannam. Whoever gives anyone the sanctuary of Allah, and he violates the sanctuary of Allah in any way without right then may the curse of Allah be upon him.' (Ahmad).

38. The *hadith* of Maᶜiz and his stoning. (Ahmad).

39. 'He is not persistent (in wrong action) who seeks forgiveness, even if he repeats it seventy times a day.' (At-Tirmidhi).

40. 'That he, may Allah bless him and grant him peace, took counsel on the command of war.' (At-Tabarani).

41. The *hadith* 'When "*Whoever does evil will be recompensed it ...*" (Qur'an 4: 123) was revealed ...' (At-Tirmidhi, Ibn Hibban and others).

42. 'You recite this *ayah*, "*O you who believe, you are responsible for your own selves ...*" (Qur'an 5: 105).' (Ahmad, the four authors of books called *Sunan* and Ibn Hibban).

43. 'What do you think of two of whom Allah is the third?' (The two Shaykhs).

44. 'O Allah, by spear-thrusts and by plague.' (Abu Yaᶜla).

45. '(*Surah*) Hud made me grey ...' (Ad-Daraqutni in *al-ᶜIlal*).

46. 'Associating partners (with Allah) among my *ummah* is more hidden than the creeping of ants ...' (Abu Yaᶜla and others).

47. 'Messenger of Allah, teach me something I can say in the morning and the evening ...' (Al-Haytham ibn Kulayb in his *Musnad*, and At-Tirmidhi and others have it among those ascribed to Abu Hurairah).

48. 'Take hold of "No god but Allah" and seeking forgiveness, because Iblis said, "I destroyed people with wrong actions and they destroyed me with 'No god but Allah' and seeking forgiveness. When I saw that, I destroyed them with whims so that they think they are guided aright."' (Abu Yaᶜla).

49. 'When, "*Do not raise your voices above the voice of the Prophet!*" (Qur'an 49: 2) was revealed, I said, "Messenger of Allah, I will not speak to you except as the decrepit do."' (Al-Bazzar).

50. 'Each one is eased to that which is created for him.' (Ahmad).

51. 'Whoever forges a lie against me intentionally or rejects something I have ordered, then let him take up his abode in Jahannam.' (Abu Ya'la).

52. 'What is the salvation of this matter ... in "No god but Allah".' (Ahmad and others).

53. '"Go out and announce among people that whoever witnessed that there is no god but Allah, the Garden becomes a must for him." So I went out and 'Umar met me ...' (Abu Ya'la. It is recorded from a *hadith* of Abu Hurairah and is most unusual as a *hadith* of Abu Bakr).

54. 'There are two types from my *ummah* who will not enter the Garden, *al-Murji'ah* and *al-Qadariyah*.' (Ad-Daraqutni in *Al-'Ilal*).

55. 'Ask Allah for health and safety.' (Ahmad, an-Nasa'i and Ibn Majah who has it by many different chains of transmission).

56. 'The Messenger of Allah, may Allah bless him and grant him peace, when he wanted some matter, used to say, "O Allah, do good to me and choose for me."' (At-Tirmidhi).

57. 'The supplication of debt is, "O Allah, the dispeller of worry ..."' (Al-Bazzar and al-Hakim).

58. 'Every body which has grown from (the nourishment of) usury, the Fire is more appropriate for it,' and in another wording, 'A body nourished on what is forbidden will not enter the Garden.' (Abu Ya'la).

59. 'There is nothing in the body which does not complain of the sharpness of the tongue.' (Abu Ya'la).

60. 'Allah descends on the midmost night of Sha'ban and in it forgives every human apart from a *kafir* or a man in whose heart there is a grudge.' (Ad-Daraqutni).

61. 'The *Dajjal* will emerge in the east from a land known as Khurasan, and peoples will follow him whose faces are as if they are shields formed of two hides, one sewn upon the other.' (At-Tirmidhi and Ibn Majah).

62. 'I have been given seventy thousand who will enter the Garden without any reckoning.' (Ahmad).

63. The *Hadith* of Intercession in its full length with people's going back and forward between prophet after prophet. (Ahmad)

64. 'Even if mankind were to travel in a valley and the *Ansar* were to travel in another valley, I would travel in the valley of the *Ansar*.' (Ahmad).

65. 'Quraysh are the masters of this authority, the best of them following the best of them and the worst of them following the worst of them.' (Ahmad).

66. The *hadith* that he, may Allah bless him and grant him peace, made a last testament about the *Ansar* at his death and said, 'Accept from their one who behaves excellently well and overlook (the behaviour of) their evil-doer.' (Al-Bazzar and at-Tabarani).

67. 'I know a land which is called Oman whose shores the sea sprinkles, and in which there is a tribe of the Arabs. If my messenger were to come to them they would not shoot him either with arrows or stones.' (Ahmad and Abu Yaᶜla).

68. The *hadith* that Abu Bakr passed by al-Hasan while he was playing with some boys and he put him upon his neck and said, 'My father! A resemblance with the Prophet and no resemblance to ᶜAli.' Ibn Kathir said: This is as if it were a *hadith* connected to the Prophet, because it has the strength of him saying, 'Truly the Prophet, may Allah bless him and grant him peace, used to resemble al-Hasan.'

69. The *hadith* that 'The Prophet, may Allah bless him and grant him peace, used to visit Umm Ayman.' (Muslim).

70. The *hadith* on the killing of the thief for the fifth theft. (Abu Yaᶜla and ad-Daylami).

71. The *hadith* of the story of Uhud. (At-Tayalisi and at-Tabarani).

72. 'While I was with the Messenger of Allah, may Allah bless him and grant him peace, I saw him pushing something away from himself but I did not see anything, so I said, "Messenger of Allah, may Allah bless him and grant him peace, what are you pushing away?" He said, "The world. It extended itself towards

me, so I said, 'Get away from me!' So it said to me, 'Why! You will not grasp me!?'"' (Al-Bazzar).

This is what Ibn Kathir narrated in *Musnad as-Siddiq* of the *hadith* which are connected back to the Prophet, may Allah bless him and grant him peace, but there escaped him other *hadith* which we will follow on with in order to complete the number which an-Nawawi mentioned.

73. 'Kill the tick (blood-sucker) whatever he may be among men.' (At-Tabarani in *al-Awsat*)

74. 'Look to whose houses you frequent, whose land you inhabit and in whose path you walk.' (Ad-Daylami).

75. 'Increase in sending blessings upon me, for Allah has appointed for my grave an angel; so that when a man of my *ummah* sends blessings, that angel will say to me, "So-and-so the son of so-and-so has this very hour sent blessings upon you."' (Ad-Daylami).

76. 'The *jumu'ah* (Friday prayer) to the *jumu'ah* is an expiation for what is between them, and the *ghusl* (complete washing of the entire body) on the day of the *jumu'ah* is an expiation.' (A *hadith* of al-ᶜAqili in *Ad-Du'afa* [weak traditions]).

77. 'The heat of Jahannam will only be for my *ummah* like the heat of the hot baths.' (At-Tabarani).

78. 'Beware of lying, for lying is remote from *iman*.' (Ibn Lal in *Makarim al-Akhlaq*).

79. 'Give the good news of the Garden to whoever took part in Badr.' (Ad-Daraqutni in *Al-Afrad*).

80. 'The *deen* is Allah's weighty banner. Who is able to carry it?' (Ad-Daylami).

81. '*Surah Yasin* is called the one which encompasses people generally in its goodness, which feeds and provides the means of living.' (Ad-Daylami, and al-Bayhaqi in *Shu'ab al-Iman*).

82. 'The humble and just ruler (*Sultan*) is the shade of Allah and His spear in the land. There will be raised up for him (in the record of his actions) every day and night the actions of sixty *siddiqs*.' (Abu'sh-Shaykh and al-ᶜAqili in *Ad-Du'afa*, and Ibn Hibban in *Kitab ath-Thawab*).

83. 'Musa said to his Lord, "What is the recompense for whoever consoles a mother bereaved of her child?" He said, "I will shade him in My shade."' (Ibn Shahin in *At-Targheeb*, and ad-Daylami).

84. 'O Allah, strengthen Islam with ʿUmar ibn al-Khattab.' (At-Tabarani in *Al-Awsat*).

85. 'Game is not caught, nor a thorny tree lopped, nor the root of a tree cut except through insufficient glorification (of Allah).' (Ibn Rahwayh in his *Musnad*).

86. 'If I had not been sent among you, ʿUmar would have been sent.' (Ad-Daylami).

87. 'If the people of the Garden had traded, they would have traded in cloth.' (Abu Yaʿla).

88. 'Whoever rebels, inviting (allegiance) to himself or to another, while there is an *Imam* (*Amir* or *Khalifah*) over people, then the curse of Allah, the angels and all men is upon him, so kill him.' (Ad-Daylami in *At-Tarikh*).

89. 'Whoever records some knowledge or a *hadith* from me, then reward will not cease being recorded for him as long as that knowledge or *hadith* remains.' (Al-Hakim in *At-Tarikh*).

90. 'Whoever walks barefoot in obedience of Allah, then Allah will not ask him on the Day of Resurrection about what He made obligatory upon him.' (At-Tabarani in *Al-Awsat*).

91. 'Whoever it would please that Allah should shade him from the boiling of Jahannam, and that He should place him in His shade, let him not be tough on the believers, and let him be compassionate to them.' (Ibn Lal in *Makarim al-Akhlaq*, Abu'sh-Shaykh, and Ibn Hibban in *Ath-Thawab*).

92. 'Whoever rises in the morning intending obedience towards Allah, Allah will record for him the reward of his day even if he disobeys Him.' (Ad-Daylami).

93. 'A people do not abandon *jihad* but that Allah will envelop them in punishment.' (At-Tabarani is *Al-Awsat*).

94. 'One who forges a lie will not enter the Garden.' (Ad-Daylami without an *isnad*).

95. 'Do not despise any one of the Muslims because the small one of the Muslims is, with Allah, great.' (Ad-Daylami).

96. 'Allah says, "If you wish for My mercy then show mercy to My people (My creation)."' (Abu'sh-Shaykh, Ibn Hibban and ad-Daylami).

97. 'I asked the Prophet, may Allah bless him and grant him peace, about the lower garment and he took hold of the calf muscle. I said, "Messenger of Allah, increase me!" He took hold of the forepart of the muscle. I said, "Increase me," and he said, "There is no good in what is lower than that." I said, "We are destroyed, Messenger of Allah!" He said, "Abu Bakr, aim for and take a middle course and you will be safe."' (Abu Nu'aym in *Hilyah al-Awliya*).

98. 'My palm and the palm of 'Ali are equal in justice.' (Ad-Daylami and Ibn 'Asakir).

99. 'Do not neglect to seek refuge from the *shaytan*, for if you do not see him, he is not unaware of you.' (Ad-Daylami who did not quote a chain of transmission).

100. 'Whoever builds a mosque for Allah, then Allah will build a house for him in the Garden.' (At-Tabarani in *Al-Awsat*).

101. 'Whoever has eaten of this foul-smelling herb (garlic) then let him not approach our mosque.' (At-Tabarani in *Al-Awsat*).

102. The *hadith* of the raising of the hands in the opening, the bowing, the prostration and the rising. (Al-Bayhaqi in *As-Sunan*).

103. 'That he, may Allah bless him and grant him peace, gave a camel as a gift to Abu Jahl.' (Al-Isma'ili in his *Mu'jam*).

104. 'Looking at 'Ali is an act of worship.' (Ibn 'Asakir).

That which is narrated from as-Siddiq in commentary on the Qur'an

Ibn Abi Mulaykah said: Abu Bakr was asked about an *ayah* and he said, 'What land would hold me or what sky would shade me if I were to say about an *ayah* of the Book of Allah that which Allah did not wish?'

Ibrahim at-Taymi said: Abu Bakr was asked about His words, exalted is He, '*And fruits and herbage*,' (Qur'an 80: 31) and he said, 'Which sky would shade me and what land would sustain me if I were to say about the Book of Allah that which I do not know?'

Abu Bakr was asked about *al-Kalalah* and he said, 'I will say my view on it and if it is correct it is from Allah, and if it is wrong it is from me and from *Shaytan*. I think that it is the one who has no child nor parent (surviving to inherit from him).' When ʿUmar was appointed *khalifah* he said, 'I am shy of rejecting something which Abu Bakr said.'

Al-Aswad ibn Hilal said: Abu Bakr said to his companions, 'What do you say about these two *ayats*, "*Truly, the ones who say, 'Our Lord is Allah', and then go straight, ...*" (Qur'an 41: 30) and "*And the ones who believe and do not clothe their belief in wrongdoing ...*"? (Qur'an 6: 82).' They said, 'Then they go straight and do not do wrong actions and do not clothe their belief in error.' He said, 'You have made it to carry a meaning which it cannot carry.' Then he said, 'They say, "*Our Lord is Allah,*" and then *they go straight*, so they do not incline towards a god other than Him and do not clothe their belief in *shirk* (associating others as partners with Him)."

ʿAmir ibn Saʿd al-Bajili related from Abu Bakr as-Siddiq about His words, exalted is He, '*For the ones who do excellently well there is the very best and more*,' (Qur'an 10: 26) that he said, 'Gazing on the face of Allah, exalted is He.'

Abu Bakr said about His words, exalted is He, '*Truly the ones who say, "Our Lord is Allah," and then they go straight, ...*' (Qur'an 41: 30), that he said, 'People have said it. So whoever dies upon that is of those who go straight.'

What is narrated from as-Siddiq of traditions which stop short at him, sayings, judgements, *khutbahs*, and prayers

Ibn ʿUmar said: A man came to Abu Bakr and said, 'Do you see adultery as a decree (of Allah)?' He said, 'Yes.' He said, 'So Allah has decreed it for me and then later He will punish me for it?' He said, 'Yes, son of the uncircumcised woman. By Allah, if there were anybody with me, I would order him to cut off your nose.'

Az-Zubayr narrated that Abu Bakr said, while he was delivering the *khutbah* to people, 'People, be shy and modest before Allah. By the One in Whose hand my self is, I shade myself when I go to the toilet in the open spaces, covering my head out of modesty towards Allah.'

ᶜAmr ibn Dinar said: Abu Bakr said, 'Be shy before Allah. By Allah, I enter the toilet and I lean my back against the wall out of modesty before Allah.'

Abu ᶜAbdullah as-Sunabihi related that he once prayed the prayer after sunset behind Abu Bakr as-Siddiq and he recited in the first two sets of bowing and prostration the Fatihah and a *surah* from among the small *surahs* (at the end of the Qur'an) and that he recited in the third, '*Our Lord, do not cause our hearts to deviate after You have guided us.*' (Qur'an 3: 8)

Ibn ᶜUyaynah said: Abu Bakr used to say, when he was consoling a man for a bereavement, 'There is no harm in patience, and no benefit in impatience, and death is less serious than what comes before it and more severe than what comes after it. Remember the loss of the Prophet, may Allah bless him and grant him peace, your affliction will seem little to you, and Allah will magnify your reward.'

Salim ibn ᶜUbayd, and he was a Companion, said: Abu Bakr as-Siddiq used to say to me, 'Stand between me and the dawn so that I can take the pre-dawn meal (preparatory to fasting).'

Abu Qilabah and Abu's-Safar both said: Abu Bakr as-Siddiq used to say, 'Shut the door until we have eaten the pre-dawn meal.'

Hudhayfah ibn Usayd said: I observed Abu Bakr and ᶜUmar and what they would make apparent (of their actions), wishing to set *sunnahs*.

Ibn ᶜAbbas said: I bear witness that Abu Bakr as-Siddiq said, 'Eat the fish which float (on the surface, i.e. which have died naturally, as it is permitted to eat them).'

Abu Bakr as-Siddiq disliked trading meat for live animals.

He placed the grandfather in the same standing as the father, meaning in inheritance.

ᶜAta' narrated from Abu Bakr that he said: The grandfather has the same degree as the father as long as there is no father but him, and the son of the son is in the place of the son as long as there is no son apart from him.

Al-Qasim narrated that Abu Bakr was brought a man who had denied his father and so Abu Bakr said, 'Hit the head for the *shaytan* is in the head.'

Ibn Abi Malik said: Abu Bakr, when he prayed over the dead, used to say, 'O Allah, Your slave, whose family, property and relatives have forsaken him, the wrong action is great, and You are all-forgiving, compassionate.'

ᶜUmar narrated that Abu Bakr gave judgement that ᶜAsim ibn ᶜUmar ibn al-Khattab should go to Umm ᶜAsim (ᶜUmar's ex-wife), and that he said (to ᶜUmar), 'Her scent, her odour and her gentleness are better for him than you are.'

Qais ibn Abi Hazim said: A man came to Abu Bakr and said, 'My father wants to take my property, all of it and he will make an end of it.' Abu Bakr said to his father, 'You can only have of his property that which will be sufficient for you.' He (the father) said, '*Khalifah* of the Messenger of Allah, did the Messenger of Allah, may Allah bless him and grant him peace, not say, "You and your property belong to your father."?' So he said, 'Yes, and he only meant expenditure on maintenance by that.'

ᶜAmr ibn Shuᶜayb narrated from his father who narrated from his father that Abu Bakr and ᶜUmar would not kill a freeman (in retaliation) for (the killing of) a slave.

Ibn Abi Mulaykah narrated from his grandfather that a man bit the hand of a man and so caused his (own) incisor to fall out, and Abu Bakr declared that there was no retaliation for it.

ᶜIkrimah said that Abu Bakr gave judgement that there were fifteen camels for (cutting off or mutilating) an ear, and said, 'The hair and the turban will conceal its disfigurement.'

Abu ᶜImran al-Juni said that Abu Bakr sent troops to Syria and put in command over them Yazid ibn Abi Sufyan and said, 'I counsel you with ten qualities: do not kill a woman, nor a child, nor a feeble old man; do not cut down a fruitful tree; do not ruin cultivated land; do not slaughter a camel or a sheep except for its owner; do not destroy the date-palm, nor burn it; do not conceal plunder; and do not be cowardly.'

Abu Barzah al-Aslami said: Abu Bakr was angry with a man and his anger became very severe indeed, so I said, '*Khalifah* of the Messenger of Allah, strike off his head!' He said, 'Woe to you! That belongs to no-one after the Messenger of Allah, may Allah bless him and grant him peace.'

Al-Muhajir ibn Abi Umayyah, who was the Amir of al-Yamamah, had two women singers brought before him, one of whom had sung abuse of the Prophet, may Allah bless him and grant him peace, so he cut off her hand and pulled out her teeth; and the other had sung ridicule of the Muslims, so he cut off her hand, and pulled out her teeth. Abu Bakr wrote to him, 'It has reached me that which you have done with the woman who sang abusing the Prophet, may Allah bless him and grant him peace, and if it were not that you had preceded me I would have told you to kill her, because the *hadd* punishment for the prophets does not resemble other *hadd* punishments. Whoever of the Muslims dares to do that is a renegade, and if he is a non-Muslim who has a covenant with the Muslims then he is a treacherous and hostile enemy. As for the one who sang ridiculing the Muslims; if she was one of those who claim to be Muslims, then she should be taught manners and punished but not mutilated. If she was one of the people of the *dhimmah* (People of the Book living under the governance of the Muslims), then, by my life, that *shirk* which you have turned away from is greater (as a crime than ridicule of the Muslims). If I had previously commmanded you in a case the like of this (and then later you had done what you did) you would have reached affliction, so accept that I will let things be, and beware of mutilating people, because it is a crime and must be avoided except in retaliation (for a similar crime of mutilation).'

Safiyyah bint Abi ᶜUbaid narrated that a man had sexual intercourse with a virgin slave girl and confessed it, so he ordered that he should be whipped and then he exiled him to Fadak.

Muhammad ibn Hatib said: A man who had stolen was brought to Abu Bakr and already all his hands and feet had been cut off (for thefts), so Abu Bakr said, 'I cannot find anything for you except what the Messenger of Allah, may Allah bless him and grant him peace, decided about you on the day he ordered that you be killed, and he certainly knew better about you,' and he ordered that he be killed.

Al-Qasim ibn Muhammad said that a man from Yemen, who had a hand and a foot cut off, came and stayed with Abu Bakr. He complained to him that the governor of the Yemen had wronged him, and he used to pray at night. So Abu Bakr would say, 'By your father, your night is not the night of a thief.' Then later they missed some jewellery belonging to Asma' bint ʿUmays, Abu Bakr's wife. He began to go around with them saying, 'Allah, You must take whoever plotted against the people of this righteous house.' Then they found the jewellery with a jeweller who claimed that the man whose limbs were amputated had brought it, and he confessed or someone witnessed against him. Abu Bakr gave the command and his left hand was cut off. Abu Bakr said, 'By Allah, his supplication against himself, for me is stronger and more severe against him than his theft.'

Anas said that Abu Bakr would cut (off the hand) for a shield whose value was five *dirhams*.

Abu Salih said: When the people of the Yemen came in the time of Abu Bakr and they heard the Qur'an, they began to weep. Abu Bakr said, 'Just like this we used to be, then the hearts became hard.' Abu Nuʿaym said, 'i.e. they became strong and tranquil with the *maʿrifah* (gnosis) of Allah, exalted is He.'

Ibn ʿUmar said: Abu Bakr said, 'Be regardful of Muhammad, may Allah bless him and grant him peace, in the people of his house.'

Abu Bakr said, 'Fragrant good fortune to whoever died in the time of weakness,' i.e. in the very beginning of Islam before the stirrings of dissensions.

Qabisah said: The grandmother came to Abu Bakr as-Siddiq asking him for her inheritance and he said, 'There is nothing for you in the Book of Allah and I have not learnt that there is anything for you in the *sunnah* of the Prophet of Allah, may Allah bless him and grant him peace, so go back until I ask people.' He asked people and al-Mughirah ibn Shuᶜbah said, 'I attended the Messenger of Allah who gave her (a grandmother) a sixth.' Abu Bakr said, 'Is there anyone else with you?' Muhammad ibn Maslamah arose and said the like of what al-Mughirah had said. So Abu Bakr allocated her that.

Al-Qasim ibn Muhammad said that two grandmothers came to Abu Bakr seeking their inheritances, the mother of a mother and the mother of a father, and so he gave the inheritance to the mother of the mother. ᶜAbd ar-Rahman ibn Sahl al-Ansari, who was one of those who had been present at Badr and was a member of Bani Harithah, said to him, '*Khalifah* of the Messenger of Allah, you have given to the one from whom he would not have inherited if she had died!' And so he divided it between the two of them.

ᶜA'ishah, may Allah be pleased with her, narrated the *hadith* of the wife of Rifaᶜah who was divorced from him and married after him ᶜAbd ar-Rahman ibn az-Zubayr but he was unable to consummate the marriage, and she wanted to return to Rifaᶜah. The Messenger of Allah, may Allah bless him and grant him peace, said to her, 'No, not until you taste the sweetness of intercourse with him and he tastes the sweetness of intercourse with you.' This much is in the *Sahih*. ᶜAbd ar-Razzaq added: She remained for a while and then she came to him and informed him that he had touched her. He forbade her to return to her first husband and said, 'O Allah, if it was more expansive for her that she should return to Rifaᶜah, then her marriage to him would not be completed for her another time.' Then later she came to Abu Bakr and ᶜUmar in their *khilafahs* and they both forbade her.

ᶜUqbah ibn ᶜAmir said that ᶜAmr ibn al-ᶜAs and Shurahbil ibn Hasanah both sent him as a messenger to Abu Bakr with the head of Bannan, the Byzantine general of Syria. When he came to Abu Bakr, he disapproved of that strongly and so ᶜUqbah said to him, '*Khalifah* of the Messenger of Allah, they (the Byzantines) do that with us.' He said, 'Are they following the *sunnah* of the Persians and the Byzantines? Don't carry the head to me; a letter and news are enough.'

Qais ibn Abi Hazim said: Abu Bakr went into a woman of Ahmas called Zaynab, and he saw her not talking and he said, 'What is wrong with her that she does not talk?' They said, 'She performed the *Hajj* in silence.' He said to her, 'Speak, because this is not permitted. This is one of the acts of *Jahiliyyah*.' So she spoke and said, 'Who are you?' He said, 'I am a man of the *Muhajirun*.' She said, 'Which of the *Muhajirun*?' He said, 'From Quraysh.' She said, 'From which group of Quraysh?' He said, 'You are a real questioner—I am Abu Bakr.' She said, 'How long will we remain on this right matter which Allah has brought us, after ignorance?' He said, 'Your remaining upon it will be as long as your *imams* stay upstanding.' She said, 'Who are the *imams*?' He said, 'Do your people not have leaders and nobles who order them and they obey them?' She said, 'Of course.' He said, 'They are those people.'

ᶜA'ishah, may Allah be pleased with her, said: Abu Bakr had a slave who used to pay him his revenue. One day he brought him something and Abu Bakr ate of it. The slave said to him, 'Do you know what this is?' Abu Bakr said, 'What is it?' He said, 'I used to act as a foreteller of the future for a man in the *Jahiliyyah* and how good was the foretelling, except that I deceived. Then he met me and gave me that which you have eaten from.' So Abu Bakr thrust his hand in his mouth and vomited everything in his stomach. Ibn Sirin said, 'I know of no-one who made himself vomit food which he had eaten except for Abu Bakr,' and he told the same story.

Aslam said that ᶜUmar discovered Abu Bakr grasping his tongue, saying, 'This is the one which has brought me to so many places.'

Abu Bakr passed by ᶜAbd ar-Rahman ibn ᶜAuf while he was quarrelling with his neighbour and he said, 'Do not quarrel with your neighbour for he will remain when people have left you.'

Musa ibn ᶜUqbah related that Abu Bakr as-Siddiq used to deliver the *khutbah* saying, 'Praise belongs to Allah, the Lord of the creatures, I praise Him and seek His aid, and We ask Him for generosity for that which is after death, because my term and yours have drawn near. And I witness that there is no god but Allah alone, no partner with Him and that Muhammad is His slave and messenger whom He sent with the Truth, as a bringer of good news and a warner and an illuminating lamp so that he might warn whoever is alive and that the word would be realised on the disbelievers. Whoever obeys Allah and His Messenger is truly guided, and whoever disobeys them has gone astray into clear error. I counsel you to have fearful obedience of Allah, and to cling strongly to the command of Allah which He has laid down for you and by which He has guided you, because the comprehensive summation of the guidance of Islam after the word of sincerity (the *shahadah*) is 'hearing and obedience' to whomever Allah has given authority over your affairs, for whoever obeys Allah and those who order the well-recognised virtues and forbid what is rejected, has succeeded and prospered, and discharged that duty with which he is obliged. Beware of following the whim of passion, for he has succeeded and prospered who has been protected from the whim of passion, greed, ambition, and anger. Beware of boasting, for what boast can he have who is created from dust, and then he will later return to dust, then later maggots will eat him, and he is today alive and tomorrow dead? So know a day by a day (the Last Day) and an hour by an hour (the Hour of the end). Protect yourselves from the supplication of the wronged one, and count yourselves among the dead, and be patient, for all action is by patience, and be on your guard for watchfulness is useful. And act, and action will be accepted. Guard yourselves from that which Allah cautioned you about of His torment, and hasten to that which Allah promised you of His mercy. Understand and you will be understood, have fearful obedience (*taqwa*; literally—self-protecting) and you will be guarded, for Allah has made clear to you that by which He destroyed those who were before you, and that by which He saved whomever He saved before you. He has made clear to you in His book His *halal* and His *haram*, and which actions He loves and which He deplores. I will not neglect you and myself, and Allah is the One from Whom aid is sought. And there is no power (to prevent evil) and strength (to do right) but by Allah. Know that as long as you are sincere towards your Lord in your actions then your Lord you have obeyed and your portion you have protected and guarded, and you will be in a state of well-being. And that which you offer voluntarily for your *deen,* then make it a free-will offering (which you send) before you and you will receive fulfillment for your loan, and you will be given your permanent daily allowance of food during your poverty and in your (time of) need of it. Then reflect, slaves of Allah, on your brethren and your companions who have passed away. They have come to that which they sent before them and they are established upon that, and they are alone in the grief and the happiness in that which is after death. Allah has no partner, and there is no relationship between Him and any one of His creatures by which He will give him good or avert evil, excepting by obedience to Him and following His command. Truly, there is no good in a good after which comes the Fire, nor any evil in an evil after which comes the Garden. I say this word of mine and I seek the forgiveness of Allah, for me and for you. Send blessings on your Prophet, may Allah bless him and grant him peace, and peace be on him, the mercy of Allah and His blessings.'

ᶜAbdullah ibn Hakim said: Abu Bakr as-Siddiq addressed a *khutbah* to us and in it he praised Allah as He is worthy and then said, 'I counsel you with fearful obedience of Allah, that you praise Him as He is worthy, and that you mix longing with fear, because Allah, exalted is He, praised Zakariyya and the people of his family saying, "*They used to hasten competitively in doing good actions, and they would supplicate Us, full of longing and fear, and they were humble to Us.*" (Qur'an 21: 90). Then know, slaves of Allah, that Allah has taken, by His right, your selves as a pledge, and He has taken on that basis your covenants, and He has bought from you the transient little with the everlasting much. This Book of Allah is among you; its light does not become snuffed out and its wonders never end, so take illumination from its light, accept the sincere advice of His Book, and seek light from it for the Day of darkness; for He has only created you for His worship and service, and He has entrusted over you noble scribes who know what you are doing. Then know, slaves of Allah, that you go out in the mornings and come back in the evenings for a period of time (the life-span) the knowledge of which He has concealed from you; so if you are capable that your life-spans should come to an end while you are on the work of Allah, then do so, and you will not be able to but by the permission of Allah. Race in your life-spans before they pass away and return you to the worst of your actions, for some people have given their lives to others and forgotten themselves and I forbid you to be like them. Make haste! Make haste! Be quick! Be quick! For behind you there is a nimble pursuer whose command is very fast.'

Yahya ibn Abi Kathir narrated that Abu Bakr used to say in his *khutbah*, 'Where are the handsome fair of face, conceited with their youth? Where are the kings who built the cities and fortified them? Where are those who used to be given conquests in battles? Their strongest were humbled when time betrayed them and they awoke in the darknesses of the graves. Make haste! Make haste! Be quick! Be quick!'

Salman said: I came to Abu Bakr and said, 'Counsel me!' He said, 'Salman, have fearful obedience of Allah, and know that there will be conquests, but I do not know what your portion of them will be, that which you put in your belly or throw upon your back (clothing). Know that whoever prays the five prayers enters the morning in a covenant with Allah, exalted is He, and enters the evening in a covenant with Allah, exalted is He. Do not kill anyone of the people who is in a covenant with Allah and thus behave treacherously towards Allah concerning His covenant, for then Allah will throw you down in the Fire upon your face.'

Abu Bakr, may Allah be pleased with him, also said, 'The right-acting people will be taken away, the foremost and then the next foremost until there only remain of the people chaff, husks and dregs like those left over from dates and barley, whom Allah will not be concerned for or care for.'

Mu'awiyyah ibn Qurrah narrated that Abu Bakr as-Siddiq, may Allah be pleased with him, used to say in his supplication, 'O Allah, make the best of my life the last of it, and the best of my action its seals and the best of my days the day I meet You.'

Al-Hasan said: It has reached me that Abu Bakr used to say in his supplication, 'O Allah, I ask You that which is best for me at the end of the affair. O Allah, make the last that You give me of good Your good pleasure and the highest ranks in the Gardens of Bliss.'

'Arfajah said: Abu Bakr, may Allah be pleased with him, said, 'Whoever is able to weep let him weep, and if not let him endeavour to weep.'

'Azrah narrated: Abu Bakr, may Allah be pleased with him, said, 'Two reds have destroyed them (women): gold and saffron.'

Muslim ibn Yasar narrated that Abu Bakr said, 'The Muslim is rewarded for everything, even a hurt (in the foot) caused by a stone, the breaking of his sandal's thong, or some article in his sleeve which he misses and fears for, then finds it in the fold (of his garment).'

Maymun ibn Mahran said: Abu Bakr was brought a crow with large wings and he turned it over and said, 'No game is caught nor tree lopped but because of the glorification it neglected.'

As-Sunabihi narrated that he heard Abu Bakr saying, 'The supplication of the brother for his brother for the sake of Allah is expected to be answered.'

Labid the poet said that he came to Abu Bakr and said, 'Every thing apart from Allah is false.' Abu Bakr said, 'You have told the truth.' He said, 'And every bliss inevitably fades away.' He (Abu Bakr) said, 'You lie! With Allah there is a bliss that does not pass away.' When he turned away Abu Bakr said, 'Perhaps the poet said the word from wisdom.'

His words indicative of the strength of his fear of his Lord

Mu'adh ibn Jabal said: Abu Bakr entered a walled garden and there was a species of pigeon in the shade of a tree, so he sighed and then said, 'Fragrant good fortune to you, bird! You eat of the trees, you find shade in the trees, and you fly off without reckoning. Would that Abu Bakr was like you.'

Al-Asma'i said: When Abu Bakr was praised he used to say, 'O Allah, You know my self better than I do, and I know my self better than they do. O Allah, make me better than what they think, and forgive me for what they don't know, and don't take me to task for what they say.'

Abu 'Imran al-Juni said: Abu Bakr said, 'I would love to be a hair in the side of a believing slave.'

Mujahid said: Ibn az-Zubayr used to be like a piece of wood, when he stood in prayer, out of fearful humility and he said, 'I have been told that Abu Bakr was like that.'

Al-Hasan said: Abu Bakr said, 'By Allah, I wish that I was this tree which is eaten (from) and chopped down.'

Qatadah said: It has reached me that Abu Bakr said, 'I wish that I was herbage which cattle eat.'

Damrah ibn Habib said: Death came to a son of Abu Bakr as-Siddiq. The young man began to glance towards a mattress. When he died they said to Abu Bakr, 'We saw your son glancing towards the mattress.' They removed him from the mattress and found underneath it five or six *dinars*. Abu Bakr struck his hand upon the other repeatedly saying, 'Truly, we belong to Allah and truly we are returning to Him. So and so, I don't think your skin would be ample enough for it.'

Thabit al-Banani narrated that Abu Bakr used to quote as a proverb this poem:

'You will not cease lamenting the death of a beloved, until you are (as) he, and the youth hopes a hope which he dies short of (attaining).'

Ibn Sirin said: No-one after the Prophet, may Allah bless him and grant him peace, was as much in awe of what he did not know as Abu Bakr. No-one after Abu Bakr was as much in awe of what he did not know as 'Umar. Sometimes a case would come before Abu Bakr for which he could find no source in the Book of Allah nor any trace or tradition in the *Sunnah* and so he would say, 'I will exert myself to arrive at my own conclusion. If it is right then it is from Allah. If it is wrong it is from me and I seek forgiveness of Allah.'

That which is narrated from him in interpretation of dreams

Sa^cid ibn al-Musayyab said: ^cA'ishah, may Allah be pleased with her, saw in a dream as if three moons fell in her room. She told it to Abu Bakr—he was one of the best of men in interpretation—and he said, 'If your dream is true, then three of the best people on the earth will be buried in your room.' When the Prophet, may Allah bless him and grant him peace, died, he said, '^cA'ishah, this is the best of your moons.'

^cUmar ibn Shurahbil said: The Messenger of Allah, may Allah bless him and grant him peace, said, 'I saw myself herding black sheep, then herding white sheep after them, until the black could not be seen among them.' Abu Bakr said, 'Messenger of Allah, as for the black sheep, they are the Arabs who will become Muslims in great numbers. The white sheep are the non-Arabs who will become Muslims until the Arabs cannot be seen among them because of their huge numbers.' The Messenger of Allah, may Allah bless him and grant him peace, said, 'In exactly the same way, the angel interpreted it before dawn.'

Ibn Abi Layla said: The Messenger of Allah, may Allah bless him and grant him peace, said, 'I saw myelf at a well drawing water from it, and black sheep came to me to drink, then later dusty white coloured sheep.' Abu Bakr said, 'Let me interpret it,' and he mentioned the like of the previous *hadith*.

Muhammad ibn Sirin said: The most skilled in interpretation of dreams of this *ummah* after its Prophet was Abu Bakr.

Ibn Shihab said: The Messenger of Allah, may Allah bless him and grant him peace, saw a dream and told it to Abu Bakr. He said, 'I saw as if I hastened to be first, I and you, up a ladder and that I beat you by two and a half steps.' He said, 'Messenger of Allah, Allah will take you to His forgiveness and mercy and I will live after you for two and a half years.'

Abu Qilabah narrated that a man said to Abu Bakr as-Siddiq, 'I saw in sleep that I was urinating blood.' He said, 'You are a man who comes to his wife (in intercourse) while she is menstruating, so ask forgiveness of Allah and don't do it again.'

A point of interest

ᶜAbdullah ibn Buraydah said: The Messenger of Allah, may Allah bless him and grant him peace, sent ᶜAmr ibn al-ᶜAs in a raiding party in which were Abu Bakr and ᶜUmar. When they reached the place of the war, ᶜAmr told them not to light a fire. ᶜUmar became angry, and he wanted to come to him, but Abu Bakr forbade him. He told him that the Messenger of Allah, may Allah bless him and grant him peace, only appointed him because of his knowledge of war. So he (ᶜUmar) became calm.

Abu Maᶜshar narrated from one of his Shaykhs that the Messenger of Allah, may Allah bless him and grant him peace, said, 'I put a man in charge of a people, among whom there is one who is better than him, because he is more alert of the eye and more perceptive about war.'

Section

Yazid ibn al-Asamm narrated that: The Prophet, may Allah bless him and grant him peace, said to Abu Bakr, 'Am I older (*akbar* literally: greater) or you?' He said, 'You are greater and more noble and I have more years than you.' This is a *mursal* and very unusual tradition. If it is authentic this answer is counted as evidence of the high degree of his intelligence and courtesy. But it is well known that this reply was made by al-ᶜAbbas, and that similarly it happened for Saᶜid ibn Yarbuᶜ in this wording: That the Messenger of Allah, may Allah bless him and grant him peace, said to him, 'Which of us is older (*akbar*)?' He said, 'You are greater and better than me and I am older.'

It was said to Abu Bakr, '*Khalifah* of the Messenger of Allah, will you not confer authority on the people of Badr?' He said, 'I know their rank, but I dislike to sully them with the world.'

Isma'il ibn Muhammad narrated that Abu Bakr divided up some property equally among the people. 'Umar said to him, 'Do you make the companions of Badr and other people equal?' Abu Bakr said to him, 'The world is only a sufficiency and the best sufficiency is the vastest. Their merit is only in their wages.'

Section

Abu Bakr ibn Hafs said: It has reached me that Abu Bakr used to fast in summertime and break his fast in wintertime.

Hayan as-Sa'igh said: The engraving on the signet ring of Abu Bakr was, 'Blessed as the One Who Decrees is Allah.'

Musa ibn 'Uqbah said, 'We don't know of four who reached the Prophet, may Allah bless him and grant him peace, and their sons as well, except for these four: Abu Quhafah, his son Abu Bakr as-Siddiq, his son 'Abd ar-Rahman and Abu 'Ateeq ibn 'Abd ar-Rahman whose name was Muhammad.

'A'ishah, may Allah be pleased with her, said: None of the *Muhajirun's* fathers became Muslims except for Abu Bakr's.

Anas said: The oldest of the companions of the Messenger of Allah, may Allah bless him and grant him peace, were Abu Bakr as-Siddiq and Suhail ibn 'Amr ibn Bayda'.

A point of interest

Asma' bint Abi Bakr said: When it was the year of the conquest (of Makkah) a daughter of Abu Quhafah went out and the cavalry met her. She was wearing a neck-ring of silver around her neck, and a man tore it off her neck. When the Prophet, may Allah bless him and grant him peace, entered the mosque, Abu Bakr stood and said, 'I adjure you (the Muslims) by Allah and Islam, (to return) my sister's neck-ring.' By Allah, no-one answered him. He said it a second time and no-one answered him. Then he said, 'Sister, hope for a recompense (from Allah) for your neck-ring, for, by Allah, trustworthiness this day among people is very scarce.'

A point of interest

I have seen in the handwriting of al-Hafidh adh-Dhahabi:

Those who were unique in their ages for their skills were: Abu Bakr as-Siddiq in genealogy, ᶜUmar ibn al-Khattab in strength in the command of Allah, ᶜUthman ibn ᶜAffan in modesty, ᶜAli in judgement, Ubayy ibn Kaᶜb in recitation, Zaid ibn Thabit in the laws of inheritance, Abu ᶜUbaydah ibn al-Jarrah in trustworthiness, Ibn ᶜAbbas in commentary (on Qur'an), Abu Dharr in truthfulness, Khalid ibn al-Walid in bravery, al-Hasan al-Basri in reminding, Wahb ibn Munabbih in stories, Ibn Sirin in interpretation (of dreams), Nafiᶜ in recitation, Abu Hanifah in *fiqh*, Ibn Ishaq in the battles, Muqatil in allegorical interpretation, al-Kalbi in the stories of the Qur'an, al-Khalil in the measures and metres of poetry, Fudail ibn ᶜIyad in worship, Sibawih in grammar, Malik in knowledge, Yahya ibn Maᶜin in knowledge of the men (i.e. the transmitters of knowledge and *hadith*), Abu Tamam in poetry, Ahmad ibn Hanbal in *Sunnah*, Al-Bukhari in criticism of the *hadith*, al-Junayd in *at-Tasawwuf*, Muhammad ibn Nasr al-Marwazi in those matters of *fiqh* on which there is disagreement, al-Jabani on al-Ashaᶜri ᶜitizal in theology, Muhammad ibn Zakariyya ar-Razi in medicine, Abu Maᶜshar in astronomy, Ibrahim al-Karmani in interpretation (of dreams), Ibn Nabatah in *khutbahs*, Abu'l-Farj al-Asbahani in public speaking, Abu'l-Qasim at-Tabarani in adjustments in cases of inheritance, Ibn Hazm in the apparent meanings (*adh-Dhahir*), Abu'l-Hasan al-Bakri in lies, al-Hariri in his *al-Maqamat*, Ibn Mandah in the breadth of his travelling, al-Mutanabbi in poetry, al-Mausili in singing, as-Suli in chess, al-Khatib al-Baghdadi in swiftness of reading, ᶜAli ibn Hilal in calligraphy, ᶜAta' as-Sulaimi in fear, the Qadi al-Fadil in composition, al-Asmaᶜi in anecdotes, Ashᶜab in ambition, Muᶜabbad in singing and Ibn Sina' in philosophy.

^cUmar ibn al-Khattab
may Allah be pleased with him

U mar ibn al-Khattab ibn Nufail ibn ^cAbdu'l-^cUzza ibn Riyah ibn Qart ibn Razah ibn ^cAdi ibn Ka^cb ibn Lu'ayy, Amir al-Muminin, Abu Hafs, al-Qurashi, al-^cAdawi, al-Faruq.

He accepted Islam in the sixth year of prophecy when he was twenty-seven years old, says adh-Dhahabi.

An-Nawawi says: ^cUmar was born thirteen years after the El-ephant, he was one of the nobility of Quraysh, and he had the role of ambassador in the *Jahiliyyah*; Quraysh, whenever war broke out among them or between them and others, would send him as an ambassador, i.e. a messenger, and when someone called them to judgement—often over a matter of standing or lineage—then they sent him as a response to that.

He accepted Islam very early on, after forty other men and eleven women. Some say that it was after thirty-nine men and twenty-three women, and some say, after forty-five men and eleven women. But it was only after he accepted Islam that Islam was shown openly in Makkah and the Muslims rejoiced in him.

He said: He was one of the outstripping first ones, one of the ten for whom it was witnessed that they were for the Garden, one of the *khulafa'* who took the right way, one of the in-laws of the Prophet, may Allah bless him and grant him peace, one of the great men of knowledge of the Companions and one of their abstinent people.

There are related from him five hundred and thirty-nine *hadith* from the Prophet, may Allah bless him and grant him peace. ^cUthman ibn ^cAffan narrated from him, ^cAli (ibn Abi Talib), Talhah (ibn ^cUbaydillah), Sa^cd (ibn Abi Waqqas), ^cAbd ar-Rahman ibn

ʿAuf, Ibn Masʿud, Abu Dharr, ʿAmr ibn ʿAbasah and his son ʿAbdullah, Ibn ʿAbbas, Ibn az-Zubayr, Anas, Abu Hurairah, ʿAmr ibn al-ʿAs, Abu Musa al-Ashʿari, al-Baraʾ ibn ʿAzib, Abu Saʿid al-Khudri, and a great number of the Companions and others, may Allah be pleased with them.

I say: I attach here some sections in which there are some sections of interest connected to his biography.

The reports on his acceptance of Islam

Ibn ʿUmar narrated that: The Prophet, may Allah bless him and grant him peace, said, 'O Allah, strengthen Islam with whoever is more beloved to You of these two men: ʿUmar ibn al-Khattab or Abu Jahl ibn Hisham.' This has been narrated from *hadith* of Ibn Masʿud and Anas, may Allah be pleased with them.

Ibn ʿAbbas related that the Prophet, may Allah bless him and grant him peace, said, 'O Allah, strengthen Islam by ʿUmar ibn al-Khattab especially.' This has been narrated in *hadith* of Abu Bakr as-Siddiq and Thawban.

ʿUmar said: I went out to confront the Messenger of Allah, may Allah bless him and grant him peace, and found that he had preceded me to the mosque (of Makkah). I stood behind him and he began by reciting *Suratu'l-Haqqah*. I was astonished by the composition of the Qurʾan, so I said, 'By Allah, this is a poet as Quraysh say.' Then he recited, '*It is truly the saying of a noble messenger, and it is not the saying of a poet, how little you believe...*' (Qurʾan 69: 40) to the end of the *ayah*, and Islam came about in my heart.

Jabir said: The beginning of ʿUmar's Islam was that ʿUmar said, 'My sister's time to give birth came to her at night so I went out of the house, and entered the precincts of the Kaʿbah. Then the Prophet, may Allah bless him and grant him peace, came and entered the *hijr* (the low-walled, semi-circular area to one end of the Kaʿbah) and on him there were two rough cloths. He prayed to Allah as much as Allah willed, then he turned away and I heard something I had not heard the like of. He went out and I followed him and he said, "Who is this?" I said, "ᶜUmar." He said, "ᶜUmar, will you not leave me alone, either by night or by day?" I became afraid that he might supplicate against me, so I said, "I witness that there is no god but Allah and that you are the Messenger of Allah." He said, "ᶜUmar, keep it secret." I said, "No, by the One Who sent you with the truth, I will openly declare it just as I openly declared idolatry."'

Anas, may Allah be pleased with him, said: ᶜUmar went out wearing his sword, and a man from Bani Zuhrah met him and said, 'Where do you intend going, ᶜUmar?' He said, 'I want to kill Muhammad.' He said, 'How will you be safe from Bani Hashim and Bani Zuhrah if you have killed Muhammad?' He said, 'I can only believe that you have converted.' He said, 'Shall I show you something astonishing; your brother-in-law and your sister have converted and abandoned your *deen*.' ᶜUmar walked on and came to the two of them while Khabbab was with them. When he heard the sound of ᶜUmar he hid in the house, and then he (ᶜUmar) entered and said, 'What is this murmur of lowered voices?' They had been reciting *Taha*. They said, 'Nothing but some conversation which we were holding.' He said, 'Perhaps you two have converted?' His brother-in-law said to him, 'ᶜUmar, what if the truth were outside of your *deen*?' So ᶜUmar leapt upon him and struck him severely. His sister came to push him away from her husband and he struck her a blow with his hand so that her face bled. Then she said, and she was angry, 'And if the truth were outside of your *deen*? I witness that there is no god but Allah and that Muhammad is His slave and His Messenger.' ᶜUmar said, 'Give me the writing which you have and I will read it,'— and ᶜUmar used to read. His sister said to him, 'You are dirty, and no-one reads it but the purified (so stand and bathe yourself or perform *wudu*).' He stood and performed *wudu'*, then he took the writing and read *Taha* until it came to, '*Truly I, I am Allah there is no god except Me, so worship Me and establish the prayer for My remembrance.*' (Qur'an 20: 14). ᶜUmar said, 'Show me the way to Muhammad.' When Khabbab heard the words of ᶜUmar he came out and said, 'Rejoice, ᶜUmar! Because I hope that you are the (answer to the) supplication which the Messenger of Allah made for you on the night of Thursday, "O Allah, strengthen Islam with ᶜUmar ibn al-Khattab or with ᶜAmr ibn Hisham."' The Messenger of Allah, may Allah bless him and grant him peace, was in the lower part of the house which was at the foot of Safa and ᶜUmar went off until he came to the house, at the door of which were Hamzah, Talhah and others. Hamzah said, 'This is ᶜUmar; If Allah wants good for him he will become a Muslim; and if He wishes other than that, then killing him will be a little thing for us.' He said: And the Prophet, may Allah bless him and grant him peace, was inside receiving revelation. He came out when ᶜUmar arrived, took hold of the folds of his clothes and the straps of his sword, and said, 'You won't give up, ᶜUmar, until Allah visits you with disgrace and punishment like he did al-Walid ibn al-Mughirah.' ᶜUmar said, 'I witness that there is no god but Allah and that you are the slave of Allah and His Messenger.'

Aslam said: ᶜUmar said to us, 'I was the most severe of people against the Messenger of Allah, may Allah bless him and grant him peace. Then one hot day at midday I was in one of the pathways of Makkah, and a man met me and said, "I am amazed at you, Ibn al-Khattab. You claim that you are like this and like this, and this matter has entered your own house." I said, "What is that?" He said, "Your sister has become a Muslim." So I went back in a fury and struck the door. Someone said, "Who is it?" I said, "ᶜUmar." They hurried and hid from me. They had been reciting a page which they had and they abandoned it and forgot it. My sister got up to open the door, and I said to her, "Enemy of her own self, have you converted?" I struck her upon the head with something that I had in my hand so that the blood flowed and she cried. She said, "Ibn al-Khattab, whatever you are going to do, then do it, for I have converted." I entered and sat down on the couch. Then I glanced at the page and said, "What is this? Give it to me." She said, "You are not one of its people, you don't clean yourself after intercourse, and this is a writing which none touches except for those who have purified themselves."

But I wouldn't give up until she gave it to me. I opened it and there in it was, "*In the name of Allah, the Merciful, the Compassionate.*" When I passed by one of the names of Allah, exalted is He, I became afraid of it and I put down the page. Then I came back to myself and picked up the page and there in it was, "*There glorifies Allah that which is in the heavens and the earth,*" and I became afraid. I read up until, "*believe in Allah and His messenger!*" (Qur'an 57: 1-7) and so I said, "I witness that there is no god but Allah," and so they all came out to me hastily, saying, "*Allahu Akbar!*" and said, "Rejoice! Because the Messenger of Allah, may Allah bless him and grant him peace, supplicated on Monday and said, 'O Allah strengthen Your *deen* with whoever is the more beloved of the two men to You, either Abu Jahl ibn Hisham or ᶜUmar.'" They directed me to the Prophet, may Allah bless him and grant him peace, in a house at the foot of As-Safa, and I went to it and knocked on the door. They said, "Who is it?" I said, "Ibn al-Khattab." They knew my severity against the Messenger of Allah, may Allah bless him and grant him peace, so nobody moved to open the door until he said, may Allah bless him and grant him peace, "Open it for him." They opened it for me, two men grabbed hold of me by the upper arms and brought me to the Prophet, may Allah bless him and grant him peace, who said, "Leave him alone." Then he grabbed me by my shirt and dragged me forcibly towards him and said, "Accept Islam, Ibn al-Khattab. O Allah guide him," and I bore witness and the Muslims said, "Allahu Akbar!" so loudly that it was heard in the valleys of Makkah.

They had been concealing themselves. I did not wish to see a man striking and being struck but that I experienced it myself and none of that touched me. I went to my uncle Abu Jahl ibn Hisham, who was one of the nobility, and knocked on his door. He said, "Who is it?" I said, "Ibn al-Khattab, and I have converted." He said, "Don't do it," and slammed the door on me. I said, "This isn't anything," and went to one of the great ones of Quraysh, called out to him and he came out to me. I said to him the same as I had said to my uncle, he said to me the same as my uncle had said to me, went in and slammed the door on me. I said, "This isn't anything, the Muslims are being struck and I am not being struck." A man said to me, "Would you like your acceptance of Islam to be known?" I said, "Yes." He said, "When people are seated in the *hijr* go to so-and-so, a man who cannot possibly conceal a secret, and say to him, just between yourself and him, 'I have converted,' for it is very rarely that he has ever concealed a secret." I went and people had already gathered in the *hijr*. I said, just between me and him, "I have converted." He said, "Did you really do that?" I said, "Yes." He cried at the top of his voice, "Ibn al-Khattab has converted." They ran up to me; I was hitting them, they were hitting me and people gathered around me. Then my uncle said, "What is this group?" Someone said, "ʿUmar has converted." He stood upon the *hijr* and indicated with the palm of his hand, "I have helped the son of my sister." They dispersed from around me. I did not want to have seen any of the Muslims being struck and striking without seeing it myself, so I said, "This which has happened to me is nothing." I went to my uncle and said, "Your help is returned to you," and I continued to hit and be hit until Allah strengthened Islam.'

Ibn ʿAbbas, may Allah be pleased with both of them, said: I asked ʿUmar, may Allah be pleased with him, 'For what reason were you called Al-Faruq?' He said, 'Hamzah accepted Islam three days before me. I went to the mosque, and Abu Jahl hurried up to abuse the Prophet, may Allah bless him and grant him peace, and Hamzah was told about it. He took his bow and came to the mosque, up to the circle of Quraysh in which Abu Jahl was. He leant upon his bow facing Abu Jahl and looked at him, and Abu Jahl recognised the mischief in his face, and said, "What is wrong with you, Abu ʿUmarah?" He raised his bow and with it struck one of the veins in his neck, cutting it so that blood flowed. Quraysh rectified that from fear of mischief and trouble.' He said, 'The Messenger of Allah, may Allah bless him and grant him peace, was concealed in the house of Al-Arqam al-Makhzumi so Hamzah went off and accepted Islam. I went out three days after him and there was so-and-so son of so-and-so al-Makhzumi, and I said to him, "Do you yearn to get out of the *deen* of your ancestors and follow the *deen* of Muhammad?" He said, "If I did, then one who has much greater right upon you has also done it." I said, "Who is he?" He said, "Your sister and your brother in-law." I went off, found the door locked and heard the murmur of lowered voices. Then the door was opened for me. I entered and said, "What is this I hear with you?" They said, "You didn't hear anything," and the conversation continued between us until I took hold of my brother in-law's head and hit him, making him bleed. My sister stood up to me and took hold of my head and said, "That has happened despite you." I was ashamed when I saw the blood, so I sat down and said, "Show me this writing." My sister said, "No-one touches it except for the purified. If you are truthful then get up and bathe yourself." I got up and bathed myself, then I returned and sat down. They brought me a page in which was, "*In the name of Allah, the Merciful, the Compassionate.*" I said, "Wholesome and pure names!" "*Taha. We have not revealed the Qur'an to you for you to grieve, ...*" up to His words, "*... His are the most beautiful names.*" (Qur'an 1-8). It became a great matter in my heart and I said, "From this Quraysh have fled!" I accepted Islam and said, "Where is the Messenger of Allah, may Allah bless him and grant him peace?" She said, "He is in the house of al-Arqam." I went to the house and knocked on the door. The people gathered and Hamzah said to them, "What is wrong with you." They said, "ʿUmar." He said, "And if it is ʿUmar? Open the door for him. If he has accepted, then we will accept that from him, and if he turns his back, we will kill him." The Messenger of Allah, may Allah bless him and grant him peace, heard that and came out. I pronounced the *shahadah* and the people of the house said, "*Allahu Akbar!*" in such a way that the people of Makkah heard it. I said, "Messenger of Allah, are we not upon the truth?" He said, "Of course." I said, "Why do we conceal it?" We went out in two ranks, in one of which I was and in the other Hamzah, until we entered the mosque, and Quraysh looked at me and at Hamzah. There came upon them gloom and depression the like of which had never before come upon them. The Messenger of Allah, may Allah bless him and grant him peace, named me on that day "al-Faruq" because Islam had been shown openly and a separation made between the truth and falsehood.'

Dhakwan said: I said to ᶜA'ishah, 'Who named ᶜUmar "al-Faruq"?' She said, 'The Prophet, may Allah bless him and grant him peace.'

Ibn ᶜAbbas, may Allah be pleased with them both, said: When ᶜUmar accepted Islam, then Jibril descended and said, 'Muhammad, the inhabitants of heaven rejoice in ᶜUmar's acceptance of Islam."

Ibn ᶜAbbas, may Allah be pleased with them both, said: When ᶜUmar accepted Islam, the idolators said, 'The people have been split in half from us today,' and Allah revealed, '*O Prophet, Allah is enough for you; and whoever follows you of the believers.*' (Qur'an 8: 64).

Ibn Masᶜud, may Allah be pleased with him, said: We did not cease to become mighty since the acceptance of Islam by ᶜUmar.

Ibn Masᶜud, may Allah be pleased with him, said: The Islam of ᶜUmar was an opening, his emigration was a help and his *imamate* was a mercy. I saw us unable to pray towards the House until ᶜUmar accepted Islam. When ᶜUmar accepted Islam, he fought them until they left us alone and we prayed.

Hudhayfah said: When ᶜUmar accepted Islam, Islam was like the man advancing towards you, only increasing in nearness. When ᶜUmar was killed, Islam was like the man backing away from you, only increasing in distance.

Ibn ᶜAbbas, may Allah be pleased with them both, said: The first man to be open about Islam was ᶜUmar ibn al-Khattab.

Suhaib said: When ᶜUmar, may Allah be pleased with him, accepted Islam, he was open about it, invited people to it openly; we sat around the House in circles, we made circuits around the House, we took our rights from whoever was tough with us, and we retaliated against him for some of what he brought us.

Aslam the freed slave of ᶜUmar said: ᶜUmar accepted Islam in Dhu'l-Hijjah of the sixth year of prophethood while he was twenty-six years old.

His emigration

ʿAli said: I don't know of anyone who didn't emigrate in secret except for ʿUmar ibn al-Khattab; because when he wanted to emigrate he strapped on his sword, put his bow over his shoulder, carried his arrows in his hand, and came to the Kaʿbah where the nobles of Quraysh were in the courtyard. He performed seven circuits, and then prayed two *rakaʿat* at the Station (of Ibrahim). Then he approached their circle one step at a time and said, "What ugly faces! Whoever wishes to bereave his mother, orphan his children and widow his wife then let him meet me behind this valley." Not one of them followed him.

Al-Bara', may Allah be pleased with him, said: The first of the *Muhajirun* who came to us was Musʿab ibn ʿUmayr, then Ibn Umm Maktum, then ʿUmar ibn al-Khattab mounted among twenty others. We said, 'What has the Messenger of Allah, may Allah bless him and grant him peace, done?' He said, 'He is right behind me.' Then later, the Prophet, may Allah bless him and grant him peace, came and Abu Bakr, may Allah be pleased with him, along with him.

An-Nawawi said: ʿUmar attended, along with the Messenger of Allah, may Allah bless him and grant him peace, all of the battles, and he was one of those who stood firm beside him on the Day of Uhud.

The *hadith* on his merit, other than those already quoted in the chapter on as-Siddiq

Abu Hurairah, may Allah be pleased with him, said: The Prophet, may Allah bless him and grant him peace, said, 'While I was asleep I saw myself in the Garden, and there was a woman performing *wudu'* beside a palace. I said, "Whose is this palace?" They said, "It belongs to ʿUmar." Then I remembered your jealousy and turned away.' ʿUmar wept and said, 'Could I be jealous of you, Messenger of Allah?'

Ibn ʿUmar narrated that the Messenger of Allah, may Allah bless him and grant him peace, said, 'While I was asleep I drank—

meaning milk—until I saw satiation flowing in my nails, and then I passed it to ᶜUmar.' They said, 'How did you interpret it, Messenger of Allah?' He said, 'Knowledge.'

Abu Saᶜid al-Khudri, may Allah be pleased with him, said: I heard the Prophet, may Allah bless him and grant him peace, saying, 'While I was sleeping I saw people being shown to me and they had shirts on. Some of them reached to the breast, and some of them reached lower than that. ᶜUmar was shown to me and he had on a shirt which he was dragging along.' They said, 'How did you interpret it, Messenger of Allah?' He said, 'The *deen*.'

Saᶜd ibn Abi Waqqas said: The Prophet, may Allah bless him and grant him peace, said, 'Ibn al-Khattab, by Him in Whose hand is my self, the *shaytan* never met you travelling on a road but that he would travel on a road other than your road.'

Abu Hurairah said: The Prophet, may Allah bless him and grant him peace, said, 'There were in the nations before you people who were inspired, and if there is one in my *ummah* it is ᶜUmar.'

Ibn ᶜUmar related that the Prophet, may Allah bless him and grant him peace, said, 'Allah has put the truth upon ᶜUmar's tongue and (in) his heart.' Ibn ᶜUmar said: No affair ever happened among people and they spoke about it and ᶜUmar spoke about it but that the Qur'an was revealed confirming what ᶜUmar said.

ᶜUqbah ibn ᶜAmir said: The Prophet, may Allah bless him and his family and grant them peace, said, 'If there were to be a prophet after me it would be ᶜUmar ibn al-Khattab.' This *hadith* has been narrated by Abu Saᶜid al-Khudri, ᶜIsmah ibn Malik and Ibn ᶜUmar.

ᶜA'ishah, may Allah be pleased with her, said: The Prophet, may Allah bless him and grant him peace, said, 'I am looking at the *shaytans* of the Jinn and men who have fled from ᶜUmar.'

Ubayy ibn Kaᶜb said: The Prophet, may Allah bless him and grant him peace, said, 'The first one whom the Truth will shake hands with is ᶜUmar, the first He will greet (with the greeting of peace), and the first He will take by the hand and enter into the Garden.'

Abu Dharr said: The Prophet, may Allah bless him and grant him peace, said, 'Truly Allah has placed the truth upon the tongue of ᶜUmar, it speaks by him (or he speaks by it).'

Abu Hurairah said: The Prophet, may Allah bless him and grant him peace, said, 'Truly Allah has placed the truth on the tongue of ᶜUmar and (in) his heart.' This *hadith* has been narrated by ᶜUmar ibn al-Khattab, Bilal, Muᶜawiyah ibn Abi Sufyan, ᶜA'ishah, and Ibn ᶜUmar, may Allah be pleased with them.

ᶜAli, may Allah be pleased with him, said: We, the Companions of Muhammad, used not to doubt that the *sakinah* (tranquility or Divine presence) spoke by the tongue of ᶜUmar.

Ibn ᶜUmar said: The Prophet, may Allah bless him and grant him peace, said, 'ᶜUmar is the lamp of the people of the Garden.' This *hadith* was narrated by Abu Hurairah and As-Saᶜb ibn Juththamah.

ᶜUthman ibn Madhᶜun said: The Prophet, may Allah bless him and grant him peace, said, 'This one is the lock upon the *fitnah* (sedition and trials),' and he indicated ᶜUmar with his hand. 'There will remain a door strongly locked between you and the *fitnah* as long as this one lives among you.'

Ibn ᶜAbbas, may Allah be pleased with both him and his father, said: Jibril came to the Prophet, may Allah bless him and grant him peace, and said, 'Greet ᶜUmar with the greeting of peace and inform him that his anger is might and his good pleasure is judgement.'

ᶜA'ishah, may Allah be pleased with her, said that the Prophet, may Allah bless him and grant him peace, said, 'The *shaytan* is afraid of ᶜUmar.'

Buraydah said that the Prophet, may Allah bless him and grant him peace, said, 'The *shaytan* is afraid of you, ᶜUmar.'

Ibn ᶜAbbas, may Allah be pleased with both of them (i.e. Ibn ᶜAbbas and his father ᶜAbbas), said: The Prophet, may Allah bless him and grant him peace, said, 'There is no angel in the heaven that does not respect ᶜUmar, and no *shaytan* on the earth but that he is afraid of ᶜUmar.'

Abu Hurairah, may Allah be pleased with him, said: The Prophet, may Allah bless him and grant him peace, said, 'Allah glories in the people of ʿArafah generally and He glories in ʿUmar particularly.' It has been narrated in a *hadith* of Ibn ʿAbbas, may Allah be pleased with them both.

Al-Fadl ibn ʿAbbas said: The Prophet, may Allah bless him and grant him peace, said, 'The truth, after me, is with ʿUmar wherever he is.'

Ibn ʿUmar and Abu Hurairah, may Allah be pleased with both of them, said: The Prophet, may Allah bless him and grant him peace, said, 'While I was asleep I saw myself at a well upon which was a bucket, so I drew from it as long as Allah willed. Then later Abu Bakr took it and drew a full bucket or two, and in his drawing there was some weakness, and Allah will forgive him. Then ʿUmar ibn al-Khattab came and drew water and it became transformed in his hand into a large bucket, and I have not seen a chief of the people do wonderful deeds such as he did, until the people had satisfied their thirst and settled down (there by the water).'

An-Nawawi said in his *Tahdhib*: The men of knowledge say, 'This points to the *khilafahs* of Abu Bakr and ʿUmar, and to the great number of conquests and the victory of Islam in the time of ʿUmar.'

Sadisah said: The Prophet, may Allah bless him and grant him peace, said, 'The *shaytan* has not met ʿUmar since he accepted Islam but that he fell upon his face.' This *hadith* has been narrated also by Sadisah from Hafsah.

Ubayy ibn Kaʿb said: The Prophet, may Allah bless him and grant him peace, said, 'Jibril said to me, "Let Islam weep over the death of ʿUmar."'

Abu Saʿid al-Khudri said: The Prophet, may Allah bless him and grant him peace, said, 'Whoever is angry with ʿUmar is angry with me. Whoever loves ʿUmar loves me. Allah glories in the people on the evening of ʿArafah generally, and He glories in ʿUmar particularly. Allah has not sent a prophet except that he put among his *ummah* an inspired man and if there is one such in my *ummah* then it is ʿUmar.' They said, 'Prophet of Allah, how inspired?' He said, 'The angels speak by his tongue.'

Sayings of the Companions and first generations on him

Abu Bakr as-Siddiq, may Allah be pleased with him, said: There is not on the face of the earth a man more beloved to me than Umar.

Someone said to Abu Bakr during his (last) illness, 'What will you say to your Lord, when you have appointed Umar?' He said, 'I will say to Him, "I have appointed over them the best of them."'

Ali, may Allah be pleased with him, said: When the right-acting ones are mentioned then begin with Umar. We did not think it unlikely that *as-Sakinah* (the Divine Presence) spoke with the tongue of Umar.

Ibn Umar, may Allah be pleased with him, said: I have never seen anyone after the Prophet, may Allah bless him and grant him peace, from the time he died, more perceptive and more liberally generous than Umar.

Ibn Masud, may Allah be pleased with him, said: Even if the knowledge of Umar were to be put in one scale of a balance and the knowledge of every living being on the earth were put in the other scale, the knowledge of Umar would outweigh their knowledge. They used to hold the view that he had gone (i.e. died) with nine-tenths of knowledge.

Hudhayfah, may Allah be pleased with him, said: It is as if the knowledge of mankind was concealed in the understanding of Umar.

Hudhayfah, may Allah be pleased with him, said: By Allah, I do not know a man whom the blame of the one who blames, for the sake of Allah, does not overcome, except for Umar.

A'ishah, may Allah be pleased with her, said—and she mentioned Umar—'He was, by Allah, skilful in managing affairs, absolutely unique.'

Mucawiyah, may Allah be pleased with him, said: As for Abu Bakr, he did not want the world and it did not want him. As for Umar, the world wanted him but he did not want it. As for us, we have rolled over in it (like an animal in the dust).

Jabir, may Allah be pleased with him, said: Ali entered upon Umar—and he was shrouded—and said, 'The mercy of Allah upon you! There is no-one I would prefer to meet Allah with that which is in his page (the record of his actions), after the companionship of the Prophet, may Allah bless him and grant him peace, than this shrouded one.'

Ibn Mas^cud, may Allah be pleased with him, said: When the right-acting ones are remembered, then begin with ^cUmar. Truly ^cUmar was the most knowledgeable of us of the Book of Allah, and the most understanding (literally: having the most *fiqh*) of us of the *deen* of Allah, exalted is He.

Ibn ^cAbbas was asked about Abu Bakr and he said, 'He was the good, all of it.' He was asked about ^cUmar and said, 'He was like the apprehensive bird which thinks that on every path there is a snare to catch it.' He was asked about ^cAli and he said, 'He was full of resolve, sound judgement, knowledge and valour.'

^cUmayr ibn Rabi^cah related that ^cUmar ibn al-Khattab said to Ka^cb al-Ahbar, 'How do you find my description?' He said, 'I find your description to be a horn of iron.' He asked, 'What is a horn of iron?' He said, 'A strong commander who, for the sake of Allah, the censure of the one who blames does not overcome.' He said, 'Then what?' He said, 'There will be after you a *khalifah* whom a wrong-doing group will kill.' He said, 'Then what?' He said, 'Then there will be the trial (affliction).'

Ibn Mas^cud, may Allah be pleased with him, said: ^cUmar ibn al-Khattab excelled people in four: the affair of the prisoners on the Day of Badr, he ordered that they should be killed and Allah revealed, '*If it were not for a decree of Allah which had preceded ...*' (Qur'an 8: 68) to the end of the *ayah*; and in the matter of the *hijab*, he ordered the women of the Prophet, may Allah bless him and grant him peace, to veil themselves, so Zaynab said to him, 'And really you are responsible over us Ibn al-Khattab, and the revelation descends upon us in our houses?' So Allah revealed, '*Then if you ask them for some item ...*' (Qur'an 33: 53) to the end of the *ayah*; and by the supplication of the Prophet, may Allah bless him and grant him peace, 'O Allah, help Islam with ^cUmar'; and in his view of Abu Bakr, for he was the first one to pledge allegiance to him.

Mujahid said: We used to say that the *shaytans* were chained and shackled during the amirate of ᶜUmar, then when he was struck they spread abroad.

Salim ibn ᶜAbdullah said: News of ᶜUmar was slow in reaching Abu Musa so he went to a woman who had a *shaytan* in her, and asked her about him. She said, 'Wait until my *shaytan* comes to me.' Then he came and she asked him about him. He said, 'I left him dressed with a piece of cloth as a waist-wrapper, smearing the camels of the *sadaqah* (of the *zakah*) with tar (against the mange or scab). And that is a man whom a *shaytan* does not see but that he falls flat on his nostrils; the angel is between his two eyes and the *Ruh al-Quds* (Jibril) speaks with his tongue.'

Section

Sufyan ath-Thawri said: Whoever claimed that ᶜAli had more right to authority than Abu Bakr and ᶜUmar has made a mistake and has accused Abu Bakr, ᶜUmar and all the *Muhajirun* and the *Ansar* of making a mistake.

Sharik said: No-one in whom there is any good advances ᶜAli before Abu Bakr and ᶜUmar.

Abu Usamah said: Do you grasp who Abu Bakr and ᶜUmar were? They were the father and mother of Islam.

Jaᶜfar as-Sadiq said: I am quit of whoever mentions Abu Bakr and ᶜUmar with anything but good.

The agreements of (the views of) ᶜUmar (with subsequent confirmatory revelations of Qur'an)

Some of them make them amount to more than twenty.

Mujahid said: ᶜUmar used to hold a view and Qur'an would be revealed with (confirmation of) it.

ᶜAli said: In the Qur'an there are some of the views of ᶜUmar.

Ibn ᶜUmar said: When people said one thing and ᶜUmar said another, the Qur'an would be revealed with the like of what ᶜUmar said.

ᶜUmar said: I agreed with my Lord in three things; I said, 'Messenger of Allah, if only we were to take the Station of Ibrahim as a place of prayer,' and there was revealed, '... *and take the Station of Ibrahim as a place of prayer.*' (Qur'an 2: 125). I said, 'Messenger of Allah, both good and bad people come to visit your wives; if only you would order them to wear *hijabs*,' and the *ayah* of the *hijab* was revealed. The wives of the Prophet, may Allah bless him and grant him peace, united in jealousy, and so I said, 'Perhaps his Lord, if he divorces you, will give him in exchange wives better than you, ...' and it was revealed just like that (with exactly the same words, see Qur'an 66: 5).

In another *hadith* ᶜUmar said, 'I agreed with my Lord in three things: in the *hijab*, in the prisoners at Badr, and in the Station of Ibrahim.' In this *hadith* is a fourth instance.

In *at-Tahdhib* of an-Nawawi, 'The Qur'an was revealed in agreement with him on the prisoners at Badr, on the *hijab*, on the Station of Ibrahim and on the prohibition of wine.' He added a fifth instance. Its *hadith* is that he said, 'O Allah, make clear to us about wine with an explanation which relieves us from all doubt.' Then Allah revealed its prohibition.

Anas said: ᶜUmar said, 'I was in agreement with my Lord in four things: this *ayah* was revealed, "*And certainly We have created man from an extraction of clay,*" (Qur'an 23: 12) and when it was revealed I said, "So blessed be Allah the best of creators," and then it was revealed, "*So blessed be Allah the best of creators.*"' (Qur'an 95: 8). Here he mentioned a sixth instance. The *hadith* has another chain of transmission from Ibn ᶜAbbas.

Then I saw in the book *Fada'il al-Imamayn* of Abu ᶜAbdullah ash-Shaybani that he said, 'ᶜUmar agreed with his Lord in twenty-one situations,' and he mentioned these six (aforementioned). He augmented as a seventh the story of ᶜAbdullah ibn Ubayy. I say: Its *hadith* is in the sound traditions from him (ᶜUmar). He said, 'When ᶜAbdullah ibn Ubayy died, the Messenger of Allah, may Allah bless him and his family and grant them peace, was invited to perform the funeral prayer over him so he stood up for that. I rose up until I stood up close to his chest and said,

"Messenger of Allah, is it over the enemy of Allah, Ibn Ubayy, who said one day such-and-such?" Then, by Allah, it wasn't very long until it was revealed, "*And do not pray over one of them ever ...*" (Qur'an 9: 84) to the conclusion of the *ayah*.'

8. '*They ask you about wine ...*' (Qur'an 2: 219) to the end of the *ayah*.

9. '*O you who believe, do not approach the prayer ...*' (Qur'an 4: 43) to the end of the *ayah*. I say that the two of them, along with the *ayah* from *Al-Ma'idah,* are one instance, and the three are in the preceding *hadith*.

10. When the Messenger of Allah, may Allah bless him and grant him peace, increased in seeking forgiveness for a people, 'Umar said, 'It is equal to them.' Then Allah revealed, '*It is equal to them whether you seek forgiveness for them . . .*' (Qur'an 63: 2) to the end of the *ayah*. This *hadith* has been narrated of Ibn 'Abbas.

11. When he, may Allah bless him and grant him peace, sought the advice of the Companions about the expedition to Badr, 'Umar was in favour of the expedition and so it was revealed, '*Just as your Lord brought you out of your house by the truth ...*' (Qur'an 8: 5) to the end of the *ayah*.

12. When he, may Allah bless him and grant him peace, sought the advice of the Companions with respect to the story of the slander (of 'A'ishah) 'Umar said, 'Who married you to her, Messenger of Allah?' He said, 'Allah.' He said, 'Do you think that your Lord would conceal a defect of hers from you? *Glory be to You, this is huge slander!* (Qur'an 24: 16). Then the revelation came down just like that.

13. His story in the fast when he made love to his wife after waking from sleep (before the pre-dawn meal)—and that was forbidden in the beginning of Islam—and so it was revealed, '*It is permitted to you on the night of the fast ...*' (Qur'an 2: 187) to the end of the *ayah*.

14. His words, Exalted is He, '*Whoever is an enemy to Jibril ...*' (Qur'an 2: 97) to the end of the *ayah*. I say that it has been narrated from many different narrators the best of which is from

ᶜAbd ar-Rahman ibn Abi Layla that: A Jew met ᶜUmar and said, 'Jibril, whom your companion mentions, is an enemy to us.' So ᶜUmar said, '*Whoever is an enemy to Allah and His angels and His messengers and Jibril and Mika'il, then truly Allah is an enemy to the disbelievers.*' So it was revealed on the tongue of ᶜUmar.

15. His words, Exalted is He, '*Then no! By your Lord, they do not believe ...*' (Qur'an 4: 65) to the end of the *ayah*. I say that its story has been narrated from Abu'l-Aswad. He said: Two men brought a dispute to the Prophet, may Allah bless him and his family and grant them peace, and he gave judgement between them. The one who had judgement given against him said, 'Let us go to ᶜUmar ibn al-Khattab,' and so the two of them went to him. The man said, 'The Messenger of Allah, may Allah bless him and grant him peace, gave judgement in my favour against this man and he said, "Let us go to ᶜUmar."' ᶜUmar said, 'Is it like that?' He said, 'Yes.' So ᶜUmar said, 'Stay where you are until I come out to you.' Then he came out to them wrapping his sword in his garment and struck the one who had said, 'Let us go to ᶜUmar,' and killed him. The other returned and said, 'Messenger of Allah, ᶜUmar killed—by Allah!—my companion.' So he said, 'I wouldn't have thought that ᶜUmar would have ventured to kill a believer.' Then Allah revealed, '*Then no! By your Lord they do not believe ...*' to the end of the *ayah*. He declared, there was to be no retaliation or compensation for the blood of the man and declared ᶜUmar free from any wrong in his killing. There is another text that supports this story which I have related in *At-Tafsir al-Musnad*.

16. Seeking permission to enter. That was because his servant entered his room when he was sleeping and he said, 'O Allah, forbid entrance.' Then the *ayah* of seeking permission to enter was revealed.

17. His saying about the Jews, 'They are a confounded people.'

18. His words, exalted is He, '*Many of the first ones and many of the latter ones.*' (Qur'an 56: 39-40). I say that Jabir ibn ᶜAbdullah narrated its story and that it is in the *Asbab an-Nuzul*.

19. The lifting (abrogation) of the recitation of, '*The older man and the older woman when they commit adultery ....*' to the end of the *ayah* (an *ayah* whose judgement remains valid although it is not in the *mushaf* and is not recited).

20. His words on the Day of Uhud when Abu Sufyan said, 'Is so-and-so among the people?' (ᶜUmar said) 'We will not answer him,' and the Prophet, may Allah bless him and grant him peace, agreed with him.

Ash-Shaybani said: We join to this that Kaᶜb al-Ahbar said, 'Woe to the king of the earth from the King of heaven.' Then ᶜUmar said, 'Except for whoever takes himself to account.' Kaᶜb said, 'By the One in Whose hand is my soul it is in the Tawrah. You have carried it on (the words of the verse) consecutively.' Then ᶜUmar fell prostrate.

Then I have seen in *Al-Kamil* of Ibn ᶜAdi from ᶜUmar that Bilal used to say, when he called the *adhan*, 'I witness that there is no god but Allah. Come to prayer.' Then ᶜUmar said to him, 'Say after it, "I witness that Muhammad is the Messenger of Allah."' The Prophet, may Allah bless him and grant him peace, said, 'Say as ᶜUmar said.'

His miracles

Ibn ᶜUmar said: ᶜUmar sent an army and he put at the head of them a man called Sariyah. While ᶜUmar was delivering the *khutbah* he began to cry out, 'Sariyah, the mountain!' three times. Then later the messenger of the army came and he asked ᶜUmar, '*Amir al-Muminin*, we were being defeated and in that situation we heard a voice crying out, "Sariyah, the mountain!" three times. We put the mountain to our rear, and then Allah defeated them.' Someone said to ᶜUmar, 'You cried out with those words.' That mountain, where Sariyah was, is close to Nahawand in the land of the non-Arabs (Persian Iraq).

Ibn ᶜUmar, in another version of the *hadith*, said: ᶜUmar was delivering the *khutbah* on the day of *Jumuᶜah* and then he turned aside during his *khutbah* and said, 'Sariyah, the mountain! He who asks the wolf to be a shepherd will be wronged.' People looked about, one to another. Then ᶜAli said to them, 'Let him explain what he meant.' When he had finished they asked him and he said, 'It occurred to me in my mind that the idolators were defeating our brothers who were passing by a mountain, and that if they were to turn towards it, they would fight on one front only, but if they passed by it they would be destroyed. So there came out of me that which you claim you heard.' He said: The messenger came a month later and mentioned that they had heard the voice of ᶜUmar on that day, and he said, 'We turned towards the mountain, and Allah gave us victory.'

ᶜAmr ibn al-Harith said: While ᶜUmar (ibn al-Khattab) was upon the *mimbar* delivering the *khutbah* on the day of *jumuᶜah* suddenly he left off the *khutbah* and said, 'Sariyah, the mountain!' two or three times. Some of those present said, 'He has gone mad, he is insane.' ᶜAbd ar-Rahman ibn ᶜAuf went in to see him—and he had confidence in him—and he said, 'You give them room to talk against you. While you were giving the *khutbah,* suddenly you cried out, "Sariyah, the mountain!" What sort of thing is this?' He said, 'By Allah, I could not control it. I saw them fighting near a mountain and they were being attacked from in front of them and from behind them. I could not stop myself from saying, "Sariyah, the mountain!" so that they would reach the mountain.' Then they waited some time until Sariyah's messenger came with his letter, 'The people met us (in battle) on the day of *jumuᶜah,* and we fought them until, when it was time for *jumuᶜah,* we heard someone cry out, "Sariyah, the mountain!" twice, so we reached the mountain. We continued victorious over our enemy until Allah defeated them and killed them.' Then those people who had accused him said, 'Leave this man alone, because he is in collusion with him.'

Ibn ᶜUmar in another *hadith* said: ᶜUmar ibn al-Khattab said to a man, 'What is your name?' He said, 'Jamrah (a live coal).' He asked, 'Whose son?' He said, 'The son of Shihab (flame).' He asked, 'From what tribe?' He said, 'From al-Hurqah (a state of burning).' He asked, 'Where is your dwelling?' He said, 'At al-Harrah (the heat).' He asked, 'In which of them?' He said, 'Dhat

Ladha (the blazing one).' ᶜUmar said, 'Go to your family for they have been burnt.' The man returned to his family and found that they had been burnt. This *hadith* is narrated of Yahya ibn Saᶜid by Malik and by a number of other compilers of *hadith*.

Qais ibn al-Hajjaj, from someone he related from, said: When Egypt was conquered, its people came to ᶜAmr ibn al-ᶜAs, when the first day of one of their months arrived, and they said to him, 'Amir, this Nile of ours has a year in which it does not flow without it.' He asked, 'And what is that?' They said, 'When eleven nights have elapsed of this month we seek a young virgin from her parents, we obtain the consent of the parents, then we dress her in the best possible clothing and ornaments, and then we throw her in this Nile.' So ᶜAmr said to them, 'This will never be in Islam. Islam demolishes what precedes it.' They left, and neither did the Nile flow a little nor a lot, until they intended to emigrate. When ᶜAmr saw that, he wrote to ᶜUmar ibn al-Khattab about it. He wrote back to him, 'You were right in what you said. Truly, Islam demolishes what precedes it.' He sent a slip of paper inside his letter and wrote to ᶜAmr, 'I have sent you a slip of paper inside my letter, so throw it in the Nile.' When ᶜUmar's letter reached ᶜAmr ibn al-ᶜAs, he took the slip and opened it, and there in it was, 'From the slave of Allah ᶜUmar ibn al-Khattab *Amir al-Muminin* to the Nile of Egypt. Now, if *you* used to flow before, then don't flow! If it was Allah who made you flow, then I ask the Overwhelming One to make you flow.' He threw the slip into the Nile a day before (the Festival of) the Cross. They woke up in the morning, and Allah, Exalted is He, had made it flow (and it rose) sixteen cubits in one night. Allah cut off this *sunnah* (custom) of the people of Egypt right up to this day.

Tariq ibn Shihab said: A man was in conversation with ᶜUmar ibn al-Khattab and told him a lie, and he would say, 'Withhold this.' Then later he told him something else and he said, 'Withhold this.' He said to him, 'Everything I told you was true except for what you told me to withhold.'

Al-Hasan said: If there was anyone who recognised a lie when he was told it, then it was ᶜUmar ibn al-Khattab.

Abu Hudbah al-Himsi said: ᶜUmar was told that the people of Iraq had pelted their *amir* with pebbles and he went out angry. He performed the prayer but was forgetful in his prayer. When he had completed the prayer, he said, 'O Allah, they have made me confused, so make them confused, and hasten with the youth of (the tribe of) Thaqif who will pass judgement among them with the judgement of *Jahiliyyah*, who will not accept from their good-doers and he will not pass over their wrong-doers with pardon.' I say that this indicates al-Hajjaj. Ibn Lahiᶜah said, 'Al-Hajjaj was not yet born at that time.'

Some particulars of his biography

Al-Ahnaf ibn Qais said: We were sitting at ᶜUmar's door and a slave girl passed by, and they said, 'The concubine of the Amir al-Muminin.' He said, 'She is not the concubine of the Amir al-Muminin, and she is not permitted to him. She is of the property of Allah.' So we said, 'Then what is permitted to him of the property of Allah, exalted is He?' He said, 'There is only permitted to ᶜUmar of the property of Allah two garments, a garment for the winter and a garment for the summer, what I can perform the *Hajj* and the ᶜ*Umrah* with (i.e. an *ihram*), my sustenance and the sustenance of my family, as a man of Quraysh who is not the wealthiest of them nor the poorest, then I am, after that, a man among the Muslims.'

Khuzaymah ibn Thabit said, 'Whenever ᶜUmar appointed a governor, he wrote to him and made a condition on him that he should not ride a *birdhaun* (a large heavy non-Arabian horse from Asia Minor or Greece), nor eat delicacies, nor dress in finery, nor lock his door against the needy. Then if he did that it would be permitted to punish him.'

ᶜIkrimah ibn Khalid and others said: Hafsah, ᶜAbdullah and others spoke to ᶜUmar and said, 'If only you were to eat wholesome food it would strengthen you upon the truth.' He asked, 'Are you all of this view?' They said, 'Yes.' He said, 'I have learnt what your sincere advice is. However, I have left my two companions on a highway, and if I abandon their highway I will not reach them in the house.' He (ʿIkrimah) said: An affliction befell the people one year, and that year he did not eat clarified butter nor fat.

Ibn Mulaykah said: ʿUtbah ibn Farqad spoke to ʿUmar about his food and he said, 'Mercy on you! Should I eat up my wholesome sweet things in my worldly life and seek to enjoy myself with them?'

Al-Hasan said: ʿUmar entered in upon his son ʿAsim when he was eating meat and he said, 'What is this?' He said, 'We had a craving for it.' He said, 'Every time you crave something, do you eat it? It is sufficient wasteful extravagance for a man that he eats everything he has an appetite for.'

Aslam said: ʿUmar said, 'There occurred to my heart a desire for fresh fish.' He (Aslam) said: Yarfaʾ mounted his camel and rode four miles there, four miles back, buying a basketful and bringing it back. Then he went to his camel, washed it, and went to ʿUmar. He said, 'Let us go and I will look at the camel.' He said, 'Did you forget to wash this sweat beneath its ears? Have you tormented an animal for the appetite of ʿUmar? No! by Allah! ʿUmar will not taste of your basket.'

Qatadah said: ʿUmar used to dress, while he was *khalifah*, with a garment of wool patched in parts with leather, and he would go around in the markets with a whip over his shoulder with which he would correct people. He would pass bits of rags and pieces of date-stones, which he would stumble on unexpectedly, and he would throw them into people's houses for them to make use of.

Anas said: I saw between ʿUmar's shoulder-blades, four patches in his shirt. Abu ʿUthman an-Nahdi said: I saw ʿUmar wearing a waist-wrapper patched with leather. ʿAbdullah ibn ʿAmir ibn Rabiʿah said: I performed the *Hajj* with ʿUmar and he did not pitch a tent of goat's hair nor of wool. He used to throw the upper part of his *ihram* and his leather mat over a bush and seek shelter underneath it. ʿAbdullah ibn ʿIsa said: There were two dark furrows in ʿUmar's face from his weeping. Al-Hasan said: ʿUmar used to pass by an *ayah* in his *wird* (daily portion set aside to recite) and he would fall down (in a faint) until he revived after some days. Anas said: I entered a walled garden and heard ᶜUmar saying, while there was a wall between us, 'ᶜUmar ibn al-Khattab, Amir al-Muminin. Well done! Well done! By Allah, you will fear Allah, Ibn al-Khattab or Allah will punish you.' ᶜAbdullah ibn ᶜAmir ibn Rabiᶜah said: I saw ᶜUmar take up a straw from the ground and say, 'I wish I was this straw. I wish I was nothing. I wish that my mother had not given birth to me.' ᶜAbdullah ibn ᶜUmar ibn Hafs said: ᶜUmar carried a skin full of water upon his neck. Someone spoke to him about that and he said, 'My self was filling me with conceit and I wished to humble it.' Muhammad ibn Sirin said: An in-law of ᶜUmar's came to see him and asked him to give him something from the *bait al-mal* and ᶜUmar refused him and said, 'Do you want me to meet Allah as a treacherous King?' Then he gave him from his own property ten thousand dirhams. An-Nakhaᶜi said: ᶜUmar used to trade while he was *khalifah*. Anas said: ᶜUmar's stomach rumbled from eating olive oil the year of the drought—he had forbidden himself clarified butter—and he tapped on his stomach with his finger and said, 'There is nothing else for us, until the people have the means of living.' Sufyan ibn ᶜUyaynah said: ᶜUmar ibn al-Khattab said, 'The person I like most is the one who points out to me my defects.' Aslam said: I saw ᶜUmar ibn al-Khattab taking hold of the ear of the horse, taking hold, with the other hand, of his own ear and leaping up on the back of the horse. Ibn ᶜUmar said: I never saw ᶜUmar become angry, and then Allah was mentioned in his presence or he was made to fear, or a person would recite an *ayah* from the Qur'an in his presence, but that he stopped short of what he meant to do. Bilal said to Aslam, 'How do you find ᶜUmar?' He said, 'The best of people, except that when he becomes angry it is a mighty matter.' Bilal said, 'If I was with him when he became angry, I would recite Qur'an to him until his anger went.' Al-Ahwas ibn Hakim said, narrating from his father: ᶜUmar was brought meat dressed with clarified butter and he refused to eat the two of them. He said, 'Both of them are seasonings.' All of the aforegoing are from Ibn Saᶜd.

Al-Hasan said: ᶜUmar said, 'It is an easy thing by which I put right a people, that I exchange them an *amir* in place of an *amir*.'

His description

Zirr said: I went out with the people of Madinah on the day of *ᶜEid* and I saw ᶜUmar walking barefoot, an old man, balding, of a tawny colour, left-handed, tall, towering over people as if he were on a riding beast. Al-Waqidi said: It is not known among us that ᶜUmar was tawny, unless he saw him in the year of the drought, because his colour changed when he ate olive oil.

Ibn ᶜUmar described ᶜUmar and said: A man of fair complexion, with a ruddy tint prevailing, tall, balding and grey-haired.

ᶜUbaydah ibn ᶜUmayr said: ᶜUmar used to overtop the people in height.

Salimah ibn al-Akwaᶜ said: ᶜUmar was left and right-handed, meaning that he used both hands together.

Abu Raja' al-ᶜUtaridi said: ᶜUmar was a tall stout man, extremely bald, fair but extremely ruddy, in the two sides of his beard a lightness, his moustache was large, and at its extremities there was a redness at the roots of which there was black.

From various sources it is known that the mother of ᶜUmar ibn al-Khattab was Hantamah the daughter of Hisham ibn al-Mughirah and she was the sister of Abu Jahl ibn Hisham, so that Abu Jahl was his maternal uncle.

His khilafah

He took on the *khilafah* through the covenant of Abu Bakr in Jumada al-Akhirah in the year 13 A.H.

Az-Zuhri said, 'ᶜUmar was appointed *khalifah* on the day that Abu Bakr died which was Tuesday eight days before the end of Jumada al-Akhirah.' He undertook the command most fully, and there were very many conquests in his days.

In the year 14 A.H., Damascus was conquered partly both by treaty and force, and Homs (ancient Emessa) and Baalbek by treaty, and Basrah and Ubullah by force.

'In that year ᶜUmar united people in one *jamaᶜah* in *salat at-tarawih* (the optional prayers said at night in Ramadan),' said al-ᶜAskari in *Al-Awa'il* (Firsts).

In the year 15 A.H., all of Jordan was conquered by force except for Tiberias which was by treaty. In this year were the battles of Yarmuk and Qadisiyyah.

Ibn Jarir said: In it Saᶜd founded Kufa, and ᶜUmar instituted regular wages (for the fighting men), registers, and gave allowances according to priority.

In the year 16 A.H., Ahwaz and Mada'in were conquered, and in the latter Saᶜd established the *jumuᶜah* in the great hall of Khosrau, and this was the first *jumuᶜah* to be held in Iraq. That was in the month of Safar. In it, was the battle of Jalula in which Yezdajird the son of Khosrau was defeated and he retreated back to Rai. In it, Takrit was taken, ᶜUmar travelled and took Al-Bait al-Maqdis (Jerusalem) and gave his famous *khutbah* in al-Jabiyyah. Kinnasrin, Aleppo, and Antioch were taken by force, Manbij by treaty, and Saruj by force. In that year, Qirqisiya' was taken by treaty. In Rabiᶜ al-Awwal, dating was begun from the *Hijrah* on the advice of ᶜAli.

In the year 17 A.H., ᶜUmar increased the size of the Prophet's Mosque. In it there was drought and famine in the *Hijaz* and it was called the Year of Destruction, and ᶜUmar prayed for rain for people by means of al-ᶜAbbas.

Niyar al-Aslami narrated that ᶜUmar, when he came out to pray for rain, came out with the cloak of the Prophet, may Allah bless him and grant him peace, upon him.

Ibn ᶜAun said: ᶜUmar took hold of the hand of al-ᶜAbbas and raised it up, saying, 'O Allah, we approach You by means of the uncle of Your Prophet (asking) that You drive away from us the drought, and that You give us to drink from the rain,' and they didn't leave before they were given to drink. The sky poured down upon them for days. In that year Ahwaz was taken by treaty.

In the year 18 A.H., Jundaysabur was taken by treaty, and Hulwan by force. In it, was the plague of Emaus; Urfa (Edessa) and Sumaysat were taken by force; Harran, Nasibin and a part of Mesopotamia by force, and it has been said, by treaty; and Mosul and its environs by force.

In the year 19 A.H., Cæsarea was taken by force.

In the year 20 A.H., Egypt was conquered by force. It is also said that all of Egypt was taken by treaty except for Alexandria which was taken by force. ᶜAli ibn Rabah said, 'The whole of the *Maghrib* (north-western Africa) was taken by force.' In that year Tustar was taken, Caesar (Heraclius), the great man of the Byzantines, died. In it also, ᶜUmar expelled the Jews from Khaybar and Najran, and he apportioned Khaybar and Wadi'l-Qurra' (between those who had been present there at the original battles of the Prophet, may Allah bless him and grant him peace).

In the year 21 A.H., Alexandria was taken by force, and Nahawand, after which the Persians could not muster an army, and Barqah and other places.

In the year 22 A.H., Azerbaijan was taken by force, and it has been said, by treaty, and Dinaur by force, Masabdhan and Hamadan by force, and Tripoli of North Africa, Rai, ᶜAskar and Qumas.

In the year 23 A.H., there were the conquests of Kirman, Sijistan, Makran in the mountainous lands, and also Isfahan and its environs.

In the end of this year there was the death of Sayyiduna ᶜUmar, may Allah be pleased with him, after his return from the *Hajj*; he was killed as a martyr.

Saᶜid ibn al-Musayyab said: When ᶜUmar returned from Mina (to Makkah), he made his camel kneel down in the watercourse, then he threw himself down, raised his hands to the sky and said, 'O Allah! I am advanced in years, my strength has weakened, and my subjects have increased, so take me to You without (my) being wasteful or falling short.' Dhu'l-Hijjah had not gone before he was killed.

Abu Salih as-Saman said: Kaᶜb al-Ahbar said to ᶜUmar, 'I find you in the Tawrah killed as a martyr.' He said, 'How can I be a martyr when I am in the peninsula of the Arabs?'

Aslam said: ᶜUmar said, 'O Allah provide me with martyrdom in Your way, and make my death to be in the city of Your Messenger.'

Maᶜdan ibn Abi Talhah: ᶜUmar gave a *khutbah* and said, 'I saw (in a dream) as if a cock pecked at me once or twice, and I can only believe that it means that my term has come. There are people who tell me to appoint a successor, and Allah will not cause His *deen* to go to waste nor His *khilafah*. If the matter is hastened for me, then the *khilafah* is a matter of consultation between these six whom the Messenger of Allah, may Allah bless him and grant him peace, was pleased with when he died.'

Az-Zuhri said: ᶜUmar would not permit a captive who had reached the age of puberty to enter Madinah until al-Mughirah ibn Shuᶜbah wrote to him—and he was the governor of Al-Kufah—mentioning to him a slave who had a number of crafts and asking permission that he enter Madinah, saying, 'He has many trades which are useful to people. He is a blacksmith, engraver and carpenter.' He gave permission to him to send him to Madinah. Al-Mughirah put a demand for revenue on him (the slave) of one hundred dirhams per month, so the slave came to ᶜUmar to complain of the severity of that imposition. He said, 'Your demand for revenue is not that much,' and he turned away in anger and threateningly. ᶜUmar waited some days and then he called him and said, 'Have I not been informed that you say, "If I wished, I could make a mill which will grind by means of the wind."' Then he turned his face to ᶜUmar with a frown and said, 'I will make for you a mill which people will talk about.' When he turned away, ᶜUmar said to his companions, 'The slave threatened me just now.' After a while Abu Lu'lu'ah wrapped his garments around a dagger with two heads (to the blade) whose handle was in the middle of it, hid in one of the corners of the mosque in the darkness of the last part of the night, and there he waited until ᶜUmar came out waking people up for the prayer. When he drew near to him, he stabbed him three times.

ᶜAmr ibn Maymun al-Ansari said: Abu Lu'lu'ah, the slave of al-Mughirah, stabbed ᶜUmar with a dagger which had two heads, and he stabbed, along with him, twelve other men of whom six died, then a man from Iraq threw over him a robe. When he became tangled up in it, he killed himself.

Abu Rafi* said: Abu Lu'lu'ah, the slave of al-Mughirah, used to make mills. Al-Mughirah used to demand as revenue from him four *dirhams* a day. He met *Umar and said, 'Amir al-Muminin, al-Mughirah is being very heavy on me, so speak to him.' He said, 'Behave well towards your master,'—and *Umar's intention was to speak to al-Mughirah about it—so he (the slave) became angry and said, 'His justice encompasses all of the people except for me,' and he secretly decided to kill him. He took a dagger, sharpened it and poisoned it. *Umar used to say, 'Straighten your ranks,' before he pronounced the *takbir*. He came and stood opposite him in the rank, stabbed him in his shoulder and side, and *Umar fell. Then he stabbed thirteen other men with him, of whom six died. *Umar was carried to his family. The sun was about to rise so *Abd ar-Rahman ibn *Auf led the people in prayer with the two shortest *surahs*. *Umar was brought some *nabidh* (a drink made from dates left to soak in water) and he drank it and it came out of his wound, but it wasn't yet distinct (from the blood). So they gave him some milk to drink, and it came out of his wound and they said, 'There's no great harm with you.' He said, 'If there is any harm in killing, then I have been killed.' People began to praise him, saying, 'You were such and such and you were such and such.' He said, 'By Allah, I wish that I had gone out of it, independent of others, with nothing against me and nothing for me, and that the companionship of the Messenger of Allah, may Allah bless him and his family and grant them peace, was secure for me.' Ibn *Abbas praised him, so he said, 'Even if I had that gold which would fill the earth, I would ransom myself by it from the terror of the rising. I have made it (the *khilafah*) a matter of consultation between *Uthman, *Ali, Talhah, az-Zubayr, *Abd ar-Rahman ibn *Auf and Sa*d.' He ordered Suhayb to lead people in prayer, and gave the six a period of three (days in which to decide).

Ibn *Abbas said: Abu Lu'lu'ah was a Magian.

133

ᶜAmr ibn Maimun said: ᶜUmar said, 'Praise be to Allah Who did not make my decree of death to be at the hands of a man who claimed Islam.' Then he said to his son, 'ᶜAbdullah, look and see what debts I have.' They calculated it and found it to be eighty-six thousand or thereabouts. He said, 'If the wealth of the family of ᶜUmar is enough, then pay it. If it is not, then ask among Bani ᶜAdi, and if their wealth is not enough, then ask among Quraysh. Go to the Mother of the Believers, ᶜA'ishah, and say, "ᶜUmar asks permission to be buried with his two companions."' He went to her and she said, 'I wanted it—meaning the burial plot—for myself, but I will definitely prefer him over myself, today.' ᶜAbdullah came and said, 'She has given permission,' so he praised Allah. Someone said to him, 'Make bequest, Amir al-Muminin, and appoint a successor.' He said, 'I see no-one with more right to this command than these six with whom the Prophet, may Allah bless him and grant him peace, was pleased when he died,' and he named the six, and said, 'ᶜAbdullah ibn ᶜUmar will be present with them but he has no part in the command. If the office should fall to Saᶜd, then he it is, and if not, then let whoever of you is appointed seek help from him, for I did not remove him (from his office) because of any incapacity or treachery.' Then he said, 'I counsel the *khalifah* after me to have fearful obedience of Allah; I counsel him to pay particular care to the *Muhajirun* and the *Ansar*, and I counsel him to treat the people of the provinces well,' and other similar counsels. When he died, we went walking with him, ᶜAbdullah ibn ᶜUmar called out the greeting and said, 'ᶜUmar seeks permission to enter.' ᶜA'ishah said, 'Bring him in.' He was brought in and placed there with his two companions.

When they finished burying him and had returned, that group gathered and ᶜAbd ar-Rahman ibn ᶜAuf said, 'Delegate your authority to three among you.' Az-Zubayr said, 'I delegate my authority to ᶜAli.' Saᶜd said, 'I delegate my authority to ᶜAbd ar-Rahman.' Talhah said, 'I delegate my authority to ᶜUthman.' He continued: so there remained these three. ᶜAbd ar-Rahman said, 'I don't want it. Which of you two will be quit of this matter and we will entrust it to him (the remaining one)? And Allah is his witness and Islam, let him consider in himself who is the best of them and let him be eager for the benefit of the *ummah*.' The two Shaykhs, ᶜAli and ᶜUthman were silent. ᶜAbd ar-Rahman said, 'Delegate me and, Allah is my witness, I will not fail you in choosing the best of you.' They said, 'Yes.' Then he went apart with ᶜAli and said, 'You have that precedence in Islam and kinship with the Prophet, may Allah bless him and grant him peace, which you know. Allah is your witness; if I give you authority, will you be just, and if I give authority (to ᶜUthman) over you, will you hear and obey?' He said, 'Yes.' Then he went apart with the other and said to him the same thing. When he had their agreement, he pledged allegiance to ᶜUthman and ᶜAli pledged allegiance to him.

ᶜUmar said: If my term overtakes me, and Abu ᶜUbaydah al-Jarrah is still alive, then I would appoint him as *khalifah*. If my Lord asked me, I would say, 'I heard the Prophet, may Allah bless him and grant him peace, saying, "Every Prophet has a trustworthy (companion), and my trustworthy (companion) is Abu ᶜUbaydah ibn al-Jarrah."' If my term overtakes me, and Abu ᶜUbaydah al-Jarrah has died, I would appoint Muᶜadh ibn Jabal as *khalifah*. If my Lord asked me, 'Why did you appoint him as *khalifah*?' I would say, 'I heard the Prophet, may Allah bless him and grant him peace, saying, "He will be raised up on the Day of Resurrection a distance in front of the men of knowledge."' They had both died during his *khilafah*.

Abu Rafiᶜ narrated that someone spoke to ᶜUmar at his death about the appointment of a *khalifah*, so he said, 'I have seen among my companions an unfortunate eagerness. If one of two men had reached me, and then I had entrusted this command to him, I would have been sure of him: Salim the freed slave of Abu Hudhayfah and Abu ᶜUbaydah ibn al-Jarrah.'

ᶜUmar was struck on the Wednesday, four days before the end of Dhu'l-Hijjah, and he was buried on Sunday, the day of the new moon of al-Muharram, the Sacred (month). He was sixty-three years old. It has also been said that he was sixty-six, sixty-one, sixty (which al-Waqidi preferred). It has been said that he was fifty-nine, fifty-five and fifty-four. Suhayb performed the (funeral) prayer over him in the mosque.

In the *Tahdhib* of al-Mazini, there is that the engraving on the seal-ring of ᶜUmar was, 'Death is enough of an admonisher, ᶜUmar.'

Tariq ibn Shihab said: Umm Ayman said, on the day ᶜUmar was killed, 'Today Islam has been rent.'

ᶜAbd ar-Rahman ibn Yasar said, 'I witnessed the death of ᶜUmar ibn al-Khattab and the sun was eclipsed on that day.' The men who transmitted (this *hadith*) were trustworthy.

The things in which he was first

Al-ᶜAskari said: He was the first to be called 'Amir al-Muminin', the first to date events from the *Hijrah*, the first to take a *bait al-mal* (see the chapter on Abu Bakr), the first to establish as a *sunnah* the standing (for prayer) in the month of Ramadan, the first who patrolled at night, the first who punished satire, the first who punished wine-drinking with eighty (lashes), the first who declared *al-mutᶜah* (temporary marriage) *haram* (rather the Prophet, may Allah bless him and grant him peace, forbade it on the Day of Khaybar—see the *Muwatta'* of Imam Malik), the first to forbid the sale of female slaves who had borne children to their masters, the first to assemble for prayers over the dead with four *takbirs*, the first to have a register, the first to make conquests, the first to survey the *Sawad* (the cultivated land of Iraq), the first to convey food from Egypt upon the Aylah Sea (Gulf of ᶜAqabah) to Madinah, the first who dedicated *sadaqah* (purely for the sake of Allah) in Islam, and the first who adjusted the division of inheritances (in cases where the calculated portions add up to more than the total inheritance), the first to take the *zakah* of horses, the first to say, 'May Allah lengthen your life,' (he said it to ᶜAli) and the first to say, 'May Allah help you,' (he said it to ᶜAli). This is the end of what al-ᶜAskari mentioned.

An-Nawawi said in his *Tahdhib* that he was the first to adopt the whip. Ibn Saᶜd mentions it in the *Tabaqat,* and he said: It used to be said, after him, 'The whip of ʿUmar is more terrible than your sword.' He (an-Nawawi) continued: He was the first to appoint Qadis in the provinces, the first who established the provinces of (the cities of) Kufah, Basrah, and of Mesopotamia, Syria, Cairo (Egypt), and Mosul.

Ismaʿil ibn Ziyad said: ʿAli ibn Abi Talib passed by the mosques in Ramadan and in them there were lamps, so he said, 'May Allah illuminate ʿUmar in his grave, as he has illuminated our mosques for us.'

Ibn Saʿd said: ʿUmar appointed a meal (flour) house and put flour in it, parched barley meal, dates, raisins and necessities, in order to help the traveller whose journey was interrupted (through need or other causes), and he established between Makkah and Madinah on the road that which would be useful to travellers whose journeys were interrupted. He demolished the Mosque of the Prophet, added to it, expanded it and floored it with pebbles. He was the one who evicted the Jews from the *Hijaz* (and sent them) to Syria, and evicted the people of Najran (and sent them) to Kufah. He was the one who moved the Station of Ibrahim back (from the Kaʿbah) to where it is today, and it used to be adjoining the House.

Some accounts of him and of his judgements

ʿUmar ibn ʿAbd al-ʿAziz asked Abu Bakr ibn Sulayman ibn Abi Hathamah what was the reason that it used to be written, 'From the *Khalifah* of the Messenger of Allah, may Allah bless him and grant him peace,' in the time of Abu Bakr, then later ʿUmar used to write at first, 'From the *Khalifah* of Abu Bakr.'? Then who was the first to write, 'From the Amir al-Muminin (the Commander of the Believers)'? He said, 'Ash-Shifa, who was one of the women of the *Muhajirun*, told me that Abu Bakr used to write, "From the *Khalifah* of the Messenger of Allah," and ʿUmar used to write, "From the *Khalifah* of the *Khalifah* of the Messenger of Allah," until one day ʿUmar wrote to the governor of Iraq, to send him two strong men whom he could ask about Iraq and its inhabitants. He sent to him Labid ibn Rabiᶜah and ᶜAdi ibn Hatim, and they came to Madinah and entered the mosque where they found ᶜAmr ibn al-ᶜAs. They said, 'Get permission for us (to visit) the Amir al-Muminin.' ᶜAmr said, 'You two, by Allah, have hit upon his name!' Then ᶜAmr went in to him and said, 'Peace be upon you, Amir al-Muminin.' He said, 'What occurred to you about this name? You must explain what you have said.' He told him and said, 'You are the *amir* (commander) and we are the *muminun* (the believers).' Thus letters have continued to be written with that from that day.

An-Nawawi said in his *Tahdhib*: ᶜAdi ibn Hatim and Labid ibn Rabiᶜah named him thus when they came as a deputation from ᶜIraq. It has been said that al-Mughirah ibn Shuᶜbah named him with this name. It has also been said that ᶜUmar said to people, 'You are the believers and I am your *amir*,' and so he was called Amir al-Muminin, and before that he was known as the *Khalifah* of the *Khalifah* of the Messenger of Allah, but they changed from that expression because of its length.

Muᶜawiyyah ibn Qurrah said: It used to be written 'From Abu Bakr the *Khalifah* of the Messenger of Allah,' and then when it was ᶜUmar ibn al-Khattab they wanted to say, 'The *Khalifah* of the *Khalifah* of the Messenger of Allah.' ᶜUmar said, 'This is lengthy.' They said, 'No. But we have appointed you as *amir* over us, so you are our *amir*.' He said, 'Yes, and you are the believers, and I am your *amir*.' Then it became written Amir al-Muminin.

Ibn al-Musayyab said: The first to write the date was ᶜUmar ibn al-Khattab two and a half years into his *khilafah*, and it was written down as the sixteenth year of the *Hijrah*, through the advice of ᶜAli.

Ibn ᶜUmar related from ᶜUmar that he wished to record the *sunan* (customary practices of the Prophet, may Allah bless him and grant him peace, and of his companions), so he sought Allah's choice in the matter (through the supplication known as the *istikharah*) for a month. Then he arose one morning with a clear resolve and said, 'I remembered a people who were before you who wrote a book, and then they turned to it and abandoned the Book of Allah.'

Shaddad said: The first words that ᶜUmar would say when he ascended the *mimbar* were, 'O Allah, I am severe, so make me gentle, I am weak, so strengthen me, and I am miserly, so make me generous.'

ᶜUmar said, 'I have placed myself in respect to Allah's property in the same relation as the guardian of the orphan to his (the orphan's) wealth. If I am in good circumstances, I will refrain from it, and if I am in need I will eat of it in moderation, and if (again later) I am in good circumstances, I will repay.'

Ibn ᶜUmar said that when ᶜUmar ibn al-Khattab was in need, he used to go to the man in charge of the *bait al-mal* and seek a loan from him. Often he might be in difficulty and the man in charge of the public treasury would come to him, seek repayment of the debt and would oblige him to pay it, and ᶜUmar would be evasive to him. Then often ᶜUmar would receive his stipend and so pay his debt.

Al-Bara' ibn Maᶜrur said that ᶜUmar went out one day until he came to the *mimbar* and he had been suffering from a complaint. The good qualities of honey were mentioned to him, and there was a receptacle (made of kid-skin) of it in the *bait al-mal*. He said, 'If you give me permission I will take it, but if not then it is *haram* for me.' They gave him permission.

Salim ibn ᶜAbdullah said that ᶜUmar used to insert his hand into the saddle sore of his camel and say, 'I fear that I will be asked about what is (wrong) with you.'

Ibn ᶜUmar said: When ᶜUmar meant to forbid people from some wrong action, he would come to his family and say, 'If I come to know of anyone who becomes involved in something I have forbidden, I will double the punishment for him.'

ᶜUmar ibn al-Khattab went out one night to patrol Madinah—and he used to do that a lot—when he came upon one of the women of the Arabs whose door was bolted against her (locking her in) and she was saying:

'This night, whose stars creep slowly, is wearisome and makes me sleepless, because I have no bedfellow with whom to sport,

For, by Allah, if it were not that Allah's punishments are feared, his rights would have been removed from this couch. However, I fear a Watchful One Who is in charge of our selves and Whose recorder is not negligent for an instant. Fear of my Lord and modesty prevent me, and I honour my husband (too much) that his noble station should be conferred (on another).'

So he (ʿUmar) wrote to his governors about military expeditions that no-one should be absent for more than four months.

Salman said that ʿUmar said to him, 'Am I a king or a *khalifah*?' Salman said to him, 'If you collect a *dirham* from the land of the Muslims, or less or more, then you put it to an improper use, you are a king, not a *khalifah*.' ʿUmar took warning from it.

Sufyan ibn Abi'l-ʿArja' said: ʿUmar ibn al-Khattab said, 'By Allah, I do not know whether I am a *khalifah* or a king, for if I am a king then this is a tremendous matter.' Someone said, 'Amir al-Muminin, there is a distinction between the two of them.' He said, 'What is it?' He said, 'A *khalifah* does not take except what is due and he does not use it except in the right way, and you, praise be to Allah, are like that. The king treats people unjustly, and takes from this one and gives to that one.' ʿUmar was silent.

Ibn Masʿud, may Allah be pleased with him, said: ʿUmar mounted a horse and his robe disclosed his thigh. The people of Najran saw on his thigh a black mole and said, 'This is the one whom we find in our Book will exile us from our land.'

Kaʿb al-Ahbar said to ʿUmar, 'We find you in the Book of Allah at one of the gates of Jahannam preventing people from falling into it. When you die, they will carry on plunging into it until the Day of Resurrection.'

Abu Mashʿar said: Our Shaykhs told us that ʿUmar said, 'This matter will not be correct but with the severity that has no haughtiness in it, and with the gentleness that has no weakness in it.'

Hakim ibn 'Umayr said: 'Umar ibn al-Khattab said, 'Let not the *amir* of an army or a raiding party whip anyone for a *hadd* punishment until he arrives at Darb (*Derbe* near the Cilician Gates, a mountain pass through which the Muslims passed returning from raids into Byzantine territory) so that the rage of the *shaytan* does not carry him to the point that he joins with the *kuffar.*'

Ash-Sha'bi said: The Byzantine Emperor wrote to 'Umar ibn al-Khattab, 'My messengers have come to me from you claiming that among you there is a tree which is not like anything else among trees: it produces something like the ears of the ass, it opens out (to reveal) something like a pearl, it becomes green so that it is like the green emerald, it reddens until it is like the red ruby, then later it ripens and matures so that it becomes like the sweetest honey-cake ever eaten, then later it dries until it becomes a defence (against want) for the house-dweller and a provision for the traveller. If my messengers have told me the truth, I can only imagine that this is one of the trees of the Garden.' 'Umar wrote to him, 'From the slave of Allah, 'Umar, the Amir al-Muminin, to Caesar, the king of the Byzantines. Truly your messengers have told you the truth. This tree, which is with us, is the tree which Allah made to grow over Maryam when she gave birth to 'Isa her son. So fear Allah and do not take 'Isa as a god apart from Allah, for truly, "*The likeness of 'Isa with Allah is as the likeness of Adam, He created him from dust, ...*"' (Qur'an 3: 59) to the end of the *ayah*.

Ibn 'Umar narrated that 'Umar ordered his governors, so they recorded their properties, and among them was Sa'd bin Abi Waqqas. Then 'Umar shared with them in their properties and took a half and gave them a half.

Ash-Sha'bi said that when 'Umar used to appoint a governor he would record his property.

Abu Imamah ibn Sahl ibn Hunayf said: 'Umar remained some time not eating anything at all from the property of the *bait al-mal*, until poverty and constriction came upon him in that. He sent for the Companions of the Prophet, may Allah bless him and grant him peace, to seek their advice. He said, 'I have occu-

pied myself with this command, so what is fitting for me from it?'
ᶜAli said, 'The midday and evening meals.' ᶜUmar took that.

Ibn ᶜUmar narrated that ᶜUmar performed the *Hajj* in the year
twenty-three (A.H.) and spent sixteen *dinars* upon his *Hajj*. He
said, 'ᶜAbdullah we have been extravagant with this property.'

Qatadah and ash-Shaᶜbi said: A woman came to ᶜUmar and
said, 'My husband stands at night (in prayer) and fasts during the
day.' ᶜUmar said, 'You have praised your husband excellently
well.' Kaᶜb ibn Sawwar said, 'She was complaining.' ᶜUmar said,
'How?' He said, 'She claims that she has no share in her husband
(in his time).' He said, 'If you understood that much, then you
decide between them.' He said, 'Amir al-Muminin, Allah has permitted him four (wives). So she has one day of every four days,
and one night of every four nights.'

Ibn Jarir said: One I trust informed me that ᶜUmar, while he
was patrolling, heard a woman saying:

> 'This night stretches out and is grievous, and that I have no
> intimate to sport with has made me sleepless,
> For, if it were not for fear of Allah Whom nothing is like,
> his rights would have been removed from this couch.'

ᶜUmar said, 'What is wrong with you?' She said, 'You sent my
husband on an expedition some months ago, and I long for
him.' He said, 'Do you mean to do wrong?' She said, '(I seek) the
refuge of Allah!' He said, 'So restrain yourself; it is only (a matter
of) the post to him.' He sent a message to him. Then he went to
Hafsah and said, 'I want to ask you about a matter which con-
cerns me, so dispel it for me. How long does a woman long for
her husband?' She lowered her head and was shy. He said, 'Truly
Allah is not shy of the truth.' She gestured with her hand, indicat-
ing three months, and if that is not possible, then four months.
ᶜUmar wrote that armies must not be kept on service for more
than four months.

Jabir ibn ᶜAbdullah narrated that he came to ᶜUmar to complain
to him of the treatment he received from his women-folk. ᶜUmar
said to him, 'We also find that, so much so that when I intend

(going out for) some necessity, she says to me, "You are only going to the girls of Bani so-and-so to look at them."' ʿAbdullah ibn Masʿud said to him, 'Has it not reached you that Ibrahim, peace be upon him, complained to Allah about Sarah's character and it was said to him, "She has been created from a rib so have the enjoyment of her company as long as you don't see in her any unsoundness in her *deen*."'

ʿIkrimah ibn Khalid said: One of ʿUmar ibn al-Khattab's sons went in to see him. He had combed and oiled his hair and dressed up in the very best clothing. ʿUmar struck him with a whip until he made him weep. Hafsah asked him, 'Why did you strike him?' He said, 'I saw that his self had made him conceited, and I wanted to make it (his self) small for him.'

Layth ibn Abi Salim narrated that ʿUmar said, 'Do not name yourselves with the name al-Hakam (the ruler and judge) nor Abu'l-Hakam (possessor of judgement) for truly Allah, He is al-Hakam (the ruler) and don't call a road a *sikkah*.' (*Sikkah* is literally both a 'row' and a 'plough' and it is possible there is a reference to the tradition that 'The *sikkah* (plough) has not entered the abode of a people but that it humiliated them.')

Ad-Dahhak said: Abu Bakr said, 'By Allah, I wish that I were a tree by the side of the road which a camel passed by, and it took me into its mouth, chewed me, swallowed me, passed me out as dung, and that I were not a man.' ʿUmar said, 'Would that I were my family's ram, which they were fattening as much as seemed right to them, until when I became as fat as could be, some people whom they love visit them, and they sacrifice me for them, make some of me into roasted meat, some of me into sun-dried meat, then eat me, and that I were not a human being.'

Abu'l-Bakhtari said: ʿUmar ibn al-Khattab used to give the *khutbah* on the *mimbar*. Al-Hussein ibn ʿAli, may Allah be pleased with him, stood up before him and said, 'Come down from my father's *mimbar*.' ʿUmar said, 'It is the *mimbar* of your father and not the *mimbar* of my father. Who told you to do this?' ʿAli stood and said, 'By Allah, no-one told him to do this. I will certainly cause you (al-Hussein) some pain, traitor.' He (ʿUmar) said, 'Don't hurt the son of my brother, for he has told the truth, it is the *mimbar* of his father.'

Abu Salamah ibn ʿAbd ar-Rahman and Saʿid ibn al-Musayyab narrated that ʿUmar ibn al-Khattab and ʿUthman ibn ʿAffan were arguing over a certain question until an onlooker said, 'They will never reach an agreement.' Yet they only separated on the best and most beautiful terms.

Al-Hasan said: The first *khutbah* which ʿUmar delivered, he praised Allah and then said, 'Right. I have been tested by you and you have been tested by me, and I have succeeded to the *khilafah*, amongst you, after my two companions. Whoever is here present, we will manage their affairs in person, and whoever is not here with us, we will appoint over him strong and trustworthy people. Whoever acts excellently well, we will increase him in excellent treatment, and whoever acts wrongly we will punish, and may Allah forgive us and you.'

Jubayr ibn al-Huwayrith narrated that ʿUmar ibn al-Khattab, may Allah be pleased with him, sought the advice of the Muslims on the recording of a register. ʿAli said to him, 'Divide up every year what is collected for you of property, and don't keep any of it.' ʿUthman said, 'I see much wealth, which is sufficient for the people and if it is not counted so that whoever takes is distinguished from whoever does not take, I am afraid that the matter will become confused.' Al-Walid ibn Hisham ibn al-Mughirah said, 'Amir al-Muminin, I went to Syria and I saw that its kings had recorded registers and organised the troops, so record registers and organise the troops.' He took his advice, and he called ʿAqil ibn Abi Talib, Makhramah ibn Naufal and Jubayr ibn Mutʿim, who were genealogists of Quraysh, and said, 'Record people according to their ranks.' They recorded them beginning with Banu Hashim, then they followed with Abu Bakr and his people, then ʿUmar and his people, according to the order of their *khilafahs*. When ʿUmar saw it, he said, 'Begin with the close relatives of the Prophet, may Allah bless him and grant him peace, the closest, then the next closest until you place ʿUmar where Allah placed him.'

Saʿid ibn al-Musayyab said: ʿUmar recorded the register in *al-Muharram* of the year 20 A.H.

Al-Hasan said: ʿUmar wrote to Hudhayfah, 'Give the people their stipends and their provisions.' He wrote back to him, 'We have done that and a great deal remains.' ʿUmar wrote to him, 'It is their spoils which Allah has given them. It is not ʿUmar's nor ʿUmar's family's. Divide it up among them.'

Jubayr ibn Mutʿim said: While ʿUmar was standing on the mountain of *ʿArafah* he heard a man calling out, saying, '*Khalifah* of Allah!' Another man heard him, and they were taking provisions for the way, so he said, 'What is wrong with you, may Allah split your uvulas?' I went towards the man and shouted at him. Jubayr continued: Then the next morning, I was standing with ʿUmar at al-ʿAqabah (the major pillar of stones in *Mina*) and he was stoning it, when there came a stray pebble and split (the skin on) ʿUmar's head. I turned that way and heard a man from the mountain saying, 'I make it known, by the Lord of the Kaʿbah, that ʿUmar will not stand in this place after this year,' and it was the one who had called out among us the day before, and that disturbed me greatly.

ʿA'ishah, may Allah be pleased with her, said: At the time of the last *Hajj* which ʿUmar performed with the Mothers of the Believers (the wives of the Prophet, may Allah bless him and grant him peace), when we returned from *ʿArafah*, I passed by al-Muhassab and I heard a man upon his camel saying, 'Where was ʿUmar, the Amir al-Muminin?' I heard another man saying, 'Here was the Amir al-Muminin.' He made the camel kneel down upon its breast, then he raised his voice in a wail saying:

'Upon you peace from an *imam* and may the hand of Allah bless that much-rent skin,
Whoever hurries on or mounts the two wings of the ostrich, in order to overtake what you sent ahead the day before, will be outstripped.
You decided matters, then after them you left behind trials and misfortunes in their sleeves, not yet unloosed.'

That rider did not move and it was not known who he was, and we used to say that he was one of the *Jinn,* for ᶜUmar came back from that *Hajj,* was stabbed by the dagger and died.

ᶜAbd ar-Rahman ibn Abza said that ᶜUmar said, 'This authority is among the people of Badr as long as one of them remains, then it is among the people of Uhud as long as one of them remains, and among such and such, and such and such, and there is no part in it for a freed captive, nor the son of a freed captive, nor those who became Muslims at the Conquest (of Makkah).'

An-Nakhaᶜi narrated that a man said to ᶜUmar, 'Will you not appoint ᶜAbdullah ibn ᶜUmar as *khalifah?*' He said, 'May Allah fight you! By Allah, I never wanted this of Allah. Shall I appoint as *khalifah* a man who did not know how to divorce his wife properly?'

Kaᶜb said: There was among the Tribe of Isra'il a king whom, when we remember him we are reminded of ᶜUmar, and when we remember ᶜUmar we are reminded of him. He had by his side a prophet who received revelation. Allah revealed to the prophet, peace be upon him, to say to him, 'Make your covenant and write your testament to me, for you are dead after three days.' The prophet informed him of that. When it was the third day, he fell down (dead) between the wall and the couch. He came to his Lord and said, 'O Allah, if You knew that I was just in my rule; that when matters differed, I followed Your guidance; and I was such and such, and such and such, then increase my life-span until my infant son grows up and my nation increases.' Allah revealed to the prophet that, 'He has said such and such—and it is true—and I have added fifteen years to his life-span. That is enough for his infant son to grow up and his nation to increase.' When ᶜUmar was stabbed, Kaᶜb said, 'If ᶜUmar were to ask his Lord, Allah would definitely let him stay.' ᶜUmar was told about that. He said, 'O Allah take me back to You without (my) being powerless and incapable or blameworthy.'

Sulayman ibn Yasar related that the *Jinn* wailed in mourning for ᶜUmar.

Malik ibn Dinar said: A voice was heard on the mountain of *Tabalah* when ʿUmar, may Allah be pleased with him, was killed:

'Let him weep for Islam, whoever would weep, for they are on the point of being thrown to the ground and (their) appointed time has not been exceeded,
And the world has declined and the best of it has gone, turning its back, and whoever is sure of the promise has become weary of it.'

Yahya ibn Abi Rashid al-Basri said: ʿUmar said to his son, 'Be economical with my shroud, for if there is good for me with Allah, He will exchange it for me for that which is better than it. If I have been otherwise, He will strip me and be very fast in stripping me. Be economical in the grave you dig for me, for if there is good for me with Allah, He will expand it for me as far as my sight can reach. If I have been otherwise, He will tighten it upon me until my ribs interlace. Let not a woman go out with me (to the grave), and do not attribute to me a purity that I do not have, for Allah has more knowledge of me. When you go out (with me to the grave) then hasten your pace, for if there is good for me with Allah, you will send me on to what is better for me. If I am otherwise, you will throw an evil you have been carrying down from your necks.'

Section

Ibn ʿAbbas related that al-ʿAbbas said: I asked Allah, one year after ʿUmar had died, to show me him in dream. I saw him after a year and he was wiping the sweat from his brow, so I said, 'May my father and my mother be your ransom, Amir al-Muminin! How is it with you?' He said, 'This is the time I have just finished. The house of ʿUmar had almost been violently demolished if it had not been that I met a pitying, compassionate One (*Ra'uf Rahim*).'

Zayd ibn Aslam related that ʿAmr ibn al-ʿAs saw ʿUmar in his sleep and asked, 'How have you done?' He asked, 'When did I

147

leave you?' He answered, 'Twelve years ago.' He said, 'I have only finished my accounting now.'

Salim ibn ᶜAbdullah ibn ᶜUmar said: I heard a man of the *Ansar* saying, 'I asked Allah to show me ᶜUmar in my sleep, then I saw him after ten years, and he was wiping sweat from his brow. I said, 'Amir al-Muminin, what have you done?' He said, 'Right now I have finished, and if it were not for the mercy of my Lord I would have been destroyed.'

Ash-Shaᶜbi said: ᶜAtikah bint Zayd ibn ᶜAmr ibn Nufayl eulogised ᶜUmar, saying:

'Eye! let your tears and weeping be abundant, and do not weary over the noble *imam*.
The fate of the inspired horseman distressed me on the day of combat and harsh reproach;
The protection of the *deen*, the helper against fate, succour of the troubled and the distressed.
Say to the people of hardship and misfortune, "Die! since fate has given us to drink the cup of division and disunion."'

Those of the Companions who died during his days

During the *khilafah* of ᶜUmar, may Allah be pleased with him, those of the notable companions who died were: ᶜUtbah ibn Ghazwan, al-ᶜAla' ibn al-Hadrami, Qais ibn as-Sakan, Abu Quhafah the father of as-Siddiq, may Allah be pleased with him, Saᶜd ibn ᶜUbadah, Suhayl ibn ᶜAmr, Ibn Umm Maktum the *mu'adhdhin*, ᶜAyyash ibn Abi Rabiᶜah, ᶜAbd ar-Rahman the brother of az-Zubayr ibn al-ᶜAwwam, Qais ibn Abi Saᶜsaᶜah one of those who memorised all of the Qur'an, Naufal ibn al-Harith ibn ᶜAbd al-Muttalib, his brother Abu Sufyan, Mariyah the mother of the *Sayyid* Ibrahim (the son of the Prophet, may Allah bless him and grant him peace, who died in infancy), Abu ᶜUbaydah ibn al-Jarrah, Muᶜadh ibn Jabal, Yazid ibn Abi Sufyan, Shurahbil ibn Hasanah, al-Fadl ibn al-ᶜAbbas, Abu Jandal ibn Suhayl, Abu Malik al-Ashᶜari, Safwan ibn al-Muᶜattal, Ubayy ibn Kaᶜb, Bilal the *mu'adhdhin*, Usayd ibn al-Hudhayr, al-Bara' ibn Malik the brother of Anas, Zaynab bint Jahsh, 'Iyad ibn Ghanam, Abu'l-Haytham ibn at-Tayyihan, Khalid ibn al-Walid, al-Jarud the chief of Bani 'Abd al-Qais, an-Nu'man ibn Muqarran, Qatadah ibn an-Nu'man, al-Aqra' ibn Habis, Saudah bint Zam'ah, 'Uwaym ibn Sa'idah, Ghilan ath-Thaqafi, Abu Mihjan ath-Thaqafi, and other Companions, may Allah be pleased with all of them.

ᶜUthman ibn ᶜAffan

may Allah be pleased with him

U thman ibn ᶜAffan ibn Abi'l-ᶜAs ibn Umayyah ibn ᶜAbd Shams ibn ᶜAbd Manaf ibn Qusayy ibn Kilab ibn Murrah ibn Kaᶜb ibn Lu'ayy ibn Ghalib, al-Qurashi, al-Amawi (al-Makki and then later al-Madani) Abu ᶜAmr, and it has been said Abu ᶜAbdullah and Abu Layla.

He was born in the sixth year of the Elephant, and he accepted Islam very early on, being one of those whom as-Siddiq called to Islam. He emigrated on both emigrations: the first to Abyssinia and the second to Madinah.

He married Ruqayyah the daughter of the Messenger of Allah, may Allah bless him and grant him peace, before prophethood, and she died with him during the nights of the Battle of Badr. He was held back from Badr, because of her becoming ill, with the permission of the Messenger of Allah, may Allah bless him and grant him peace, who assigned a portion of the spoils to him and rewarded him, and so he is counted among the people of Badr because of that.

The messenger brought the good news of the victory of the Muslims at Badr on the same day that they buried her in Madinah. The Messenger of Allah, may Allah bless him and grant him peace, married him to her sister Umm Kulthum after her, and she later died with him in the ninth year of the *Hijrah.*

The men of knowledge said: We don't know of anyone who married two daughters of a prophet apart from him, and for that reason he is known as *Dhu'n-Nurayn*—the Possessor of Two Lights.

He was one of the first outstrippers (*as-Sabiqun al-Awwalun*), the first of the *Muhajirun*, one of the ten for whom it was witnessed that they were destined for the Garden, and one of the six with whom the Messenger of Allah, may Allah bless him and grant him peace, was pleased when he died. He was one of the Companions who memorised all of the Qur'an, and indeed Ibn ᶜAbbad said, 'None of the *khulafa'* memorised all of the Qur'an except for him and al-Ma'mun.'

Ibn Saᶜd said: The Messenger of Allah, may Allah bless him and grant him peace, appointed him as his deputy in charge of Madinah during the military expeditions to *Dhat ar-Riqaᶜ* and *Ghatafan*.

One hundred and forty-six *hadith* of his from the Messenger of Allah, may Allah bless him and grant him peace, have been narrated.

The following related *hadith* from him: Zaid ibn Khalid al-Juhani, Ibn az-Zubayr, as-Sa'ib ibn Yazid, Anas ibn Malik, Zaid ibn Thabit, Salamah ibn al-Akwaᶜ, Abu Umamah al-Bahili, Ibn ᶜAbbas, Ibn ᶜUmar, ᶜAbdullah ibn Mughaffal, Abu Qatadah, Abu Hurairah and other Companions, may Allah be pleased with them, and a great number of others of the Followers (of them Abban ibn ᶜUthman, ᶜUbaydullah ibn ᶜAdi, Humran and others).

ᶜAbd ar-Rahman ibn Hatib said: I saw none of the companions of the Messenger of Allah, may Allah bless him and grant him peace, who, when he narrated a *hadith*, narrated it more completely and more excellently than ᶜUthman ibn ᶜAffan, unless it was a man who was in awe of the *hadith*.

ᶜUthman was the most knowledgeable of them in the rites of the *Hajj*, and then after him, Ibn ᶜUmar.

ᶜAbdullah ibn ᶜUmar ibn Abban al-Juᶜfi said: My maternal uncle Hussein al-Juᶜfi said, 'Do you realise why ᶜUthman was called the Possessor of Two Lights?' I said, 'No.' He said, 'No-one has ever been united to two daughters of a prophet since Allah created Adam (nor will be) until the Hour arises other than ᶜUthman, and for that reason he was called the Possessor of Two Lights.'

Al-Hasan said: ᶜUthman was only called the Possessor of Two Lights because no-one is known of who closed his door upon two daughters of a prophet other than him.

ʿAli ibn Abi Talib was asked about ʿUthman and he said: That was a man who is called in the Highest Assembly (of the angels) the Possessor of Two Lights. He was the son-in-law of the Messenger of Allah, may Allah bless him and grant him peace, with two of his daughters.

Sahl ibn Saʿd said: It is said about ʿUthman 'the Possessor of Two Lights' because he will pass from one abode to another in the Garden and there will gleam forth for him two flashes of lightning, and it is for that reason that is said about him.

It is said that he was given the *kunya* of Abu ʿAmr in the *Jahiliyyah*, then in the time of Islam, Ruqayyah gave birth to ʿAbdullah for him, and he took his *kunya* from him (Abu ʿAbdullah).

His mother was Arwa bint Kurayz ibn Rabiʿah ibn Habib ibn ʿAbd Shams (ibn ʿAbd Manaf) and her mother was Umm Hakim al-Baida' bint ʿAbd al-Muttalib ibn Hashim and she was the twin sister of the father of the Messenger of Allah, may Allah bless him and grant him peace. The mother of ʿUthman was the daughter of the paternal aunt of the Prophet, may Allah bless him and grant him peace.

Ibn Ishaq said: He was the first to accept Islam after Abu Bakr, ʿAli and Zaid ibn Harithah.

ʿUthman was of middle stature—he was not short, nor was he tall—with a beautiful face, a fair complexion tinged with red, on his face the marks of small-pox, with a full beard, large-limbed, broad-shouldered, plump in the shank, long in the forearms, hair covering both his forearms, curly-haired but balding to the fore of his head, the most beautiful of people in the fore-teeth, his locks fell beneath his ears and he coloured them with yellow, and he had strengthened his teeth with gold.

ʿAbdullah ibn Hazm al-Mazini said: I saw ʿUthman ibn ʿAffan and I have never seen a man or a woman with a more beautiful face than him.

Musa ibn Talhah said: ʿUthman ibn ʿAffan was the most beautiful of people.

Usamah ibn Zaid said: The Messenger of Allah, may Allah bless him and grant him peace, sent me to ʿUthman's house with a dish in which was meat. I went in, and there was Ruqayyah, may Allah be pleased with her, seated. I began to look at the face of Ruqayyah one time and another time at the face of ʿUthman. When I returned, the Messenger of Allah, may Allah bless him and grant him peace, questioned me and asked me, 'Did you go in to them?' I said, 'Yes.' He said, 'Have you seen a couple more beautiful than them?' I said, 'No, Messenger of Allah.'

Muhammad ibn Ibrahim ibn al-Harith at-Taymi said: When ʿUthman bin ʿAffan became a Muslim, his paternal uncle, al-Hakam ibn Abi'l-ʿAs ibn Umayyah took hold of him, bound him with rope, and said, 'Do you wish to leave the religion of your fathers for an innovated *deen*? By Allah, I will not leave you until you give up that which you are involved in.' ʿUthman said, 'By Allah, I will not give it up nor abandon it.' When al-Hakam saw his firmness in his *deen* he left him.

Anas said: The first one to emigrate with his family to the Abyssinians was ʿUthman ibn ʿAffan. The Prophet, may Allah bless him and grant him peace, said, 'May Allah accompany the two of them. ʿUthman is the first to emigrate with his family for the sake of Allah since Lut.'

ʿA'ishah, may Allah be pleased with her, said: When the Prophet, may Allah bless him and grant him peace, married away his daughter Umm Kulthum, he said to her, 'Your husband, of all men, is the one who most resembles your grandfather Ibrahim and your father Muhammad.'

Ibn ʿUmar said: The Messenger of Allah, may Allah bless him and grant him peace, said, 'We find a resemblance in ʿUthman to our father Ibrahim.'

The *ahadith* related on his merit apart from what have already been quoted

ʿA'ishah, may Allah be pleased with her, related that the Prophet, may Allah bless him and grant him peace, gathered his garments around him when ʿUthman entered and said, 'Should I not feel shy of a man of whom the angels are shy?'

Abu ᶜAbd ar-Rahman as-Sulami related that ᶜUthman, when he was besieged, looked out over them, and said, 'I adjure you by Allah, and I adjure none but the Companions of the Prophet, may Allah bless him and grant him peace, do you not know that the Messenger of Allah, may Allah bless him and grant him peace, said, "Whoever equips the Army of Difficulty (of Tabuk) then there is the Garden for him."? And I equipped it. Do you not know that the Messenger of Allah, may Allah bless him and grant him peace, said, "Whoever has the well of *Rumah* dug, then the Garden is for him."? And I had it dug.' They affirmed what he said.

ᶜAbd ar-Rahman ibn Khabbab said: I witnessed the Prophet, may Allah bless him and grant him peace, urging (people to) support the Army of Difficulty, and then ᶜUthman ibn ᶜAffan said, 'Messenger of Allah, I will be responsible for one hundred camels with their saddle blankets and their saddles, in the way of Allah.' Then he further urged people to support the army and ᶜUthman said, 'Messenger of Allah, I will be responsible for two hundred camels with their saddle blankets and their saddles, in the way of Allah.' Then he further urged people to support the army and ᶜUthman said, 'Messenger of Allah, I will be responsible for three hundred camels with their saddle blankets and their saddles, in the way of Allah.' Then the Messenger of Allah, may Allah bless him and grant him peace, came down (from the *mimbar*) saying, 'There will be nothing at all against ᶜUthman whatever he does after this.'

Anas and ᶜAbd ar-Rahman ibn Samurah both said: ᶜUthman came to the Prophet, may Allah bless him and grant him peace, with one thousand *dinars* when he equipped the Army of Difficulty and poured them into his lap. The Messenger of Allah, began turning them over, saying, 'Nothing ᶜUthman does after this day will harm him,' twice.

Anas said: When the Messenger of Allah, may Allah bless him and grant him peace, ordered the Pledge of Allegiance of *Ridwan* (at Hudaybiyah) ᶜUthman ibn ᶜAffan was the messenger of the Messenger of Allah, may Allah bless him and his family and grant them peace, to the people of Makkah. So people pledged allegiance. The Prophet, may Allah bless him and his family and grant them peace, said, 'Uthman ibn 'Affan is upon the business of Allah and the business of His Messenger,' and he struck one of his two hands upon the other, so that the hand of the Messenger of Allah, may Allah bless him and grant him peace, was better for 'Uthman than their hands were for them themselves.

Ibn 'Umar said: The Messenger of Allah, may Allah bless him and grant him peace, mentioned a *fitnah* (a trial or sedition) and said, 'This one will be killed wrongfully in it,' about 'Uthman.

Murrah ibn Ka'b said: I heard the Prophet, may Allah bless him and grant him peace, mentioning a trial which he thought to be near. A man passed by, muffled up in his garment, and he (the Prophet) said, 'This one on that day will be upon the guidance.' I stood up and went to him and it was 'Uthman ibn 'Affan. I turned, faced him (the Prophet) and said, 'This one?' He said, 'Yes.'

'A'ishah, may Allah be pleased with her, related that the Prophet, may Allah bless him and grant him peace, said, ''Uthman, perhaps Allah will robe you in a garment, so if the hypocrites wish to strip it off you do not take it off until you meet me.'

'Uthman said, on the day of the House (the site of his siege), 'The Prophet, may Allah bless him and grant him peace, made a covenant with me and I will be patient with it.'

Abu Hurairah said: 'Uthman bought the Garden from the Prophet, may Allah bless him and grant him peace, twice: when he had the well of *Rumah* dug and when he equipped the Army of Difficulty.

Abu Hurairah, may Allah be pleased with him, said that the Prophet, may Allah bless him and grant him peace, said, ''Uthman, of my companions, most resembles me in character.'

'Asmah ibn Malik said: When the daughter of the Messenger of Allah, may Allah bless him and his family and grant them peace, died under (the roof of) 'Uthman, the Messenger of Allah, may Allah bless him and grant him peace, said, 'Get 'Uthman married. Even if I had a third (daughter) I would have got him married, and I did not get him married except through revelation from Allah.'

ʿAli, may Allah be pleased with him said: I heard the Prophet, may Allah bless him and grant him peace, say to ʿUthman, 'Even if I had forty daughters I would marry them to you, one after another, until none of them remained.'

Zaid ibn Thabit said: I heard the Prophet, may Allah bless him and grant him peace, saying, 'ʿUthman passed by me while one of the angels was with me, and he said, "A martyr whose people will kill him. We are shy of him."'

Ibn ʿUmar related that the Prophet, may Allah bless him and grant him peace, said, 'The angels are shy of ʿUthman, just as they are shy of Allah and His Messenger.'

Al-Hasan related that the modesty of ʿUthman was mentioned in his presence. He said, 'If he were in the middle of the house—and the door locked—then he put off his clothes in order to pour water over himself, modesty would prevent him from raising (straightening) his backbone.'

His khilafah

He was pledged allegiance as *khalifah* three nights after the burial of ʿUmar. It is related that people got together, during those days, with ʿAbd ar-Rahman ibn ʿAuf, advising him and talking confidentially with him. Not one person of judgement who sat alone with him saw any to equal ʿUthman. When ʿAbd ar-Rahman sat to pledge allegiance, he praised Allah and said, during his speech, 'I saw that people refuse anybody but ʿUthman.' This is narrated from al-Miswar ibn Makhramah. In another narration, 'Now! ʿAli, I have researched among people and I don't see them regarding anyone equal to ʿUthman. Therefore, do not make a way against yourself.' He took the hand of ʿUthman and said, 'We pledge allegiance to you according to the *Sunnah* of Allah, the *Sunnah* of His Messenger and the *Sunnah* of the two *khalifahs* after him.' ʿAbd ar-Rahman pledged allegiance to him and the *Muhajirun* and the *Ansar* pledged allegiance to him.

Anas said: ᶜUmar sent for Abu Talhah al-Ansari an hour before he died and said, 'You be among fifty of the *Ansar* along with this group, the companions of the counsel, because they, as I believe, will gather in a house. Stand at that door with your companions, allow no-one to enter, and do not leave them to allow the third day to pass without their appointing one of themselves to the command.'

Abu Wa'il said: I said to ᶜAbd ar-Rahman ibn ᶜAuf, 'How could you have sworn allegiance to ᶜUthman and neglected ᶜAli?' He said, 'Where was my wrong action? I started with ᶜAli and I said, "Shall I swear allegiance to you according to the Book of Allah, the *Sunnah* of His Messenger and the conduct of Abu Bakr and ᶜUmar?" He said, "In what I am able." Then later I offered the same to ᶜUthman and he said, "Yes."'

It has been related that ᶜAbd ar-Rahman said to ᶜUthman in private, 'If I don't pledge allegiance to you who would you point out to me?' He said, 'ᶜAli.' He said to ᶜAli, 'If I don't pledge allegiance to you who would you point out to me?' He said, 'ᶜUthman.' Then he called for az-Zubayr and said, 'If I don't pledge allegiance to you who would you point out to me?' He said, 'ᶜAli or ᶜUthman.' Then later he called for Saᶜd and said, 'Whom would you indicate to me? For, as for me and you, we don't want it.' He said, 'ᶜUthman.' Then ᶜAbd ar-Rahman sought the counsel of all the notables and saw that most of them were inclined to ᶜUthman.

It is related of Ibn Masᶜud, may Allah be pleased with him, that he said, when ᶜUthman was pledged allegiance, 'We have charged with command the best of those remaining and we have not been negligent.'

In this year of his *khilafah,* Rai was taken, and it had been taken previously and subsequently lost. In that year many nose-bleeds occurred among people, so that it was known as, 'The year of the nose-bleeds.' ᶜUthman was afflicted by nose-bleeds to such an extent that he stayed away from the *Hajj* and deputed someone in his place. In that year many Byzantine fortresses were taken. In it ᶜUthman appointed Saᶜd ibn Abi Waqqas as governor of Kufah and removed al-Mughirah.

In the year 25 A.H., ᶜUthman removed Saᶜd from Kufah and appointed al-Walid ibn ᶜUqbah ibn Abi Muᶜayt—and he was a Companion, and a brother of ᶜUthman on his mother's side— and that was the first thing for which he was disliked; because he appointed his relatives to posts of authority. *It has been told as a tale* (as-Suyuti very deliberately chose this wording) that al-Walid led them in prayer for the dawn prayer with four *rakaᶜat* when he was drunk, and that then he turned to them and said, 'Shall I do more (*rakaᶜat*) for you?'

In the year 26 A.H., ᶜUthman enlarged and extended *al-Masjid al-Haram*, and bought sites (adjoining it) for the enlargement. In the same year Sabur (possibly Shahpur) was taken.

In the year 27 A.H., Muᶜawiyah went on a military expedition to Cyprus, taking the armies by sea. ᶜUbadah ibn as-Samit was with them and his wife, Umm Haram bint Milhan al-Ansariyah (of the Ansar). She fell from her riding beast, and died there as a martyr, and the Prophet, may Allah bless him and grant him peace, had foretold for her this army. He had supplicated for her that she should be of them. She was buried in Cyprus. In that same year Arrajan and Darabjird were taken. ᶜUthman removed ᶜAmr ibn al-ᶜAs from Egypt and appointed ᶜAbdullah ibn Saᶜd ibn Abi Sarh over it, who led an expedition against northern Africa and conquered it, both on the plains and in the mountains, and every man in the army received one thousand *dinars*, and it has also been said, three thousand *dinars*. Then Andalucia was taken in this same year.

An observation

Muᶜawiyah had pressed ᶜUmar ibn al-Khattab very persistently about raiding Cyprus and doing so by sea, so ᶜUmar wrote to ᶜAmr ibn al-ᶜAs, 'Describe to me the sea and the one who travels on it.' He wrote to him, 'I have seen a great creation which a small creation mounts. If it is still it pierces the hearts, and if it moves it awes the intellects. In it the intellects grow in littleness, and wrong actions in muchness, and in it they are like grubs upon a timber. If it leans over, it sinks, and if it is swift, it enters into the wave and dives therein.' When ʿUmar read the letter he wrote to Muʿawiyah, 'By Allah I will never convey a Muslim upon it.' Ibn Jarir said, 'Muʿawiyah carried out the expedition against Cyprus during the time of ʿUthman, and its people made a treaty with him on the basis of their paying the *jizyah*.'

In the year 29 A.H., Persepolis was taken by force of arms, and Fasa and other places. In that year, ʿUthman added to the mosque of Madinah, extended it, and rebuilt it with sculpted stone, making its pillars of stone and its roof of teak. He made its length one hundred and sixty cubits and its breadth one hundred and fifty cubits.

In the year 30 A.H., Jur was taken and many provinces of the land of Khurasan; Naysabur was taken by treaty, and it has been said, by force. Tus and Sarkhas were both taken by treaty, and similarly Marw and Bayhaq. When these extensive provinces were taken, ʿUthman's revenues became abundant, and wealth came to him from every direction, until he established treasuries and made provisions to flow abundantly. He would order for a man one hundred thousand purses in each of which there were four thousand ounces (of silver).

In the year 31 A.H., Abu Sufyan ibn Harb, the father of Muʿawiyah, died, and also al-Hakam ibn Abi'l-ʿAs the paternal uncle of ʿUthman, may Allah be pleased with him.

In the year 32 A.H., al-ʿAbbas ibn ʿAbd al-Muttalib, the paternal uncle of the Prophet, may Allah bless him and grant him peace, died, and ʿUthman led the (funeral) prayer over him. In that year ʿAbd ar-Rahman ibn ʿAuf died, one of the ten from the first outstrippers who had once given away as *sadaqah* forty thousand and an entire caravan which had come from Syria, just as it was. In that year, ʿAbdullah ibn Masʿud al-Hudhali died, one of the four reciters, one of the earliest in Islam, and one of the men of knowledge, among the Companions, who were famous for the vast extent of their knowledge. In that year the wise and abstinent Abu'd-Darda' al-Khazraji died; he had been appointed to the position of Qadi of Damascus under Muʿawiyah. In that year Abu Dharr Jundub ibn Jinadah al-Ghiffari, the truthful in speech, died. In that year, Zaid ibn ʿAbdullah ibn ʿAbd-Rabbihi al-Ansari died, the one who was shown the *adhan* in a dream.

In the year 33 A.H., al-Miqdad ibn al-Aswad died at his land at al-Jurf, and he was carried to Madinah (for burial). In that year, Abdullah ibn Saʿd ibn Abi Sarh mounted a military expedition against Abyssinia.

In the year 34 A.H., the people of Kufah ejected Saʿid ibn al-ʿAs and were pleased with Abu Musa al-Ashʿari.

In the year 35 A.H., there occurred the killing of ʿUthman.

Az-Zuhri said: ʿUthman ruled the *khilafah* for twelve years. For six years he ruled without people criticising him at all. To Quraysh he was preferrable to ʿUmar ibn al-Khattab, because ʿUmar was severe against them, but when ʿUthman ruled over them he was gentle with them and made his connections close with them. Then later he flagged in their affair, and appointed his relatives and family in the last six (years of his rule). He decreed for Marwan the *khums* (the fifth share of the spoils of *jihad* that goes to the ruler) of North Africa, and he gave his relatives and family wealth. In that he was interpreting the 'making close connections (with family)' which Allah has ordered. He said, 'Abu Bakr and Umar gave up and abandoned what of that was theirs (by right), and I have taken it and divided it among my relatives,' but people rejected and repudiated that from him.

Az-Zuhri also said in another narration: I said to Saʿid ibn al-Musayyab, 'Can you tell me how the killing of ʿUthman was? What were people up to and what was he up to? And why did the Companions of Muhammad, may Allah bless him and grant him peace, fail to help him?' Ibn al-Musayyab said, 'ʿUthman was killed unjustly, whoever killed him was wrongdoing, and whoever failed to help him is free of blame.' I said, 'How was that?' He said, 'When Uthman was appointed, a group of the Companions disliked his appointment, because Uthman used to love his people. He ruled people for twelve years. He used to appoint people from Bani Umayyah who had not kept company with the Prophet, may Allah bless him and grant him peace. His *amirs* used to produce matters which the Companions of Muhammad, may Allah bless him and grant him peace, would repudiate. ᶜUthman used to ask people to have good will for them and he would not remove them. That was in the year 35 A.H. During the six last years he chose in preference the tribe of his paternal uncle. He appointed them and did not let anyone share with them. He ordered them to fear Allah, he appointed ᶜAbdullah ibn Abi Sarh in charge of Egypt and he remained in control there for years. The people of Egypt came to complain of him and to complain of his wrongdoing. There had been slights before from ᶜUthman to ᶜAbdullah ibn Masᶜud, Abu Dharr and ᶜAmmar ibn Yasir. Banu Hudhayl and Banu Zuhrah had what they had in their hearts because of the state of Ibn Masᶜud. Banu Ghiffar, their allies and whoever was angry because of Abu Dharr, had in their hearts what they had in them. Banu Makhzum were furious at ᶜUthman because of the condition of ᶜAmmar ibn Yasir.

The people of Egypt came to complain of Ibn Abi Sarh, so he wrote a letter to him in which he threatened him, but Ibn Abi Sarh refused to accept what ᶜUthman forbade him, he struck one of those of the people of Egypt who came to him from ᶜUthman, one of those who had gone to Uthman, and he killed him. Seven hundred men left Egypt and dwelt in the mosque (of Madinah). They complained to the Companions at the times of the prayers about what Ibn Abi Sarh had done. Talhah ibn ᶜUbaydullah stood and addressed ᶜUthman very severely. ᶜA'ishah, may Allah be pleased with her, sent a message to him saying, 'The Companions of Muhammad, may Allah bless him and grant him peace, came to you and they asked you to remove this man and you refused? This one has killed a man from among them so treat them with justice (in their complaint) against your governor.' ᶜAli ibn Abi Talib came to him and said, 'They are only asking you for a man in place of (in retaliation for) a man and they have claimed from him (retaliation for the spilling of) blood. Remove him from over them and give a (just) decision between them. If there is anything due against him, be just to them.' He (ᶜUthman) said to them (the Egyptians), 'Choose from amongst yourselves a

man whom I shall appoint over you in his (Ibn Abi Sarh's) place.'
The people indicated to him Muhammad ibn Abi Bakr. They
said, 'Appoint Muhammad ibn Abi Bakr over us.' He wrote his
covenant and appointed him. A number of the *Muhajirun* and
Ansar went with them to look into that (dispute) which was
between the people of Egypt and Ibn Abi Sarh. Muhammad went
and those with him. When they were about three days' journey
from Madinah they came upon a black slave on a camel beating
the camel so much that it was as if he was pursuing or being
pursued. The Companions of Muhammad, may Allah bless him
and grant him peace, said to him, 'What is your story? What is
your business? It is as if you were fleeing or pursuing someone.'
He said to them, 'I am the slave of the Amir al-Muminin and he
has directed me to the governor of Egypt.' A man said to him,
'This (Muhammad ibn Abi Bakr) is the governor of Egypt.' He
said, 'It is not this one I want.' Muhammad ibn Abi Bakr was told
of his affair and so he sent a man in search of him who took him
and brought him to him. He said, 'Slave, who are you?' He began
to say, one time, 'I am the slave of the Amir al-Muminin,' and
another time, 'I am the slave of Marwan,' until one man recognised that he was the slave of ʿUthman. Muhammad said to him,
'To whom are you sent?' He said, 'To the governor of Egypt.' He
said, 'With what?' He said, 'With a message.' He said, 'Do you
have a letter with you?' He said, 'No.' They searched him and
didn't find a letter with him. He had with him an ewer which
was dry, in which was something which moved about, so they
moved it about to bring it out but it didn't come out. They broke
the ewer and there was a letter in it from ʿUthman to Ibn Abi
Sarh. Muhammad gathered those with them of the *Muhajirun*,
the *Ansar* and others, then he opened the letter in their presence. There was in it, 'When Muhammad, so-and-so, and so-
and-so come to you, then find a way to kill them, and declare his
letter to be false. Consider yourself confirmed in your governor-
ship until my advice on it comes to you, and imprison whoever
tries to come to me to accuse you of wrong-doing. My advice on
that will certainly come to you, if Allah wills.'

When they read the letter they were terrified. Then they became resolved and returned to Madinah. Muhammad sealed the letter with the signet rings of the group who were with him, and then entrusted the letter to a man who was with them. Then they went to Madinah. There they gathered together Talhah, az-Zubayr, ᶜAli, Saᶜd, and whoever there was of the Companions of Muhammad, may Allah bless him and his family and grant them peace. Then he broke (the seals of) the letter in their presence, and told them of the story of the slave. They read out the letter to them, and none of the people of Madinah was left who was not enraged at ᶜUthman. It only increased those who were angry because of Ibn Masᶜud, Abu Dharr and ᶜAmmar ibn Yasir in fury and rage. The Companions of Muhammad arose and kept to their houses. There was no-one among them who was not incoherent when he read the letter. The people beseiged ᶜUthman in the year 35 A.H., and Muhammad ibn Abi Bakr raised Bani Taym and others against him.

When ᶜAli saw that, he sent for Talhah, az-Zubayr, Saᶜd, ᶜAmmar and a group of the Companions, all of whom were at Badr. Then he went in to ᶜUthman, with him the letter, the slave and the camel. ᶜAli said to him, 'This slave is your slave?' He said, 'Yes.' He said, 'And the camel is your camel?' He said, 'Yes.' He said, 'Then you wrote this letter?' He said, 'No,' and he swore an oath, 'By Allah I did not write this letter, I did not order it, and I had no knowledge of it.' ᶜAli said, 'The seal is your seal?' He said, 'Yes.' He said, 'How does your slave go out on your camel, with a letter upon which is your seal, and you know nothing about it?' He swore again, 'By Allah, I did not write this letter, I didn't order it, and I never directed this slave to go to Egypt.' As for the handwriting, they recognised that it was that of Marwan, and they came to doubt as to ᶜUthman. They demanded that he should give them Marwan and he refused, while Marwan was with him in the house. The Companions of Muhammad, may Allah bless him and grant him peace, left him in anger, and in doubt about his affair. They knew that Uthman would not swear an oath that was false, but people said, 'ᶜUthman will never be free of guilt in our hearts unless he hands Marwan over to us for questioning, so that we know the situation of the letter, and how he could order the killing of a man of the Companions of Muhammad, may Allah bless him and grant him peace, without right. If *Uthman wrote it, we will remove him from office. If Marwan wrote it as if it had been written by *Uthman, then we will have to look seriously at what we shall do in the case of Marwan.'

They stuck to their houses, and *Uthman refused to send Marwan out to them, for he feared that he would be killed. People continued laying siege to *Uthman, and they prevented water (from reaching him). He looked over the people (from an upper floor) and said, 'Is *Ali among you?' They said, 'No.' He said, 'Is Sa*d among you?' They said, 'No.' He was silent and then he said, 'Will no-one reach *Ali and ask him to get us water to drink?' That reached *Ali, so he sent him three water-skins full of water, but they almost didn't reach him. Because of them a number of the freed slaves of Banu Hashim and Banu Umayyah were wounded in the course of the water getting to him.

It reached *Ali that it was intended to kill *Uthman, and he said, 'We only want Marwan from him. As for the killing of *Uthman, no!' He said to al-Hasan and al-Hussein, 'Go with your two swords and stand at the door of *Uthman and allow no-one to reach him.' Then az-Zubayr sent his son, Talhah sent his son and a number of the Companions of the Prophet, may Allah bless him and grant him peace, sent their sons to prevent people getting to *Uthman, and to demand the surrender of Marwan. When people saw that, they shot arrows against the door of *Uthman until al-Hasan ibn *Ali was reddened with blood at his door, an arrow struck Marwan while he was in the house. Muhammad ibn Talhah was besmeared with blood and also Qanbar, the freed slave of Ali, was wounded in the head.

Muhammad ibn Abi Bakr was afraid that Banu Hashim would become angry because of the state of al-Hasan and al-Hussein and provoke a tumult. He took the hands of two men and said to them, 'If Banu Hashim come and see blood on the face of al-Hasan they will remove these people from around *Uthman and what we wanted will be rendered useless. Let us go and scale the wall of the house and kill him, without anyone knowing about it.' Muhammad and his two men got over the wall from the house of a man of the *Ansar* and entered ᶜUthman's house, without any of those who were with him (ᶜUthman) knowing, because everyone with him was up above the houses (on the roofs). There was no-one with him but his wife. Muhammad said to the two of them, 'Stay where you are, because his wife is with him, until I first enter. When I have taken hold of him, then you come in and strike him until you have killed him.' Muhammad went in and took hold of his beard, and ᶜUthman said to him, 'By Allah, if your father could see you, your behaviour to me would cause him great distress,' and so his hand slackened (and he held back), and then the two men entered and struck him until they had killed him.

They went out in flight by the same way that they had come in, and his wife cried out, but her cry was not heard in the house because of the commotion in the house. His wife went up to the people and said, 'The Amir al-Muminin has been killed!' The people entered and they found him slaughtered. The news reached ᶜAli, Talhah, az-Zubayr, Saᶜd and whoever was in Madinah and they went out—and their intellects had gone, because of the news which had come to them—until they came in to ᶜUthman and found him killed. They repeated again and again, 'Truly we belong to Allah and truly we are returning to Him.' ᶜAli said to his two sons, 'How was the Amir al-Muminin killed while you two were at the door?' He raised his hand and slapped al-Hasan, struck the chest of al-Hussein, abused Muhammad ibn Talhah and ᶜAbdullah ibn az-Zubayr, and went out—enraged—until he came to his house.

The people came rushing to him, saying to him, 'We will pledge allegiance to you, so stretch out your hand, for there must be an *amir*.' ᶜAli said, 'That is not your business. It only belongs to the people of Badr. Whoever the people of Badr are pleased with is the *khalifah*.' Not one of the people of Badr remained without coming to ᶜAli and they said to him, 'We see no-one who has more right to it than you. Stretch out your hand and we will pledge allegiance to you.' They pledged allegiance to him. Marwan and his son fled.

ʿAli came to the wife of ʿUthman and said to her, 'Who killed ʿUthman?' She said, 'I don't know. Two men I don't know came in to him, and along with them was Muhammad ibn Abi Bakr.' She told ʿAli and the people of what Muhammad had done, so ʿAli called for Muhammad and asked him about what the wife of ʿUthman had said. Muhammad said, 'She did not lie. By Allah, I did come into him, I did want to kill him, then he reminded me of my father and I stood back from him, turning in penitence to Allah, exalted is He. By Allah, I did not kill him, and I did not hold him.' His wife said, 'He has told the truth. But he did bring the two of them in.'

Kinanah, the freed slave of Safiyyah, and others relate: An Egyptian, who was blue-eyed with a ruddy complexion, called Himar killed ʿUthman.

Al-Mughirah ibn Shuʿbah said that he entered upon ʿUthman while he was besieged and said, 'You are the *Imam* of the people, and what you see has happened to you. I offer you three courses; one of them, that you come out and fight them, for there are numbers (of men) and strength with you; you are in the right and they are in the wrong; or we should cut a door for you other than the door over which they stand guard, then you sit on your mount and take yourself to Makkah, for they will not consider it lawful to kill you when you are there; or else you should take yourself to Syria, for they are the people of Syria and among them is Muʿawiyah.' ʿUthman said, 'As for me going out and fighting, I will not be the first *khalifah* of the Messenger of Allah, may Allah bless him and grant him peace, in his *ummah* to spill (their) blood; and as for me going to Makkah, I heard the Messenger of Allah, may Allah bless him and grant him peace, saying, "A man of Quraysh will wrangle and dispute in Makkah; there will be upon him half the punishment of the world," and I shall not be him; and as for me taking myself to Syria, then I will never separate myself from the Abode of the *Hijrah* and the neighbourhood of the Messenger of Allah, may Allah bless him and grant him peace.'

Abu Thawr al-Fahmi said: I entered upon ᶜUthman while he was besieged and he said, 'I have hidden ten (things) with my Lord: I was the fourth of four in Islam; I equipped the Army of Difficulty; the Messenger of Allah, may Allah bless him and grant him peace, married me his daughter and then later she died, and he married me his other daughter, and I did not court (her) and I didn't wish (for it); I have never placed my right hand upon my private parts since I pledged allegiance with it to the Messenger of Allah, may Allah bless him and grant him peace; and no *Jumuᶜah* has passed me by since I accepted Islam without me freeing a slave, unless there was something with me (of debt), then I would free him (or her) after that; and I never committed adultery in *Jahiliyyah* or Islam; and I never stole in *Jahiliyyah* or Islam; and I memorised the entire Qur'an in the time of the Messenger of Allah, may Allah bless him and grant him peace.'

ᶜUthman was killed in the middle of the days of *Tashriq* (the days of the *ᶜEid* of *Hajj*) in the year 35 A.H.; and it has been said that he was killed on the day of *Jumuᶜah,* the 18th of Dhu'l-Hijjah. He was buried on the night before Saturday, between the sunset and night prayers, in Hash Kawkab in *al-Baqᶦ* (the cemetery of Madinah) and he was the first to be buried in it (Hawsh Kawkab). It was said that his killing was on Wednesday, and it was said that it was Monday six days before the end of Dhu'l-Hijjah. On the day he was killed, he was eighty-two years old. It has also been said that he was eighty-one years old, eighty-four, eighty-six, eighty-eight or eighty-nine, and it was said that he was ninety. Qatadah said: Az-Zubayr prayed the funeral prayer over him and buried him and he had requested him to do that.

Anas related in a *marfuᶜ hadith,* 'Allah has a sword sheathed in its scabbard as long as ᶜUthman is alive. Then when he is killed, that sword will be drawn and it will not be sheathed until the Day of Resurrection.'

Zaid ibn Abi Habib said: It has reached me that all of the mounted group who went to ᶜUthman went mad.

Hudhayfah said: The first of the trials was the killing of cUthman, and the last of the trials is the emergence of the Dajjal. By the One in Whose hand is my self, a man will not die, in whose heart there is the weight of grain of loving the killing of cUthman, but that he would follow the Dajjal if he reached him (his time), and if he did not reach him he would affirm him in his grave.

Ibn Abbas said: If people had not sought (retaliation) for the blood of cUthman they would have been stoned with stones from heaven.

Al-Hasan said: cUthman was killed while cAli was away in some land he owned. When it reached him he said, 'O Allah, I did not approve (of it) and I did not abet (it).'

Qais ibn cAbbad said: I heard cAli on the Day of the (battle of the) Camel saying, 'O Allah I am clear before You of having taken part in the (shedding of the) blood of cUthman. My intellect was shaken on the day of cUthman's killing, my soul was repulsed, and they came to me to pledge allegiance to me and I said, "By Allah, I am ashamed to take the allegiance of a people who killed cUthman, and I am ashamed before Allah to be sworn allegiance while cUthman is not yet buried," so they went away. When the people returned and asked me to accept their allegiance, I said, "O Allah, I am afraid of what I am proceeding to do." Then the determination (of the people) came, I was sworn allegiance, they said, "Amir al-Muminin!" and it was as if my heart was rent asunder. I said, "O Allah, take from me for the sake of cUthman until You are contented."'

Abu Khaldah al-Hanafi said: I heard cAli saying, 'Banu Umayyah claim that I killed cUthman. No, by Allah Whom there is no god but He! I did not kill him, I did not abet it, I forbade it but they disobeyed me.'

Samurah said: Islam was in a well fortified fortress, and they made a breach in Islam with the killing of cUthman which will not be closed until the Day of Resurrection. The *khilafah* was among the people of Madinah and they drove it out and it did not return to them.

Muhammad ibn Sirin said: The piebald horses (of the angels) were never missing from the battles and the armies until the killing of ⁱUthman. There was no disagreement on the new moons until the killing of ⁱUthman. This redness which is on the horizons was never seen until the killing of al-Hussein.

Humayd ibn Hilal said: ⁱAbdullah ibn Salam came upon those who were besieging ⁱUthman and said, 'Do not kill him, for, by Allah, any man of you kills him will meet Allah without a hand. The sword of Allah will remain sheathed, and by Allah, if you kill him, Allah will draw it out and He will never sheathe it again. A prophet was never killed but that seventy thousand were killed because of him, nor a *khalifah* but that thirty-five thousand were killed because of him before they were again united.'

ⁱAbd ar-Rahman ibn Mahdi said: There were two qualities that ⁱUthman had which neither Abu Bakr nor ⁱUmar had: his self-collectedness until he was killed, and his uniting the people upon a single *mushaf* (written copy of the Qur'an).

Ash-Shaⁱbi said: I have not heard a better elegy upon ⁱUthman than the words of Kaⁱb ibn Malik when he said:

'Then he restrained his hands and closed his door, and he was certain that Allah is not forgetful,
He said to the people of the house, "Do not kill them! May Allah pardon every man who does not fight."
So how you have seen Allah pour out upon them enmity and hatred after harmony with each other!
And how you have seen the good turning back from people after him, the way the driving winds turn (the clouds) back!'

Section

Musa ibn Talhah said: I saw ⁱUthman going out on the day of *Jumuⁱah*, upon him two yellow garments. He would sit on the *mimbar*, then the *mu'adhdhins* would call to the prayer while he would talk, asking people about their prices and their sick.

ⁱAbdullah ar-Rumi said: ⁱUthman would take care of his *wudu* (washing for prayer) at night himself. Someone said to him, 'If only you would tell one of the servants then they would take care (of it for) you.' He said, 'No! The night is for them to rest in.'

ᶜAmr ibn ᶜUthman ibn ᶜAffan said: The engraving on the seal-ring of ᶜUthman was, 'I trust in the One Who created and completed (His creation).'

Ibn ᶜUmar related that Jahjah al-Ghifari stood up against Uthman while he was (upon the *mimbar*) delivering the *khutbah*, and he took his staff from his hand and broke it over his knee. The year did not pass until Allah sent gangrene in his foot and he died from it.

The things in which ᶜUthman was first

Al-ᶜAskari said in *al-Awa'il* (The Firsts): He was the first to grant lands (taken in *jihad*), and the first who enclosed pastures (for the animals paid in *zakah* and for the horses and camels for *jihad*), the first to lower his voice in the *takbir*, the first to perfume the mosque (of Madinah), the first to command the first call to prayer on the *Jumuᶜah*, the first to provide for the *mu'adhdhins*, the first to be speechless in the *khutbah*, and then he said, 'People, the first time of mounting is hard, after today there are other days, and if I live you will have the *khutbah* in its proper manner. We were never public speakers and Allah will teach us.' He was the first to place the *khutbah* on the *ᶜEid* before the prayer, the first to entrust to the people the payment of their own *zakah*, the first to take charge of the *khilafah* during the life of his mother, the first to appoint a chief of police, and the first to set apart an enclosure in the mosque from fear that there should happen to him what happened to ᶜUmar. This is what al-ᶜAskari mentioned and he also said: The first disagreements in the *ummah* in which some would accuse others of errors were in his time, concerning things which they blamed him for. Before that they used to disagree about *fiqh* and no-one would accuse others of errors.

I say: Of his firsts there remain that he was the first of this *ummah* to emigrate with his family for the sake of Allah, as has preceded, and he was the first to unite people on one manner of recitation.

Hakim ibn ᶜAbbad ibn Hanif said: The first reprehensible thing that appeared in Madinah when the world was overflowing (with wealth) and the fatness of people reached a limit, was the flying of pigeons and archery with crossbows (firing clay bullets) (for bets), so ᶜUthman appointed a man from Banu Layth in the eighth year of his *khilafah* who clipped them (the wings of the pigeons) and broke the crossbows.

The notables who died during the time of ᶜUthman

There died during the time of ᶜUthman the following notable people: Suraqah ibn Malik ibn Jushum, Jabbar ibn Sakhr, Hatib ibn Abi Baltaᶜah, ᶜIyad ibn Zuhayr, Abu Usayd as-Saᶜidi, Aus ibn as-Samit, al-Harith ibn Naufal, ᶜAbdullah ibn Hudhafah, Zaid ibn Kharijah the one who spoke after death, Labid the poet, al-Musayyab the father of Saᶜid, Muᶜadh ibn ᶜAmr ibn al-Jamuh, Maᶜbid ibn al-ᶜAbbas, Muᶜayqib ibn Abi Fatimah ad-Dawsi, Abu Lubabah ibn ᶜAbd al-Mundhir, Nuᶜaim ibn Masᶜud al-Ashjaᶜi and others of the Companions.

Apart from the Companions there were Hutai'ah the poet and Abu Dhu'ayb the poet of the tribe of Hudhayl.

^cAli ibn Abi Talib

may Allah be pleased with him

Ali ibn Abi Talib, may Allah be pleased with him—and the name of Abu Talib was ^cAbd Manaf—Ibn ^cAbd al-Muttalib—and his name was Shaybah—ibn Hashim—and his name was ^cAmr—Ibn ^cAbd Manaf—and his name was al-Mughirah—ibn Qusayy—and his name was Zaid—ibn Kilab ibn Murrah ibn Ka^cb ibn Lu'ayy ibn Ghalib ibn Fihr ibn Malik ibn Nadr ibn Kinanah. He was Abu'l-Hasan and he was Abu Turab, a *kunya* which the Prophet, may Allah bless him and grant him peace, gave him.

His mother was Fatimah bint Asad ibn Hashim and she was the first Hashimi woman to give birth to a Hashimi child. She accepted Islam and emigrated.

^cAli, may Allah be pleased with him, is one of the ten for whom it is witnessed that the Garden is for them, he was the brother of the Messenger of Allah, may Allah bless him and his family and grant them peace, by the act of taking brothers (undertaken between the *Muhajirun* and the *Ansar* in Madinah); he was his son-in-law through (marriage to) Fatimah, the mistress of the women of the worlds, may Allah be pleased with her; he was one of the first to embrace Islam, one of the lordly learned ones, one of the famously courageous ones, one of those mentioned for being abstinent, one of the recognised deliverers of the *khutbah*, one who memorised the entire Qur'an and recited it before the Prophet, may Allah bless him and grant him peace, and Abu'l-Aswad ad-Du'ali and ^cAbd ar-Rahman as-Sulami, in turn, recited it before him. He was the first *khalifah* from Bani Hashim, the father of the two grandsons (of the Prophet, may

Allah bless him and grant him peace). He accepted Islam very early on; rather, Ibn ʿAbbas, Anas, Zaid ibn Arqam, Salman al-Farisi and a whole group of others said that he was the first to accept Islam, and some of them relate that there is a consensus on that.

ʿAli, may Allah be pleased with him, said, 'The Messenger of Allah, may Allah bless him and grant him peace, was sent (on his prophetic mission) on Monday and I accepted Islam on the Wednesday.' His age when he accepted Islam was ten years old. It has been said that it was nine, eight, and it has even been said that it was less than that. Al-Hasan ibn Zaid ibn al-Hasan said: He didn't ever worship idols, because of his youth.

When he, may Allah bless him and grant him peace, told him to remain some days behind after him in Makkah, in order to repay some things entrusted to and deposited with the Prophet, may Allah bless him and grant him peace, and for him then to join his family, he did that.

He was present with the Messenger of Allah, may Allah bless him and his family and grant them peace, at Badr, Uhud and all the rest of the battles except for Tabuk, because the Prophet, may Allah bless him and grant him peace, made him his deputy in Madinah. In all of the battles there are famous stories about him, and the Prophet, may Allah bless him and grant him peace, gave him the standard on many occasions.

Saʿid ibn al-Musayyab said: On the day of Uhud, ʿAli received sixteen wounds.

It is well established in the two *Sahih* collections, 'That he, may Allah bless him and grant him peace, gave him the standard on the day of Khaybar and told that victory would be at his hands.' The accounts of his bravery and stories of him in the wars are famous.

ʿAli, as an old man, was stout, balding over the forehead, with much hair, of middle stature inclining to shortness, full-bellied, with an extremely full beard which filled between his two shoulders and was white as if it were cotton, and he was very tawny complexioned.

Jabir ibn ʿAbdullah said: ʿAli carried the gate upon his back on the day of Khaybar until the Muslims ascended upon it and conquered it. They tried to drag it afterwards and it was only possible for forty men to carry it.

Abu Rafiʿ related: ʿAli took hold of the gate of the fortress, the fortress of Khaybar; he used it as a shield to protect himself, and it continued in his hand while he fought until Allah gave us the victory. I certainly saw eight of us struggling to turn that gate over and we were not able to turn it.

Sahl ibn Saʿd said: The name that ʿAli, may Allah be pleased with him, loved the most was 'Abu Turab ('Dusty One' or literally 'Father of Dust'), and he rejoiced in being called by it. No-one named him Abu Turab except for the Prophet, may Allah bless him and grant him peace. That was because one day, when he was angry with Fatimah, he went out and laid down against the wall of the mosque, and then the Prophet, may Allah bless him and grant him peace, came and his back was covered in dust. The Prophet, may Allah bless him and grant him peace, began to rub the dust from his back saying, 'Sit down Abu Turab.'

He related five hundred and eighty-six *hadith* from the Prophet, may Allah bless him and his family and grant them peace.

His three sons, al-Hasan, al-Hussein and Muhammad ibn al-Hanafiyyah, related from him, and Ibn Masʿud, Ibn ʿUmar, Ibn ʿAbbas, Ibn az-Zubayr, Abu Musa, Abu Saʿid, Zaid ibn Arqam, Jabir ibn ʿAbdullah, Abu Imamah, Abu Hurairah, and a great number of other Companions and Followers, may Allah be pleased with all of them.

The *ahadith* related on his merit

The *Imam* Ahmad ibn Hanbal said: That which has been related about ʿAli, may Allah be pleased with him, has not been related about any of the Companions of the Messenger of Allah, may Allah bless him and grant him peace.

Saʿd ibn Abi Waqqas related that: The Messenger of Allah, may Allah bless him and his family and grant them peace, deputised ᶜAli ibn Abi Talib (as his *khalifah* in Madinah) in the Battle of Tabuk. He said, 'Messenger of Allah, will you leave me behind with the women and children?' He said, 'Are you not pleased to be in the same relation to me as Harun was to Musa, except that there is no prophet after me?' This has also been related in *hadith* of Abu Saᶜid al-Khudri, Asma' bint Qais, Umm Salamah, Habashi ibn Jinadah, Ibn ᶜUmar, Ibn ᶜAbbas, Jabir ibn Samurah, al-Bara' ibn ᶜAzib and Zaid ibn Arqam.

Sahl ibn Saᶜd said that the Messenger of Allah, may Allah bless him and his family and grant them peace, said on the day of Khaybar, 'I will give the standard tomorrow to a man at whose hands Allah will give victory, who loves Allah and His Messenger, and whom Allah and His Messenger love.' The people spent the night wondering about and discussing who would be given it. When people awoke in the morning they went to the Messenger of Allah, may Allah bless him and his family and grant them peace, and all of them were hoping that they would be given it. He said, 'Where is ᶜAli ibn Abi Talib?' They said, 'He is complaining of an ailment in his eyes.' He said, 'Send for him.' They brought him. The Messenger of Allah, may Allah bless him and his family and grant them peace, spat in his eyes and supplicated for him and he was healed to such an extent that it was as if he had not had a pain. Then he gave him the standard.

The above *hadith* has been related by Ibn ᶜUmar, ᶜAli, Ibn Abi Layla, ᶜImran ibn Husayn and Ibn ᶜAbbas.

Saᶜd ibn Abi Waqqas said: When this *ayah* was revealed, '*Let us call our sons and your sons ...*' (Qur'an 3: 61) then the Messenger of Allah, may Allah bless him and his family and grant them peace, called for ᶜAli, Fatimah, Hasan, Hussein and said, 'O Allah, these are my family.'

Abu Surayhah or Zaid ibn Arqam related from the Prophet, may Allah bless him and grant him peace, that he said, 'He for whom I am his master (*mawla*), then Ali is his master.' This has been narrated from ᶜAli, Abu Ayyub al-Ansari, Zaid ibn Arqam, ᶜAmr ibn Dhi Murr, Abu Hurairah, Ibn ᶜUmar, Malik ibn Huwairith, Habashi ibn Jinadah, Jarir, Saᶜd ibn Abi Waqqas, Abu Saᶜid al-

Khudri, Anas, Ibn cAbbas, cAmmarah, Buraydah and in most of them there is extra, 'O Allah befriend whoever befriends him and be an enemy to whoever is his enemy.' (The Arabic equally translates as, 'O Allah befriend whomever he befriends and be an enemy to whomever he is an enemy.')

Abu't-Tufayl said: cAli gathered people together in the year 35 A.H. in the court (of the mosque) and said to them, 'I adjure you by Allah, of every Muslim man who heard the Messenger of Allah, may Allah bless him and grant him peace, saying on the day of Ghadir Khumm what he said when he arose.' Thirty men stood up and bore witness that the Messenger of Allah, may Allah bless him and grant him peace, said, 'He for whom I am his master, then Ali is his master. O Allah befriend whoever befriends him and be an enemy to whoever is his enemy.'

Buraydah said: The Messenger of Allah, may Allah bless him and grant him peace, said, 'Allah has told me to love four and informed me that He loves them.' It was said, 'Messenger of Allah, name them for us.' He said, 'cAli is of them,'—saying that three times—'And Abu Dharr, Miqdad and Salman.'

Habashi ibn Jinadah said: The Messenger of Allah, may Allah bless him and grant him peace, said, 'cAli is from me and I am from Ali.'

Ibn Umar said: The Messenger of Allah, may Allah bless him and grant him peace, made pacts of brotherhood between his companions, so cAli came with his eyes full of tears and said, 'Messenger of Allah, you made pacts of brotherhood between your companions and you did not make brotherhood between me and anyone.' The Messenger of Allah, may Allah bless him and grant him peace, said, 'You are my brother in the world and in the hereafter.'

cAli said: By the One Who split the grain and created the soul, the Unlettered Prophet promised me that no-one would love me except for a believer and that no-one would hate me except for a hypocrite.

Abu Sacid al-Khudri said: We used to recognise the hypocrites by their hatred of cAli.

Jabir ibn ᶜAbdullah and ᶜAli both said: The Messenger of Allah, may Allah bless him and grant him peace, said, 'I am the Madinah of knowledge and ᶜAli is its (the Madinah's) gate.' This is a good (*hasan*) *hadith* as is the correct position, not *sahih* as al-Hakim said, nor fabricated as Ibn al-Jawzi and an-Nawawi said.

ᶜAli said: The Messenger of Allah, may Allah bless him and grant him peace, sent me to the Yemen, so I said, 'Messenger of Allah, you have sent me, and I a youth, to judge between them (as a *Qadi*), and I don't know what the nature of judgement is.' He struck my chest with his hand and said, 'O Allah, guide his heart and make firm his tongue.' (ᶜAli said), 'By the One Who split the grain, I have not had any doubt about passing judgement (in a dispute) between two (people).'

ᶜAli said that someone said to him, 'Why is that you have the most *hadith* of the companions of the Messenger of Allah, may Allah bless him and grant him peace?' He said, 'I was such that when I asked him, he informed me, and when I was silent, he began (to teach) me.'

Abu Hurairah said: ᶜUmar ibn al-Khattab said, 'ᶜAli is the best of us in judicial decision.'

Ibn Masᶜud, may Allah be pleased with him, said: We used to say among ourselves that the best of the people of Madinah in judicial decision was ᶜAli.

Ibn ᶜAbbas said: When a trustworthy person relates to us a *fatwa* of ᶜAli, we do not go beyond it.

Saᶜid ibn al-Musayyab said: ᶜUmar ibn al-Khattab used to seek refuge with Allah from every difficult question or case for which there is no Abu Hasan (in which he was not present).

He (Saᶜid ibn al-Musayyab) also said: None of the Companions would say, 'Ask me (about anything you like)!' except for ᶜAli.

Ibn Masᶜud said: The most knowledgeable of the people of Madinah in the laws of inheritance and in judicial decisions is ᶜAli ibn Abi Talib.

ᶜA'ishah, may Allah be pleased with her, related that ᶜAli was mentioned in her presence and she said, 'As for him, he is the most knowledgeable, of those who remain, in the *Sunnah*.'

Masruq said: The knowledge of the Companions of the Messenger of Allah, may Allah bless him and grant him peace, culminated in °Umar, °Ali, Ibn Mas°ud and °Abdullah, may Allah be pleased with them.

°Abdullah ibn °Ayyash ibn Abi Rabi°ah said: °Ali had whatever you will of a cutting tooth in knowledge, he had excellence by reason of his family relations, priority in (accepting) Islam, his acquaintanceship with the Messenger of Allah, may Allah bless him and his family and grant them peace, discernment (*fiqh*) in the *Sunnah*, courage in war, and liberality with property.

Jabir ibn °Abdullah said: The Prophet, may Allah bless him and grant him peace, said, 'People are from all sorts of different stocks, and I and °Ali are from one stock.'

Ibn °Abbas said: Allah did not reveal an *ayah* beginning, '*O you who believe ...*' but that Ali is its *amir* and its eminence. Allah reproached the Companions of Muhammad in more than one place but He never mentioned °Ali but with approval.

Ibn °Abbas said: There has not been revealed about anyone in the Book of Allah what has been revealed about °Ali.

Ibn °Abbas said: Three hundred *ayat* were revealed about °Ali.

Sa°d said: The Prophet, may Allah bless him and grant him peace, said to °Ali, 'It is not permitted for anyone to be in a state of *junub* (requiring the complete washing of the body known as *ghusl*) in this mosque apart from me and you.'

Umm Salamah, may Allah be pleased with her, said: When the Messenger of Allah, may Allah bless him and his family and grant them peace, became angry, none dared to speak to him except for °Ali.

Ibn Mas°ud, may Allah be pleased with him, related that the Prophet, may Allah bless him and grant him peace, said, 'Looking at Ali is an act of worship.' It has also been narrated in *hadith* of °Imran ibn Husayn, Abu Bakr as-Siddiq, °Uthman ibn °Affan, Mu°adh ibn Jabal, Anas, Thawban, Jabir ibn °Abdullah and °A'ishah, may Allah be pleased with them.

Ibn °Abbas said: °Ali had eighteen excellences which no-one else of this *ummah* had.

Abu Hurairah said: ʿUmar ibn al-Khattab said, 'ʿAli was given three qualities any one of which I should prefer the gift of over high-bred camels.' He was asked, 'And what are they?' He said, 'He married him his daughter Fatimah; his dwelling at the mosque, wherein what is not permitted to me in it is permitted to him; and the standard on the day of Khaybar.' The like of it is narrated from Ibn ʿUmar.

ʿAli said: I have not been afflicted with swelling of the eye nor a headache since the Messenger of Allah, may Allah bless him and grant him peace, drew his hand over my face and spat lightly in my eyes on the day of Khaybar when he gave me the standard.

Saʿd ibn Abi Waqqas said: The Messenger of Allah, may Allah bless him and grant him peace, said, 'Whoever harms ʿAli, harms me.'

Umm Salamah narrated that the Messenger of Allah, may Allah bless him and grant him peace, said, 'Whoever loves ʿAli, loves me, and whoever loves me, loves Allah. Whoever hates ʿAli, hates me and whoever hates me, hates Allah.'

Umm Salamah heard the Prophet, may Allah bless him and grant him peace, saying, 'Whoever reviles ʿAli, reviles me.'

Ibn Abi Saʿid al-Khudri related that the Prophet, may Allah bless him and grant him peace, said to ʿAli, 'You will fight for the sake of the Qur'an, as I fought for the sake of its revelation.'

ʿAli said: The Messenger of Allah, may Allah bless him and his family and grant them peace, called me and said, 'ʿAli, there is in you a resemblance to ʿIsa; the Jews hated him so much that they slandered his mother, and the Christians loved him so much that they gave him a degree which wasn't his.' Now surely, two (sorts) will be destroyed because of me: a lover who goes beyond the limits, who praises me immoderately for what is not in me, and one who hates (me), whose hatred of me brings him to slander me.

Umm Salamah said: I heard the Prophet, may Allah bless him and grant him peace, saying, 'ʿAli is with the Qur'an and the Qur'an is with ʿAli, they will not separate until they come to me to drink from the Pool."

ᶜAmmar ibn Yasir related that the Prophet, may Allah bless him and grant him peace, said to ᶜAli, 'The most grievous of people are two men: the fair-complexioned one of Thamud who hamstrung the female camel, and the one who will strike you, ᶜAli, upon this—meaning his cranium above the forehead—until this becomes moistened from it (from the blood)—meaning his beard.' This has been narrated in *hadith* of ᶜAli, Suhayb, Jabir ibn Samurah and others.

Abu Saᶜid al-Khudri said: People complained about ᶜAli so that the Messenger of Allah, may Allah bless him and grant him peace, rose among us delivering an address and said, 'Do not complain about ᶜAli for, by Allah, he is somewhat rough for the sake of Allah, or in the way of Allah.'

The pledge of allegiance to ᶜAli for the *khilafah* and what came about from that

Ibn Saᶜd said: ᶜAli was pledged allegiance as *khalifah* the morning after the killing of ᶜUthman in Madinah. All of the Companions, may Allah be pleased with them, who were there pledged allegiance. It is said that Talhah and az-Zubayr pledged allegiance with displeasure and unwillingly. Then they went to Makkah and ᶜA'ishah, may Allah be pleased with her, was there. They took her and went with her to Basrah seeking retaliation for the blood of ᶜUthman. That reached ᶜAli so he went to Iraq and at Basrah met Talhah, az-Zubayr, ᶜA'ishah and whoever was with them, which is known as the Battle of the Camel, and which occurred in Jumada al-Akhirah of the year 36 A.H. Talhah, az-Zubayr and others were killed there, the dead reaching thirteen thousand. ᶜAli spent fifteen nights at Basrah and then he went to Kufah.

Then Muᶜawiyah ibn Abi Sufyan and those with him in Syria came out against him. That reached ᶜAli and he went out to meet him. They met at Siffin in Safr of the year 37 A.H. The fighting continued there for some days, until the people of Syria raised the *mushafs* calling to that which is in them, which was a trick of ᶜAmr ibn al-ᶜAs. People hated the war and they called each other to negotiate and appointed two arbiters. ᶜAli appointed Abu Musa al-Ashᶜari and Muᶜawiyah appointed ᶜAmr ibn al-ᶜAs. They signed a decree between them that they should meet at the beginning of the year at al-Adhruh where they would consider seriously the command of the *ummah*. People separated, Muᶜawiyah returning to Syria and ᶜAli to Kufah.

Then (a group known as) the *Khawarij* (the seceders—literally 'those who go out') from among his companions and those with him, went out against him. They said, 'There is no judgement but (that) of Allah', and they set up a military camp at Harura'. He sent Ibn ᶜAbbas to them, who argued with them and convinced them, so that many of them returned. A group of them stayed firm, went to an-Nahrawan and obstructed the roadway. ᶜAli went to them there and killed them at an-Nahrawan, killing Dhu'th-Thudayyah (literally, 'the possessor of the little breast', a man who had been foretold to be among the *Khawarij* by the Prophet, may Allah bless him and grant him peace). That was in the year 38 A.H.

People gathered in al-Adhruh in Shaᶜban of this year, among them Saᶜd ibn Abi Waqqas, Ibn ᶜUmar and other Companions. ᶜAmr allowed Abu Musa al-Ashᶜari to go first, as a trick he had devised. He (Abu Musa) spoke and removed ᶜAli from office. Then ᶜAmr spoke and confirmed Muᶜawiyah in office and pledged allegiance to him. People split up over this. ᶜAli disagreed with his companions to such an extent that he began to bite his fingers saying, 'I am disobeyed and Muᶜawiyah is obeyed?'

Three men of the *Khawarij* hastened to act: ᶜAbd ar-Rahman ibn Muljam al-Muradi, al-Burk ibn ᶜAbdullah at-Tamimi and ᶜAmr ibn Bukayr at-Tamimi. They gathered in Makkah and made a covenant with each other that they three would kill: ᶜAli ibn Abi Talib, Muᶜawiyah ibn Abi Sufyan and ᶜAmr ibn al-ᶜAs, and that they would give the slaves (of Allah) rest from them. Ibn Muljam said, 'I will take ᶜAli for you.' Al-Burk said, 'I will take Muᶜawiyah for you.' ᶜAmr ibn Bukayr said, 'I will suffice you for ᶜAmr ibn al-ᶜAs.' They made a covenant on that one night, either the eleventh or the seventeenth of Ramadan, and then each of them directed himself to the land in which his intended victim was. Ibn Muljam went to Kufah, met his companions of the *Khawarij* and told them secretly of what they intended to do.

On the night preceding the *Jumuʿah* of the seventeenth of Ramadan of the year 40 A.H., ʿAli woke up before dawn. He said to his son al-Hasan, 'This night I saw the Messenger of Allah, may Allah bless him and his family and grant them peace, and I said, "Messenger of Allah, what distress and argumentation I have received from your *ummah*!" He said to me, "Supplicate Allah against them." I said, "O Allah, give me in exchange for them what is better for me than they are, and give them in exchange for me what is worse for them than I am."'

Then the *mu'adhdhin* Ibn adh-Dhabbah came in to ʿAli and said, 'The prayer.' ʿAli went out the door crying out, 'People, the prayer, the prayer!' Ibn Muljam stood before him, struck him with the sword, and it hit the top of his forehead reaching the brain. People rushed upon him from every side, and he was held and bound. ʿAli lingered for the *Jumuʿah* and Saturday, and died the night before Sunday. Al-Hasan, al-Hussein and ʿAbdullah ibn Jaʿfar washed his body, al-Hasan led the prayer over him, then he was buried in the house of the Amirate in Kufah at night. Later they cut off the limbs of Ibn Muljam, he was put in a reed basket, and they burnt him in a fire.

All of the above are the words of Ibn Saʿd. He summarised excellently well all of these events and battles, and he didn't expand on them greatly as others did. This is more befitting to this occasion. He said, may Allah bless him and grant him peace, 'When my companions are mentioned, refrain yourselves (from speaking)', and he said, 'It is sufficient for my Companions (to mention) their killing.'

As-Suddi said: ʿAbd ar-Rahman ibn Muljam fell passionately in love with a woman of the *Khawarij* called Qatam, and he married her and gave her as a dowry three thousand *dirhams* and the killing of ʿAli. Al-Farazdaq said about that:

'I have not seen a dowry sent by a liberally generous one, like the dowry of Qatam, of human beings (slaves) and beasts:

Three thousand, a slave, a maidservant and the striking of ᶜAli with the penetrating sword.

There is no dowry more dear than ᶜAli even if it were very expensive, and no assassination but that it is less than the assassination by Ibn Muljam.'

Abu Bakr ibn ᶜAyyash said: The grave of ᶜAli was concealed so that the *Khawarij* would not dig up his body; and Sharik said: His son al-Hasan carried him to Madinah. Al-Mubarrad said from Muhammad ibn Habib: The first to be transferred from one grave to another was ᶜAli, may Allah be pleased with him.

Saᶜid ibn ᶜAbd al-ᶜAziz said: When ᶜAli ibn Abi Talib, may Allah be pleased with him, was killed, they carried him to bury him with the Prophet, may Allah bless him and grant him peace. While they were journeying with him at night, the camel on which he was bolted. No-one knew where it had gone, and they couldn't overtake it. For that reason the people of Iraq say, 'He is in the clouds.' Others say, 'The camel arrived in the lands of Tayy, where they took him and buried him.'

When ᶜAli was killed he was sixty-three years old. It has been said that he was sixty-four, sixty-five, fifty-seven and fifty-eight. He had nineteen women slaves.

Some fragments of accounts of ᶜAli, his judgements and his words

A Shaykh from Fazarah said: I heard ᶜAli saying, 'Praise belongs to Allah Who made our enemy ask us about something that had occurred to him in the matter of his *deen*. Muᶜawiyah wrote to me, asking me about the ambiguous hermaphrodite (i.e. does the hermaphrodite inherit property as a man or as a woman?). I wrote to him that he should make him inherit according to how he urinated.' Ash-Shaᶜbi also narrated the like of it from ᶜAli.

Al-Hasan said: When ^cAli came to Basrah, Ibn al-Kawwa' and Qais ibn ^cAbbad stood before him and said to him, 'Will you not inform us about this course which you are set upon, taking charge of the *ummah,* so that some of them are striking others; is it a covenant of the Messenger of Allah, may Allah bless him and grant him peace, which he made with you? Tell us, for you are the trusted one in whom we have confidence about that which you have heard.'

He said, 'As for there my having a covenant about that from the Prophet, may Allah bless him and grant him peace, then no. By Allah, if I was the first to affirm him, I will not be the first to attribute a lie to him. If I had had a covenant from the Prophet, may Allah bless him and grant him peace, about that, I would never have allowed the brother of Bani Taym ibn Murrah (Abu Bakr) and ^cUmar ibn al-Khattab to stand upon his *mimbar*, I would have fought them with my own hand, even if I could find nothing but this garment of mine. However, the Messenger of Allah was not killed, and he did not die suddenly, rather he lingered in his illness for days and nights, with the *mu'adhdhin* coming to him to announce the time of the prayer to him. He would order Abu Bakr, who would lead the people in prayer, while he knew my standing. One of his wives wanted to turn him away from Abu Bakr, and he refused and became angry. He said, "You are the female companions of Yusuf! Tell Abu Bakr to lead the people in prayer!" When Allah took His Prophet, may Allah bless him and grant him peace, we considered our affairs and we chose for our worldly affairs he whom the Prophet of Allah, may Allah bless him and grant him peace, was satisfied with for our *deen*. The prayer was the root of Islam and it is the *Amir* of the *deen*, and the support of the *deen*, so we pledged allegiance to Abu Bakr, for he was worthy of that, no two of us disagreed about him, none of us bore testimony against others, and nor did we deny his privilege. I discharged what was due to Abu Bakr, acknowledged the obedience that was his right, went on military expeditions with him in his troops. I would take when he gave me, go on military expeditions when he sent me on them, and I would lash for the *hadd* punishment with my whip for him.

When he died, ᶜUmar undertook it (the *khilafah*) and he took it according to the *sunnah* of his companion (Abu Bakr) and that which he knew of his affair. We pledged allegiance to ᶜUmar, no two of us disagreeing about him, nor any of us bearing testimony against any others, nor did we deny his privilege. I discharged what was due to ᶜUmar, acknowledged the obedience that was his right, and went on military expeditions with him in his armies. I would take when he gave me, go on military expeditions when he sent me on them, and I would lash for the *hadd* punishment with my whip for him.

When he died, I recalled within myself my close relationship (to the Prophet, may Allah bless him and grant him peace), my priority, my precedence and my merit, thinking that no-one would hold another equal to me. However, he (ᶜUmar) was afraid that, if the *khalifah* after him would do a wrong action, it would attach to him in his grave. He withdrew himself and his son from it, for if there had been any partiality in him he would have preferred his son for it (the *khilafah*). He quit himself of it passing it on to a group of six from Quraysh of whom I was one. When the group met, I thought that they would not consider anyone equal to me. ᶜAbd ar-Rahman ibn ᶜAuf took a compact from us that we would listen to and obey whomever Allah gave authority over us. Then later he took the hand of ᶜUthman ibn ᶜAffan and put his hand in his.

I considered my affair, and (saw that) my obedience had preceded my oath of allegiance, and my covenant had been taken for another. We therefore pledged allegiance to ᶜUthman. I discharged what was due to him, acknowledged the obedience that was his right, and went on military expeditions with him in his armies. I would take when he gave me, go on military expeditions when he sent me on them, and I would lash for the *hadd* punishment with my whip for him.

When he was struck down I considered my affair. The two *khalifahs,* who had taken hold of it through the covenant of the

Messenger of Allah, may Allah bless him and grant him peace, to the two of them respecting the prayer, had gone. This one, with whom the covenant had been taken, had been killed. The people of the two *harams* (Makkah and Madinah) pledged allegiance to me, and the people of these two provinces (Kufah and Basrah). One sprang into it who is not the like of me, his relationship not as my relationship, nor his knowledge like my knowledge, nor does he have priority like my priority, and I have more right to it than him.'

Jaʿfar ibn Muhammad related from his father that he said: Two men were brought before ʿAli in a dispute, and so he sat at the base of a wall. A man said to him, 'The wall will fall down!' ʿAli said, 'Carry on. Allah suffices as a guardian.' He passed judgement between them, stood up and then the wall fell down.

Jaʿfar ibn Muhammad related from his father that he said: A man said to ʿAli ibn Abi Talib, 'We hear you saying in the *khutbah*, "O Allah, set us right with that which You set right the *khalifahs* who followed the right course and were guided," so who are they?' His eyes filled with tears and he said, 'They are my two beloveds, Abu Bakr and ʿUmar, the two *Imams* of guidance, the two Shaykhs of Islam, the two Men of Quraysh, who are to be taken as exemplars after the Messenger of Allah, may Allah bless him and grant him peace. Whoever takes them as exemplars will be protected (from error), and whoever follows their footsteps will be guided on the straight path, and whoever clings to them is of the party of Allah.'

Hujr al-Madari said: ʿAli ibn Abi Talib said to me, 'What will you do when you are ordered to curse me?' I said, 'Will that happen?' He said, 'Yes.' I said, 'What should I do?' He said, 'Curse me, but do not forsake me.' He (Hujr) said: Muhammad ibn Yusuf, the brother of al-Hajjaj—and he was the *amir* of Yemen—ordered me to curse ʿAli, so I said, 'The *amir* has told me to curse ʿAli, so you curse him! may Allah curse him!' No-one understood it except for one man.

Zadan related that ʿAli was relating a *hadith* and a man accused him of lying. ʿAli said to him, 'Shall I supplicate against you if you are lying?' He said, 'Supplicate!' He supplicated against him and he did not leave before his eyesight went.

Zirr ibn Hubaysh said: Two men sat eating the morning meal, one of them having five small loaves and the other three small loaves. When they had placed the meal in front of them a man passed by them and greeted them. They said, 'Sit down and eat.' He sat down, ate with them and they ate equally of the eight loaves. The man stood, tossed down eight *dirhams* and said, 'Take them in place of what I have eaten from you two, and what I have consumed of your food.' The two of them quarrelled. The man who had the five loaves said, 'I have five *dirhams* and you have three.' The man who had the three loaves said, 'I will not be content unless the *dirhams* are divided in two halves between us.' They raised it before the Amir al-Muminin ᶜAli, and told him their story. He said to the man who had the three loaves, 'Your companion has offered you what he offered you. His bread was more than your bread, so be content with the three.' He said, 'By Allah, I will not be content with him except with the bitter truth.' ᶜAli said, 'There is nothing for you, in bitter truth, except for one *dirham* and he has seven *dirhams!*' The man said, 'Glory be to Allah!' He said, 'That's it!' He said, 'Show me the reason in the bitter truth so that I can accept it.' ᶜAli said, 'Do the eight loaves not have twenty-four third parts? You ate them and you were three persons, not knowing who ate more or less, so we will assume that you ate equally.' He continued, 'You ate eight thirds but you only had nine thirds. Your companion ate eight thirds and he had fifteen thirds, of which he ate eight leaving seven which the man who had the *dirhams* ate, and he ate one of your nine. You have one (*dirham*) for your one (loaf) and he has seven.' The man said, 'I am now content.'

ᶜAta' said: A man was brought to ᶜAli and two men bore witness against him that he had stolen. He took up (another) thing from people's affairs and threatened false witnesses, saying, 'If I am brought a false witness, I will do such and such with him.' Then he sought for the two witnesses but could not find them, so he let the man go.

ᶜAli related that a man was brought to him. Someone said, 'This man claims that he had a wet dream about my mother.' He said, 'Go and stand him in the sun and strike his shadow.'

Jaᶜfar ibn Muhammad related from his father that the seal-ring of ᶜAli was silver and that its engraving was, 'Blessed as the One Who Decrees is Allah.'

ᶜAmr ibn ᶜUthman ibn ᶜAffan said: The engraving on the seal-ring of ᶜAli was, 'Sovereignty belongs to Allah.'

Al-Mada'ini said: When ᶜAli entered Kufah, one of the wise men of the Arabs came to see him and said, 'By Allah, Amir al-Muminin, you have ornamented the *khilafah* and it has not ornamented you. You have raised it up and it has not raised you up. It was in more need of you than you were of it.'

Mujammiᶜ related that ᶜAli used to sweep out the *bait al-mal* and then perform a prayer, hoping that it would be evidence for him that he had not stored wealth within (keeping it) away from the Muslims.

Abu'l-Aswad ad-Du'ali said: I entered upon the Amir al-Muminin ᶜAli ibn Abi Talib, may Allah be pleased with him, and saw him with his eyes lowered, deep in thought. I said, 'What are you thinking about Amir al-Muminin?' He said, 'I have heard in this city of yours mistakes (in the use of Arabic), and I want to make a book on the principles of Arabic.' I said, 'If you do this, you will give life to us, and this language will remain among us.' Later, after three days I came to him, and he gave me a page in which was, 'In the name of Allah, the Merciful, the Compassionate. The word is noun, verb and particle. The noun is that which tells you about the named thing. The verb is that which tells you about the movement of the named thing. The particle is that which tells you of a meaning which is neither a noun nor a verb.' He said, 'Follow this up and add to it what occurs to you. Know, Abu'l-Aswad ad-Du'ali, that things are threefold: a substantive, a pronoun, and a thing which is neither a substantive nor a pronoun. The men of knowledge only have differing degrees of excellence in a recognition of what is neither substantive nor pronoun.' Abu'l-Aswad said: I compiled some things on it and I showed them to him. The particles of *nasb* (which put the noun governed by them in the accusative or the verb governed by them in the subjunctive) were in it. Of them I mentioned, *inna, anna, laita, la*c*alla*, and *ka'anna* but I did not mention *lakin*. He said to me, 'Why did you leave it out?' I said, 'I did not reckon it to be one of them.' He said, 'It is one of them so add it in among them.'

Rabi^cah ibn Najid said: ^cAli said, 'Be among people as the bee is among birds, for there is no bird that doesn't regard it (the bee) as insignificant. If the birds knew what blessing there is in its belly, they would not do that to it. Mix with people with your tongues and your persons, and be separate from them in your actions and your hearts; because a man has what he earns, and on the Day of Resurrection he will be with whomever he loves.'

^cAli said: Be more concerned for the acceptance of your action than you are for the action; for, an action with fearful obedience will not be little. How could an action which is accepted be little?

Yahya ibn Ju^cdah said: ^cAli ibn Abi Talib said, 'Carriers of the Qur'an (memorisers of it) act according to it, for the knowledgeable man (^calim) is only one who knows, then acts according to what he knows, and whose knowledge is in accord with his action. There will be people whose knowledge will not pass below their collar-bones (i.e. to their hearts), whose inner selves are at variance with their appearances, and whose actions are at variance with their knowledge. They will sit in circles competing for superiority with each other, to such an extent that a man will become angry at the man who sits beside him because he sits beside another and leaves him. Those, their actions in these assemblies of theirs will not rise up to Allah.'

^cAli said: *At-tawfiq* (being directed by Allah to the right course) is the best leader, good character is the best associate, the intellect is the best companion, courtesy the best inheritance, and there is no loneliness worse than conceit.

Al-Harith said: A man came to ^cAli and said, 'Tell me about the decree.' He said, 'It is a dark path; do not travel it.' He said, 'Tell me about the decree!' He said, 'A deep ocean; do not enter it.' He said, 'Tell me about the decree!' He said, 'The secret of Allah which is concealed from you; do not investigate it!' He said, 'Tell me about the decree!' He said, 'Questioner! Did Allah create you for what He wills or for what you will?' He said, 'Of course, for what He wills.' He said, 'Then He will make use of you for what He wills.'

ᶜAli said: Calamities have endings. Whoever suffers misfortune must go to the end of them. It is only right for an intelligent man, when some misfortune occurs to him, that he should submit to it until its time ends, because in trying to repulse it before the natural ending of its time there is increase in its unpleasantness.

It was said to ᶜAli, 'What is generosity?' He said, 'That which comes from the man as an initiative. As for that which comes in response to a request, it is only shame and feigning generosity.'

ᶜAli related that a man came to him, spoke well of him, praised him excessively, and something about him had already reached him (ᶜAli) before that. He said, 'I am not as you say. And I am better than what you believe within your self.'

ᶜAli said: The recompense of disobedience is weakness in worship, constriction in livelihood and shortcoming in pleasure.' Someone asked, 'What is a shortcoming in pleasure?' He said, 'When one obtains the fulfillment of a permitted appetite something intervenes which prevents one having the desire fulfilled.'

ᶜAli ibn Rabiᶜah related that a man said to ᶜAli, and he used to hate him, 'May Allah establish you!' ᶜAli said, 'Upon your heart.'

Ash-Shaᶜbi said: Abu Bakr used to speak poetry (i.e. compose it), ᶜUmar used to speak poetry, ᶜUthman used to speak poetry, but ᶜAli was more poetical than the three.

Nabit al-Ashjaᶜi said: ᶜAli ibn Abi Talib, may Allah be pleased with him, said,

> 'When hearts enclose despair and the wide breast is constricted with their worry,
> And calamities take up their abode and are at rest, and misfortunes take up residence in their places,

And no way is seen to remove the harm, and the cunning
one does not gain freedom by his trickery,
A helper comes to you, right upon your despair, whom the
Near, the Answerer brings,
And all misfortunes, when they reach their limit, near de-
liverance is joined with them.'

Ash-Sha°bi said: °Ali ibn Abi Talib said to a man whom he
disliked keeping the company of another man,

'Do not accompany an ignorant brother; beware of him!
How many an ignorant man has destroyed a forbearing
man when he took him as his brother.
A man is measured by another man if he walks along with
him.
One thing has measures and similarities for another thing.
The measure of a sandal is another sandal, when it is placed
beside it.
For the heart there is an indication of the heart when it
meets it.'

Al-Mubarrad said: Written on the sword of °Ali ibn Abi Talib,
may Allah be pleased with him, was,

'People have an eagerness for the world and (want) to
manage it, and its purity is mixed for you with impurity.
They are not provided it with intelligence after it had been
divided up, but rather they are provided it in measured
portions.
How many a courteous and intelligent man, it does not
help! A fool attains his world through (his) shortcoming.
If it had been from strength or conquest, then the hawks
would have flown off with the sparrows' provisions.'

Hamzah ibn Habib az-Zayyat said: °Ali ibn Abi Talib used to
say,

'Do not disclose your secret except to yourself, for every
sincere one has a sincere advisor.

I have seen deviating men who do not leave alone an unblemished skin (without trying to attack it).'

ᶜUqbah ibn Abi's-Sahba' said: When Ibn Muljam struck ᶜAli, al-Hasan went in to see him, weeping. ᶜAli said to him, 'My son, memorise from me four and four.' He said, 'What are they, father?' He said, 'Intelligence is the wealthiest of riches, the greatest poverty is folly, the loneliest solitude is conceit, and the noblest of noble qualities is good character.' He said, 'And the other four?' He said, 'Beware of keeping the company of a fool, for he wants to benefit you and he harms you; beware of befriending a liar, for he will make the remote seem near to you and the near seem remote; beware of befriending a mean person for he will sit inactively however much you are in need of him; and beware of befriending an immoral person, for he will sell you for a trifling sum.'

ᶜAli said that a Jew came to him and said to him, 'When did our Lord come into existence?' ᶜAli's face flushed with anger and he said, 'He was not, and then He was? He *is*, without existence. He *is*, without cause. He *is*, without anything before Him nor any end. All ends fall short of Him, for He is the end of every end.' Then the Jew accepted Islam.

The Qadi Shurayh said: When ᶜAli was setting out to Siffin, he found that he was missing a coat of armour of his. When the war was over and he returned to Kufah, he came across the armour in the hands of a Jew. He said to the Jew, 'The armour is mine; I have not sold it or given it away.' The Jew said, 'It is my armour and it is in my hand.' He said, 'Let us go to the Qadi.' ᶜAli went first, sat beside Shurayh, and said, 'If it was not because my opponent is a Jew, I would have sat beside him in the gathering, but I heard the Prophet, may Allah bless him and grant him peace, saying, "Humiliate them, since Allah has humiliated them."' Shurayh said, 'Speak, Amir al-Muminin.' He said, 'Yes. This armour, which this Jew has, is my armour; I did not sell it and I did not give it away.' Shurayh said, 'What do you say, Jew?' He said, 'It is my armour and it is in my possession.' Shurayh said, 'Do you have any evidence, Amir al-Muminin?' He said, 'Yes. Qanbar and al-Hasan will witness that the armour is mine.' Shurayh said, 'A son's witness is not acceptable on behalf of his father.' ᶜAli said, 'A man from the Garden, and his testimony is not acceptable? I heard the Prophet, may Allah bless him and grant him peace, saying, "Al-Hasan and al-Hussein are the two lords of the youth of the people of the Garden."' The Jew said, 'The Amir al-Muminin brought me before his Qadi, and his Qadi gave judgement against him. I witness that this is the truth, and I witness that there is no god but Allah and I witness that Muhammad is the messenger of Allah, and that the armour is your armour.'

His commentary on the Qur'an

As for his words in commentary on the Qur'an, there are many.

ᶜAli said, 'By Allah, an *ayah* has not been revealed without me knowing about what it was revealed, where it was revealed, and about whom it was revealed. My Lord has given me a very intelligent heart and a true and articulate tongue.'

Abu't-Tufayl said: ᶜAli said, 'Ask me about the Book of Allah, because there is no *ayah* but that I know whether it was revealed at night or in daytime, on the plain or in the mountain.'

Muhammad ibn Sirin said: When the Prophet, may Allah bless him and grant him peace, died, ᶜAli was slow to pledge allegiance to Abu Bakr. Abu Bakr met him and said, 'Do you dislike my (having the) authority?' He said, 'No, but I have sworn not to don my mantle, except for the prayer, until I have collected together the Qur'an.' They claimed that he wrote it in the order of its revelation. Muhammad (ibn Sirin) thus said, 'If that book were come across, there would be knowledge in it.'

Some fragments of his astonishingly concise words

ᶜAli, may Allah be pleased with him, said, 'Precaution is bad opinion.'

He said, 'The close one (i.e. the near relative) is the one whom affection renders close even if his kinship makes him distant. The distant one is the one whom enmity makes far even though his kinship makes him a near relative. There is nothing nearer to the body than the hand, and yet the hand, if it is corrupt, is cut off and if it is cut off, then it is cauterised.'

He said, 'Take five things from me: Let none of you fear anything but his wrong action; let him hope for nothing but his Lord; let one who does not know, not be shy of learning; and let one who does not know, not be shy of saying, "Allah knows best"; and patience has the same relation to *iman* as does the head to the body: when patience goes then faith goes, for when the head goes, then the body goes.'

He said: The real *faqih* is the one who does not make people despair of the mercy of Allah; who does not grant them licence to disobey Allah; who does not make them feel secure from the punishment of Allah; who does not abandon the Qur'an longing for something other than it; because there is no good in worship in which there is no knowledge, there is no knowledge unless there is understanding along with it, and there is no recitation if there is no reflection in it.

He said: The coolest thing for my liver, when I am asked about what I don't know, is to say, 'Allah knows best.'

He said: Whoever wants to give people what is due from him, let him love for them what he loves for himself.

He said: Seven things are from the *shaytan*: strong anger, strong sneezing, strong yawning, vomiting, nose-bleeds, secret discourse, and falling asleep during *dhikr* (remembrance of Allah).

He said: Eat the pomegranate with its pulp for it is *the* stomachic (literally: the tan of the stomach).

He said: A time will come to people in which the believer will be more humiliated than a female slave.

Abu'l-Aswad ad-Du'ali said, eulogising cAli,

'Eye, woe to you! Come to our aid; do you not weep for the Amir al-Muminin?
Umm Kulthum (the daughter of cAli and Fatimah, and the wife of cUmar) weeps over him with her tears, and she has seen death.

Say to the *Khawarij* wherever they are—and may the eyes of the envious not find rest—

"Is it in the month of fasting that you have distressed us, through the best of men altogether?

You have killed the best of those who mounted steeds and tamed them, and of those who mounted ships,

Of those who wore sandals and cut them to measure, and who recited the *Mathani* (the Fatihah) and the Clear (Book).

All the qualities of good were in him, and the love of the Messenger of the Lord of the Worlds."

Quraysh knew, wherever they were, that you (ʿAli) were the best of them in standing and in *deen*.

When I looked towards the face of Abu Hussein I saw the full moon over the onlookers.

Before his killing we were in good; we would see the nephew of the Messenger of Allah among us.

He was establishing the truth without doubting concerning it, and he was just to enemies and close relatives.

He would not conceal any knowledge that he had, and he did not have the character of the haughty ones.

It is as if when people lost ʿAli, they were ostriches bewildered in a land for years.

Do not rejoice at our affliction Muʿawiyah ibn Sakhr, for the rest of the *khulafa'* are from us.

Those notable people who died during his time

The following notable people died during the days of ʿAli, either natural deaths or by being killed: Hudhayfah ibn al-Yaman, az-Zubayr ibn al-ʿAwwam, Talhah, Zaid ibn Suhan, Salman al-Farisi, Hind ibn Abi Halah, Uwais al-Qarni, Khabbab ibn al-Aratt, ʿAmmar ibn al-Yasir, Sahl ibn Hanif, Suhayb ar-Rumi, Muhammad ibn Abi Bakr as-Siddiq, Tamim ad-Dari, Khawwat ibn Jubayr, Shurahbil ibn as-Samt, Abu Maysurah al-Badri, Safwan ibn ʿAssal, ʿAmr ibn ʿAnbasah, Hisham ibn Hakim, Abu Rafiʿ the freed-slave of the Prophet, may Allah bless him and grant him peace, and others.

Al-Hasan ibn ᶜAli
may Allah be pleased with him

Al-Hasan ibn ᶜAli ibn Abi Talib, may Allah be pleased with him, Abu Muhammad, the grandson of the Messenger of Allah, may Allah bless him and grant him peace, his descendant and the last of the *khulafa'* by his (the Prophet's, may Allah bless him and grant him peace) explicit words.

ᶜImran ibn Sulayman said: Al-Hasan and al-Hussein are two of the names of the people of the Garden. The Arabs did not use these names in the *Jahiliyyah*.

Al-Hasan, may Allah be pleased with him, was born in the middle of Ramadan in the third year of the *Hijrah*. *Hadith* have been related from him from the Prophet, may Allah bless him and grant him peace. ᶜA'ishah, may Allah be pleased with her, related *hadith* from him, and a great number of the Followers, of them his son al-Hasan, Abu'l-Haura' Rabiᶜah ibn Sinan, Ash-Shaᶜbi, Abu Wa'il and Ibn Sirin.

He resembled the Prophet, may Allah bless him and grant him peace. The Prophet, may Allah bless him and grant him peace, named him al-Hasan, slaughtered a sheep for him on his seventh day, shaved off his hair and ordered that the weight of the hair in silver should be given away as *sadaqah*. He was the fifth of the family of the mantle (when the Prophet, may Allah bless him and grant him peace, said, 'O Allah, these are my family.').

Abu Muhammad al-ᶜAskari said: This name was not known in the *Jahiliyyah*.

Al-Mufaddal said: Allah veiled the names of al-Hasan and al-Hussein until the Prophet, may Allah bless him and grant him peace, used them to name his two grandsons.

197

Anas said: No-one more resembled the Prophet, may Allah bless him and grant him peace, than al-Hasan ibn ʿAli.

Al-Bara' said: I saw the Prophet, may Allah bless him and grant him peace, with al-Hasan upon his shoulder, saying, 'O Allah, I love him, so love him.'

Abu Bakrah said: I heard the Prophet, may Allah bless him and grant him peace, upon the *mimbar*, with al-Hasan by his side looking at the people one time and looking at him one time, saying, 'This son of mine is a lord, and it is likely that through him Allah will make peace between two parties of the Muslims.'

Ibn ʿUmar said: The Prophet, may Allah bless him and grant him peace, said, 'They are my two descendants (literally 'my two sprigs of basil') in the world,' meaning al-Hasan and al-Hussein.

Abu Saʿid al-Khudri said: The Messenger of Allah, may Allah bless him and grant him peace, said, 'Al-Hasan and al-Hussein are the two lords of the youths of the people of the Garden.'

Usamah ibn Zaid said: I saw the Prophet, may Allah bless him and grant him peace, and al-Hasan and al-Hussein were upon his hips (one on each), and he said, 'These are my two sons and the two sons of my daughter. O Allah, I love them, so love them and love whoever loves them.'

Anas said: The Prophet, may Allah bless him and grant him peace, was asked, 'Who of the people of your house are most beloved to you?' He said, 'Al-Hasan and al-Hussein.'

Ibn ʿAbbas said: The Prophet, may Allah bless him and grant him peace, approached carrying al-Hasan on his shoulder. A man met him and said, 'What a blessed mount you have, boy!' The Prophet, may Allah bless him and grant him peace, replied, 'And what a blessed rider is he.'

ʿAbdullah ibn az-Zubayr said: The one most like the Prophet, may Allah bless him and grant him peace, of his family and the most beloved to him is al-Hasan ibn ʿAli. I saw him come while he was prostrate and mount his shoulders—or he said, 'his back'— and he did not make him get down until he himself got down. I saw him while he was bowing in prayer and he would separate his legs for him so that he could pass through the other side.'

198

Abu Salamah ibn ᶜAbd ar'-Rahman said: The Prophet, may Allah bless him and grant him peace, used to put forth his tongue for al-Hasan ibn ᶜAli, then when the infant saw the redness of the tongue, he would be merry with him.

Zuhayr ibn al-Arqam said: Al-Hasan ibn ᶜAli stood to deliver the *khutbah,* and a man from Azd Shanu'ah stood up and said, 'I witness that I saw the Prophet, may Allah bless him and grant him peace, place him in his lap (*hubwah* which denotes sitting on the haunches with the legs drawn in to the belly and often with a cloth wrapped around the legs and the back in support), saying, "Whoever loves me, let him love him, and let the one who is present convey it to whoever is absent," and if it were not for high regard for the Messenger of Allah, may Allah bless him and grant him peace, I would not have related it to anyone.'

Al-Hasan, may Allah be pleased with him, had many virtues: he was lordly, forbearing, possessing tranquillity, gravity and modesty; he was liberally generous, much praised; he disliked seditions and the sword; he married a great deal; and he would bestow upon a single man as much as one hundred thousand.

ᶜAbdullah ibn ᶜUbayd ibn ᶜUmayr said: Al-Hasan performed the *Hajj* twenty-five times walking, and the high-bred, riding beasts were led along with him.

ᶜUmayr ibn Ishaq said: No-one ever spoke in my presence who it was more preferable, when he talked, that he should not be silent than al-Hasan ibn ᶜAli. I never heard from him an improper word except for one time. There was a dispute between al-Hasan and ᶜAmr ibn ᶜUthman about some land. Al-Hasan proposed something which ᶜAmr did not like. Al-Hasan said, 'There is nothing for it with us but to act in spite of him (literally 'that his nose cleave to the dust').' This was the most improper word I ever heard from him.

ᶜUmayr ibn Ishaq said: Marwan was the amir over us, and he used to abuse ᶜAli every *Jumuᶜah* from the *mimbar*, while al-Hasan would listen and make no reply. Then he sent a man to him saying, 'I swear by ᶜAli, by ᶜAli, by ᶜAli, and by you, by you! I don't find any likeness for you except the mule, to which it is

said, "Who is your father?" and it replies, "My mother is a ma
Al-Hasan said to him, 'Return to him and say to him, "By Alla
will not efface for you anything of what you have said by al
ing you. However, you and I have an appointment together
fore Allah. Then, if you are truthful, may Allah recompense
for your truthfulness. If you are a liar, then Allah is worse
revenge."'

Ruzayq ibn Sawwar said: There were some words betweer
Hasan and Marwan, then Marwan approached him, became \
tough on him—and al-Hasan was silent. Marwan blew his r
using his right hand. Al-Hasan said to him, 'Woe to you! Do
not know that the right hand is for the face, and the left for
private parts (and for unclean matters generally)? I am disgu:
with you (literally 'filth to you')!' Marwan became silent.

Ash°ath ibn Sawwar related that a man said: A man sat do
with al-Hasan and he (al-Hasan) said, 'You have sat down v
us at the moment we were going to stand. Will you permit?'

°Ali ibn Zaid ibn Juda°an said: Al-Hasan gave forth his prop
twice for the sake of Allah, and Allah divided up his prop
and shared it with him three times, to such an extent that
used to give a sandal and keep a sandal with him, or giv
leather sock (known as *khuff*) and keep another sock.

°Ali ibn al-Hussein said: Al-Hasan was given to divorcing wom
and he did not separate from a woman but that she loved h
He married ninety women.

Ja°far ibn Muhammad related from his father that he said:
Hasan used to marry and divorce so much that I was afraid
would cause enmity towards us among the tribes.

Ja°far ibn Muhammad related from his father that he said:
said, 'People of Kufah, do not marry (your women-folk) to
Hasan because he is a man much given to divorce.' A man fr
Hamadan said, 'By Allah, we will marry him (to our wom
folk). Whosoever pleases him he can keep, and whosoever (
pleases him he can divorce.'

°Abdullah ibn Hasan said: Hasan was a man who used to ma
women a great deal, and they very rarely found favour with h

There were very few women he married who did not love him and were not passionately attached to him.

Juwayriyyah ibn Asma' said: When al-Hasan died, Marwan wept at his funeral prayer. Al-Hussein said to him, 'Do you weep when you forced him to swallow that which you did?' He said, 'I used to do that to one more forbearing than this,' and he pointed towards the mountain. (The mountain was proverbially the epitome of forbearance).

Al-Mubarrad said: Someone said to al-Hasan ibn ᶜAli, 'Abu Dharr says, "Poverty is more beloved to me than wealth, and illness more beloved to me than health."' He said, 'May Allah show mercy to Abu Dharr. As for me, I say, "Whoever is absolutely dependent on the goodness of Allah's choosing for him does not wish to be in any other state than the one which Allah has chosen for him."' This is the limit in research into the subject of contentment with that which destiny turns about.

Al-Hasan, may Allah be pleased with him, took charge of the *khilafah* after the death of his father through the pledge of allegiance of the people of Kufah, and he remained in it for six months and some days. Then Muᶜawiyah came out against him—and the matter belongs to Allah—and so al-Hasan sent a message to him to offer to surrender the *khilafah* to him, on the conditions: that the *khilafah* should be his after him, that no-one of the people of Madinah, al-Hijaz and Iraq should be sought out for revenge or retaliation for anything which had happened in the time of his father, and that he would pay off his debts for him. Muᶜawiyah agreed to what he asked, they concluded a treaty upon that basis, and the prophetic miracle became evident in his words, may Allah bless him and grant him peace, 'Allah will make peace through him between two groups of the Muslims.' He abdicated from the *khilafah* for him. Al-Balqini sought to prove from his abdication from the *khilafah*—which is the greatest rank—that it is permitted to abdicate from and renounce offices and positions. His abdication from it was in the year 41 A.H., in the month of Rabiᶜ al-Awwal. It has also been said that it was in Rabiᶜ al-Akhir, or Jumada al-Uwla. His companions said to him, 'O disgrace of the *muminin*!' and he would say, 'Disgrace is better than the Fire.'

A man said to him, 'Peace be upon you, humiliator of the believers!' He said, 'I am not the humiliator of the believers, but I disliked to kill you for the sovereignty.'

Then al-Hasan moved from Kufah to Madinah and resided there.

Jubayr ibn Nufayr said: I said to al-Hasan, 'People are saying that you want the *khilafah*.' He said, 'The chiefs of the Arabs were with me, at war with whomever I was at war with, and at peace with whomever I was at peace with. I abandoned that desiring the Face of Allah, and to prevent spilling the blood of the *ummah* of Muhammad, may Allah bless him and grant him peace. Now later, shall I take it by force with the help of the herds of goats of the people of al-Hijaz?'

Al-Hasan, may Allah be pleased with him, died in Madinah through poisoning. His wife, Ja°dah bint al-Ash°ath ibn Qais poisoned him. Yazid ibn Mu°awiyah suggested secretly to her that she should poison him and that then he would marry her, and she did so. When al-Hasan died, she sent a message to Yazid asking him for the fulfillment of what he had promised her. He said, 'We were not pleased with you for al-Hasan, so should we then be pleased with you for ourselves?'

His death was in 49 A.H. It has also been said that it was on the fifth of Rabi° al-Awwal in the year 50 A.H. And it has been said that it was in 51 A.H. His brother argued with him to get him to tell him who had given him the (poisoned) drink, but he would not tell him. He said, 'Allah is most severe in revenge if it should be the one I suspect. If not, then no innocent person must be killed in retaliation for me.'

°Imran ibn °Abdullah ibn Talhah said: Al-Hasan saw as if there were written between his eyes, *'Say, "He Allah is One,"'* (Qur'an 112: 1) and his family rejoiced at that. They told it to Sa°id ibn al-Musayyab and he said, 'If his dream is true, then he has very few days left to live.' He only lived a few days more before he died.

Abu'l-Mundhir Hisham ibn Muhammad related from his father that he said: Al-Hasan ibn °Ali was constricted (in his provision), and his stipend was one hundred thousand a year. Muʿawiyah withheld it from him one year, and he was extremely constricted. He said, 'I called for an ink-pot so that I might write to Muʿawiyah to remind him about myself, and then I controlled (myself). I saw the Messenger of Allah, may Allah bless him and grant him peace, (in a dream) and he said, "How are you, Hasan?" I said, "Well, father." And I complained to him about the withholding of the property from me. He said, "Did you call for an ink-pot to write to a created being like yourself to remind him of that?" I said, "Yes, Messenger of Allah. What should I do?" He said, "Say: O Allah, cast into my heart hope in You, and cut off my hope in everything other than You, until I don't hope for anyone other than You. O Allah, that which my strength is too weak for, and my action falls short of, my desire does not attain, my supplication does not reach, and what does not flow upon my tongue, of that certainty which You have given anyone of the ancients and the later peoples, then single me out for it, Lord of the Worlds."' He said, 'Then, by Allah, I had not persisted in it for a week before Muʿawiyah sent me one million and five hundred, and I said, "Praise be to Allah Who does not forget whoever remembers Him and doesn't disappoint whoever supplicates Him." I saw the Prophet, may Allah bless him and his family and grant them peace, in sleep and he said, "Hasan, how are you?" I said, "Well, Messenger of Allah," and I told him my story. He said, "My son, that is how it is for whoever hopes for (something) from the Creator and does not hope for (something) from the created."'

Sulaym ibn ʿIsa, the Qur'an reciter of the people of Kufah, said: When death came to al-Hasan he was overcome with agitation and grief. Al-Hussein said to him, 'My brother, what is this agitation and grief? You are going to the Messenger of Allah, may Allah bless him and his family and grant them peace, and ʿAli and they are your two fathers, and to Khadijah and Fatimah and they are your two mothers, and to al-Qasim and at-Tahir and they are your two maternal uncles, and to Hamzah and Jaʿfar and they are your two paternal uncles.' Al-Hasan said to him, 'Brother, I am entering into a matter of Allah's, exalted is

He, the like of which I have never entered, and I see a creation of Allah's the like of which I have never seen.'

Ibn ᶜAbd al-Barr said: From various sources we relate that when his time came, he said to his brother, 'My brother, your father raised his eyes to this authority and Allah averted him from it and put Abu Bakr in charge of it (the *khilafah*). Later, he raised his eyes to it, but it was turned away from him to ᶜUmar. Later again, he had no doubt at the time of the Council that it would not pass him by, but it was turned away from him to ᶜUthman. When ᶜUthman was killed, then ᶜAli was pledged allegiance. Then we were restrained until swords were unsheathed and so it (the *khilafah*) was never undisturbedly his. By Allah, I don't think that Allah will combine prophecy and *khilafah* in us. I don't know but that the fools of Kufah will try to appoint you as *khalifah* and drive you out. I have asked ᶜA'ishah, may Allah be pleased with her, that I should be buried with the Messenger of Allah, may Allah bless him and his family and grant them peace, and she said, "Yes." When I die, ask her about that, but I only anticipate that people will try to prevent you. If they do, don't bandy words with them.' When he died, al-Hussein came to the Mother of the Believers, ᶜA'ishah, may Allah be pleased with her, and she said, 'Yes, and it is an honour,' but Marwan prevented them. Then al-Hussein and those with him donned their swords, until Abu Hurairah prevented them, and so he was buried in al-Baqiᶜ by the side of his mother, may Allah be pleased with her.

Glossary of Arabic Terms

adhan – the call to prayer. *mu'adhdhin* – the one who calls to prayer.

Akhirah – what comes later, the next life.

^calim pl. *^culama'* – a man of knowledge. 'The *^calim* is only one who knows, then acts according to what he knows, and whose knowledge is in accord with his action,' Sayyiduna ^cAli.

amir – commander. *Amir al-Muminin* – the Commander of the Believers, a title of respect given to the *khalifah*. *Imarah* – amirate.

Ansar – lit. Helpers, the people of Madinah who welcomed and aided the Messenger of Allah, may Allah bless him and grant him peace. See also *Muhajirun*.

^caqiqah – at the birth of a child when the head is shaved and the hair's weight in silver given away as *sadaqah* and a sheep sacrificed and the meat shared with others and given away.

^cArafah – the plain where the pilgrims stand during the pivotal day of the *Hajj* in prayer and supplication.

ayah pl. *ayat* – a sign, miracle and a verse of the Qur'an.

al-Bait al-Maqdis – Lit. The Purified Dwelling, i.e. the mosque of Jerusalem or all of Jerusalem.

bait al-mal – Lit. House of Property, where the collected *zakah* of the Muslims and other revenues were stored while awaiting distribution.

al-Baqi^c – the graveyard of Madinah where many of the Companions, may Allah be pleased with them, are buried.

Dajjal – Lit. Liar, the false Messiah whose appearance marks the imminent end of the world.

deen – the life-transaction, lit. the debt of exchange between two parties, in this usage between the Creator and the created.

dhikr – lit. remembrance, mention. In a general sense all acts of worship are *dhikr*. In common usage it has come to mean invocation of Allah by repetition of His names or particular formulae.

dhimmah – obligation or contract, in particular a treaty of protection for non-Muslims living in Muslim territory.

dinar – a gold coin of approximate value £50 (1995).

dirham – a silver coin of approximate value £1.50 (1995).

Dunya – what is lower and closer to hand, the 'world'.

ᶜEid – the celebration at the end of Ramadan and also at the end of the Hajj, marked by a general public prayer, *dhikr* and mutual visiting and hospitality.

faqeeh pl. *fuqaha'* – a man learned in knowledge of *fiqh* (see below) who by virtue of his knowledge can give a legal judgement.

fatwa – an authoritative legal opinion or judgement made by a *faqeeh*.

fiqh – science of the application of the *shariᶜah*.

fitnah – a trial or affliction whereby one is tried or proved, a temptation, civil war and strife, faction and slaughter. Originally derived from a root meaning of burning, with the sense of the burning of a metal such as gold to remove the dross.

ghusl – a washing of the entire body in order to enter Islam, after sexual intercourse or ejaculation, or preparatory for the weekly *jumuᶜah* and *ᶜEid* prayers.

hadd pl. *hudud* – lit. the limits, Allah's boundary limits for the *halal* and the *haram*. The *hadd* punishments are the specific fixed penalties laid down by *shariᶜah* for specified crimes.

hadith pl. *ahadith* – reported speech, particularly of the Prophet Muhammad, may Allah bless him and grant him peace.

Hajj – the yearly pilgrimage to Makkah

halal – permitted by the *shariᶜah*

haram – forbidden by the *shariᶜah*; also an inviolable place or object.

hasan – lit. good, beautiful, a category of *hadith*, which is reliable, but whose *isnad* is not perfect.

hawd – the 'pond' of the Prophet Muhammad, may Allah bless him and grant him peace, on the Last Day, which is replenished by rivers from the Garden and from which he will give the believers to drink. Whoever drinks from it will not thirst again.

hijab – veil, the covering by adult women of their hair, and all of their bodies excepting the face and hands. It may also refer to the covering of the face.

Hijaz – the western area of Arabia which includes Makkah and Madinah.

Hijr – the semi-circular unroofed enclosure at one side of the Ka'bah, whose wall outlines the shape of the original building built by the Prophets Ibrahim and Isma'il, peace be upon them.

hijrah – emigration in the way of Allah. Islam takes its dating (indicated by A.H. 'After *Hijrah*') from the Hijrah of the Prophet, may Allah bless him and grant him peace, from Makkah to Madinah.

ihram – state entered to perform Hajj or 'Umrah, which includes, for males, wearing two pieces of cloth also known as *ihram*.

imam – the one who leads, often a term for the *amir* or *khalifah*. 'Leaders and nobles who order them (the people) and they obey them.' (Sayyiduna Abu Bakr). It is now more often restricted to one who leads people in prayer.

imamah – imamate, the office of *imam*.

iman – belief in the heart and affirmation on the tongue.

insha'Allah – if Allah wills.

iqamah – the act of establishing the prayer, and also the call made immediately prior to prayer in order to summon the people in the mosque.

isnad – chain of transmission of a *hadith*.

Isra' – the Night Journey of the Prophet, may Allah bless him and grant him peace, from Makkah to Jerusalem from whence he went on the *Mi'raj* (the ascension through the heavens).

'itizal – lit. withdrawal or secession, the theology of that group which withdrew from the circle of Hasan al-Basri, who became know as *Mu'tazilah*.

Jahiliyyah – the Time of Ignorance, before the coming of Islam *jama'ah* – the group, particularly referring to the group of people performing the prayer together.

jihad – struggle, particularly warfare to defend and establish Islam.

jinn – unseen beings created of smokeless fire who co-habit the earth together with mankind.

jizyah – a tax levied on people of previous revelations who make a contract to live under Muslim rule (see *dhimmah*). The tax was four *dinars* per adult male per year. It is interesting to note that this sum in present terms (1995) is approximately £200.

Jumada al-Ula – a month of the Muslim lunar calendar.

Jumada al-Akhirah – a month of the Muslim lunar calendar.

jumu'ah – Friday, and particularly the prayer performed on that day which it is necessary for all adult males to attend if they are able.

junub – condition, of impurity after sexual intercourse or ejaculation, requiring the complete washing of the body known as *ghusl*.

kafara – he covered over the truth, he showed ingratitude, he disbelieved, thus *kufr* disbelief, *kafir* disbeliever pl. *kafirun/kuffar.*

kalam – lit. speech, theology or the science of investigating religious belief.

khalifah pl. *khulafa'* – lit. successor, both the rank of Adamic man, one who stands in for Allah in His creation, and a Caliph or successor of the Prophet, may Allah bless him and grant him peace.

khilafah – the office of the *khalifah.*

Khawarij – a sect who believed that committing major wrong actions turns a Muslim into an unbeliever.

al-Khulafa' ar-Rashideen – (see *khalifah* above) the *khulafa'* who took the right way.

khutbah – public address, particulary in the mosque on Friday or one of the *'Eid* prayers.

kunya – a respectful and affectionate way of calling as the 'father of so-and-so', the 'mother of so-and-so' or the 'son or daughter of so-and-so'.

*ma*ᶜ*rifah* – lit. recognition, gnosis rather than scholastic knowledge.

Maghrib – the West, specifically north-west Africa.

al-Masjid al-Haram – the Inviolable Mosque of Makkah.

*marfu*ᶜ – a tradition from a Companion containing words thought to be those of the Prophet, may Allah bless him and grant him peace, but whose *isnad* does not trace back to him.

mawla – a master. Also, both the freed slave and his former master.

mimbar – steps on which the Imam stands to deliver the *khutbah* on the day of *Jumu*ᶜ*ah*.

Muhajirun – Companions of the Messenger of Allah, may Allah bless him and grant him peace, who accepted Islam outside Madinah and emigrated to Madinah, particularly those who came with him from Makkah.

Muharram – the first month of the Muslim lunar year.

mumin, pl. *muminun* and *muminin* – a believer (see *iman* above).

al-Murji'ah – a sect which was characterised by an indulgent attitude towards wrong action in the sense that they felt that 'believers' would not be diminished in their *iman* by the wrong actions they did.

mursal – a *hadith* attributed directly to the Prophet, may Allah bless him and grant him peace, by one of the Followers when it is not known from which Companion he got it.

mushaf – a written copy of the Qur'an.

musnad – a book of *ahadith* containing *ahadith* arranged according to their *isnad*, e.g. the author mentions the *Musnad as-Siddiq* which contains *ahadith* narrated by Abu Bakr, may Allah be pleased with him.

*al-mut*ᶜ*ah* – a temporary form of marriage common among pre-Islamic Arabs which was prohibited by the Prophet, may Allah bless him and grant him peace.

mutawatir – the strongest *isnad* possible for a *hadith*. This is when a number of Companions have narrated the text of the *hadith* to large numbers of knowledgeable Followers who each in turn transmitted it to numbers of later students, etc., so that there is no possible doubt about the *hadith*.

al-Qadariyah – sect of early Muslims who believed more in man's free-will than in predestination.

qadi – a judge.

ar-Rafidah – a group of the *Shiʿah* known for rejecting Abu Bakr and ʿUmar as well as ʿUthman (as opposed to the Zaidiyyah).

rakʿah pl. *rakaʿat* – a complete unit of *salah* consisting of standing, bowing and two prostrations.

ar-Riddah – the reneging or apostasy of the desert Arabs after the death of the Prophet, may Allah bless him and grant him peace.

Ruh al-Quds – the Spirit of Purity, the angel Jibril.

sabeel – a way, often *jihad,* 'the way of Allah'.

as-Sabiqun al-Awwalun – the First Foremost ones, i.e. those *Muhajirun* and *Ansar* who accepted Islam before the conquest of Makkah and strove with their lives and their wealth in *jihad.*

sadaqah pl. *sadaqat* – giving in the way of Allah, sometimes used synonymously with *zakah.*

sahih – authentic or sound. A technical term of the science of *hadith* which indicates the strength of the *isnad.*

as-sakinah – lit. tranquility. The presence of Allah sometimes made clear by a sign, also the feeling of peace of mind and security.

salah - the prayer of standing reciting Qur'an, bowing, prostrating and sitting.

salat at-tarawih – the prayers performed after the *ʿIsha'* (night) prayer during Ramadan.

as-Saqifah – roofed building, particularly the roofed gallery of Bani Saʿidah in which the *Ansar* and some of the *Muhajirun* met after the death of the Prophet, may Allah bless him and grant him peace, to choose a *khalifah.*

shahadah – witnessing, i.e. the first pillar of Islam.

shariʿah – lit. a road. It is the legal modality of a people based on the revelation of their Prophet. The last *shariʿah* in history is that of Islam, which abrogates all previous *shariʿahs.*

Shawwal – the month of the Islamic lunar calendar immediately following Ramadan.

Shaykh – lit. an old man. Title of respect used for a man of great knowledge or a leader among his people

shaytan – a devil, particularly Iblis (Satan).

Shi'ah – the sect which differed from the Muslims over their allegation of the prior right to the *khilafah* of ʿAli, may Allah be pleased with him, over the other *khulafa'*.

shirk – the unforgiveable wrong action of associating something in partnership with Allah and worshipping it or them along with Him.

sidq – truthfulness and thus *sadiq* – a truthful one and *siddiq* – one eminently truthful and affirmative of the truth.

siwak and *miswak* – toothstick cut from the ʿaraq tree. It is a *sunnah* to use it.

Sultan – the ruler.

Sunnah pl. *sunan* – lit. a form, the customary practice of a person or group of people. It has come to refer almost exclusively to the practice of the Messenger of Allah, Muhammad, may Allah bless him and grant him peace, but also comprises the customary practice of *al-Khulafa ar-Rashidun* and of the first generation of Muslims in Madinah. *Sunan* is also a title often used in certain collections of *hadith*.

surah – a large unit of Qur'an linked by thematic content, composed of *ayat*. There are 114 *surahs* in the Qur'an.

takbir – the declaration '*Allahu Akbar* – Allah is Greater'

talbiyah – the cry of the pilgrim to Makkah '*Labbayk Allahumma labbayk ....*' – 'At Your service, O Allah, at Your service ...'

taqwa or *tuqa* – lit. self-protecting, fearful obedience of Allah in avoiding all that is forbidden and undertaking all that is obligatory. Higher degrees then involve avoiding that which is disapproved of and undertaking that which is recommended, and so on.

at-Tasawwuf – Sufism.

at-tawfiq – being directed to the right direction, the grace of Allah.

ummah – a nation. The *Ummah* of the Prophet, may Allah bless him and grant him peace, are the Muslims.

ᶜUmrah – the lesser pilgrimage to Makkah which may be undertaken at any time of the year.

wird or *hizb* – two synonymous terms for a set portion of *dhikr*, *ayat* of Qur'an and supplications to be recited regularly at any time of the day or night. The latter often more particularly is used to refer to a portion of one sixtieth of Qur'an.

wudu' – the minor washing of the face and limbs in preparation for the *salah*.

zakah – a wealth tax. It is one of the *arkan* (indispensable pillars) of Islam. It is levied on certain storable crops, cattle and other livestock, gold and silver, items of trade, etc. and distributed among a number of categories including the needy and the bereft, travellers, the indebted, for the freeing of slaves, and in the way of Allah (*jihad*).